Into the Sound Country

For The Beaches
May They always accrete
and may The waves fall
softly upon Them —

Bland Simpson

Tom Simpson

Into the Sound Country

BLAND SIMPSON

Photography by Ann Cary Simpson

The University of North Carolina Press

Chapel Hill and London

A Carolinian's Coastal Plain

Manufactured in the United States of America

The paper in this book meets the guidelines for
permanence and durability of the Committee on
Production Guidelines for Book Longevity of the
Council on Library Resources.

Library of Congress Cataloging-in-Publication Data

Simpson, Bland.

Into the sound country: a Carolinian's coastal plain / Bland
Simpson; photographs by Ann Cary Simpson.

    p.   cm.

Includes index.

ISBN 0-8078-2381-3 (cloth: alk. paper).—

ISBN 0-8078-4686-4 (pbk.: alk. paper)

1. Albemarle Sound (N.C.)—Tours.   2. Beaufort Region
(N.C.)—Tours.   3. Albemarle Sound (N.C.)—History.
4. Beaufort Region (N.C.)—History.   5. Albemarle Sound
(N.C.)—Biography.   6. Beaufort Region (N.C.)—
Biography.   7. Simpson, Bland.   8. Simpson family.
I. Simpson, Ann Cary.   II. Title.

F262.A33S56   1997

917.56'186—dc21   97-18536

CIP

01 00 99 98 97   5 4 3 2 1

Several brief portions of this book originally appeared in
slightly different form in the *Spectator* and *Wildlife in North
Carolina*, both published in Raleigh; permission to use
these materials in *Into the Sound Country* is gratefully
acknowledged.

Pages ii–iii: Sunset at Leonard's Point, Albemarle Sound,
October 1996

FOR OUR PARENTS

Dorothy Page Simpson

Martin Bland Simpson Jr. (1922–1973)

Patricia Cary Kindell

John Robert Kindell

The night when the great run of

shad was passing through the inlet

and into the river estuary was a night,

too, of vast movements of birds into

the sound country.

Rachel Carson, *Under the Sea-Wind*

Contents

Into the Sound Country

The Sound Country

The Sound Country starts at the base of a scuppernong vine in the Great Dismal Swamp, runs south for two hundred amazing miles, taking in much of eastern America's greatest and broadest inland waters, and ends in a wet sheen *J*-hook point of sand at Cape Fear, where Onslow Bay and Long Bay meet in riptide over Frying Pan Shoals and form the Atlantic Ocean. This is the wet and water-loving land of eastern Carolina's coastal plain, where rivers go sliding off into swamps and gliding by grand bluffs, ancient forests drown slowly in the rotting shred of peat in baylands and pocosins, new grasses green up each spring in marshes both saltwater and fresh. It is the land of greater sounds—Currituck, Albemarle, Pamlico, Core, and Bogue—and lesser—Croatan, Roanoke, Back, Stump, Topsail, Middle, Greenville, Masonboro, Myrtle Grove, and Shallotte. Below them is only low country, sea islands, and Florida.

From my early years living in Pasquotank County, on a blackwater river in a town at most twelve feet above the sea, from as early as anything I can recall, I have heard and known and loved this word *sound*. The small fishing boats that appeared at our Water Street wharves in the afternoons, their holds full of the fruits of the sea, were said to have had a good day "down the Sound." My father, coming home at breakfast time with a brace of ducks from his first-light Currituck hunts, had shot his limit, our evening meal, from a blind "out on the

Sound." All rivers feed the sea, true, but in our world they all but one first feed the sounds.

What came to us from these big waters was not always as fine as good catches of fin and feather; the breeze was not always balmy and briny. I remember the sour-egg wind blowing up our way and over us in Elizabeth City on the black-water Pasquotank, a foul wind come up from across the Albemarle Sound, an overripeness in the paper-making mash at the mill way down in Plymouth. That was before anyone had learned to make such jejune apologia as "Smells like *money*!" People knew it stank, and just plain said, "Whew, you sure can smell Plymouth *today*!"

Pasquotank was my father's ancestral home, where descendants of the Indian Pocahontas and the English Blands and Swanns had drifted down through the Great Dismal Swamp and stopped—Virginians like furrier Edward Bland, who in 1650 explored the valleys of the Chowan and Meherrin and Roanoke and, astounded by two-crop corn and twenty-five-foot cane and fine tobacco there, wrote *The Discovery of New Brittaine* and proposed to settle the land of Ralegh's dreams. The first governor of these first Albemarle settlers was William Drummond, a Scot who also discovered Lake Drummond at the very heart of the Great Dismal, and, thanks to eight-times-great-grandfather Drummond (his daughter Sarah married a Swann), we came by our swamp spirits honestly.

On the south shore of the Albemarle Sound, closer to Elizabeth City than Plymouth, was the setting of my mother's family: a much smaller river town, Columbia in Tyrrell County, on a river as black as Pasquotank, perhaps even blacker, the Scuppernong. Into this swamp country in 1873, into the low part of it that had belonged to my mother's people the Spruills for nine generations already, or they to it, came a lumberman named Moore, come south to Tyrrell County from the little Pocomoke River town of Rehobeth, Maryland. Let five years pass and one of the young squires of the big Spruill farm Free and Easy would take a Moore daughter for his bride; let six more go by and this pair would give me my grandmother, Evelyn, born in Alligator in some of the last and best wild country Carolina can still lay claim to. But first let Moore slog it out in a rough-hewn Alligator River timber camp for six months, sending love and money home to Rehobeth, where his wife Priscilla and her six children languished, lonely on the Eastern Shore.

Let her write him over and over again, her appealing plea always the same: you *must* bring me and your family to North Carolina. And though he would protest, telling her repeatedly in return that the cypress and gum and juniper swamps of the eastern Carolina Sound Country were no place for a woman, or for children, that life here was rough, rugged and ragged both, that she could not come, let her insist and persist till after months of marital pressure transcending both Chesapeake and Albemarle, Moore would submit. Let this husband go back to Rehobeth on the Pocomoke River and outfit a small schooner, then pack his entire household and family onto the boat and set sail in the spring, southbound down Chesapeake, through the Dismal Swamp Canal and the vast morass that big ditch made passable, on down the Pasquotank River and across Albemarle Sound and up Alligator River to Old Cove Landing. And then let her in an instant finally see the slab-camp truth of her new home, forgetting all her pleading and insistence, and shrieking now in a brokenhearted horror over the ragged humanity and jungled nature of it all, shrieking this, my family's central question for three centuries now:

"Oh, Mister Moore, Mister Moore—what sort of place have you brought me and my children to?"

Beyond the Chowan River the land, already without hill
or accent, became flat, the land of a delta, with a high sky.
Albemarle Sound (unknown to me, even as a name, until that
moment) gave a great, continental sense of the North Carolina
coast, making me half regret that I hadn't known of it before,
and making me want to come again and be for a day in that
openness. It was one of those places where it was easy to
imagine the excitement of the early explorers, finding
themselves in what was truly a new world.

—V. S. Naipaul, *A Turn in the South*, 1989

Betsy

The Northeast

After a set of swooping serpentine curves coming from west to east, the Edenhouse bridge—the long one over the three-mile mouth of Chowan River into Albemarle Sound—lies before you. Across it is my earliest homeland, northeastern North Carolina, a batch of narrow counties boning their way like fingers down from Virginia and separated each from each by a succession of rivers all of them draining down into the Albemarle Sound and most all of them Indian-named: Chowan, Perquimans, Pasquotank, North, and at last, naturally, another sound . . . Currituck.

This is potato land, where potato hills in the fields are the highest and only hills around; cabbage land, where our pungent *Brassacae* are harvested with machetes; peach country around North River, where at the roadside stands from Poplar Branch to Powell's Point peaches are piled high in thin-slat bushelbaskets tilted toward the highway and travelers' eyes; peanut land in the sandy banks and ridges up near the Great Dismal Swamp, where, in times before the ruddy red drying wagons, the groundnuts stood in huge, breastlike shocks. Pinestands and gum woods are everywhere, and log trucks to course them and bear the latest crop of saw logs and pulpwood alike to the nearest mill, unless the logger

Chowan River cypress

is skimming and taking every third load to his own mill a county and a half away.

Among the first things I can remember, along with my grandmother Simpson's long-billed fishing cap and the coarse shelly sand and the rough deep-blue Atlantic at Nags Head, is the great reach of cornfields that once stretched out behind our place in Elizabeth City, which was no city at all and was still called by some of the *old* old-timers Betsy Town after the tavernmistress Betsy Tooley, from whom the town had acquired the Narrows Plantation in June 1794 and therewith the land and riverbend place to build itself and boom: in time Betsy would become the Eastern Emporium, the Queen of the Albemarle.

Ours was a small postwar frame house like all the rest on the outer edge of the town's old turn-of-the-century horse-racing track, a main part of that era's fairgrounds. All the houses on this oblong sat about a half a mile from the dark black Pasquotank River, and all of them were survivors of the vicious ninety-

Stacking peanuts, Northampton County, about 1939

mile-an-hour sidewinds spun at us by Hurricane Hazel as she came into Carolina on a full Hunter's Moon high tide and swept the coast below us clean of cottages and claptrap and bent our big backyard maple to the breaking point before relenting late on the eve of my sixth birthday, letting the party go on the beautiful next day, a pony come to cart us all around.

A line of great oaks with whitewashed lower trunks led along what was now called West Williams Circle down toward the creek channel into Gaither's Lagoon and the river itself. There was still a small scallop-shingled kitchen from the bygone fairground days hidden in the lagoon's jungles and, on drier ground near some small hoglots at the other end of the old horsetrack, there was the old Horner's Sawmill that burned twice before I would write my age in double ciphers—the first time at night and so hot that the heat softened the oiled dirt road of South Williams Circle two hundred yards from the blaze to where it was as malleable as pluffmud in a marsh.

Like us, our neighbors were all from around there and bore names like Daniels and Harris, Shannonhouse and Orr, Calloway, Cavanaugh, Burgess, Blanchard and Barwick, Aydlett, Gollobin, Spence, Jennette, Winder, and Owens. Hugh Marr, my second cousin, lived two doors away and slept with a human skull beneath his bed that had been given him by his apothecary grandfather. Lifting the neatly sliced top off that skull was the height of pure mortal adventure for awhile, till in fourth grade Miss Audrey Austin read us a story of mysterious disappearance and death that had happened right where we lived, right along the nearby riverside, and we learned that our playmate George Owens's grandfather Len had been a key witness in the sensational 1902 trial of Jim Wilcox for the murder of Beautiful Nell Cropsey. We played all over that old racetrack, down by the lagoon and the river as well, giving Beautiful Nell's vine-covered haunted house wide berth; we picked peanuts in the fall from a one-acre patch where the headwaters of the lagoon ran out beside Jarvis's white clapboard shed-sized grocery; and we studied the cottonpickers as they worked a patch near the low brick building at the far side of that great eastern cornfield, our brand new 1958 J. C. Sawyer Elementary School.

Beneath the windows that ran along one wall of our fourth-grade classroom at Sawyer School was a little library. Here was a dictionary, a book of the maps of the world, another of the mammals of Africa and Asia, and always a sheaf of *My Weekly Reader*s. The jewel of our collection, though, was the series of bright, blue-bound biographies that nearly filled the middle shelf.

In these books were simple tales of heroic, or at least adventurous, Americans: Ethan Allen; Thomas Jefferson; Lewis and Clark and their guide, the Indian woman Sacagawea; Jim Bridger; Dolly Madison; John Wanamaker; Clara Barton; Horace Greeley; and Susan B. Anthony. I read almost every book on the shelf, and my favorite was everyone else's favorite, too: Davy Crockett, frontiersman, yarnspinner, congressman, staunch and sturdy defender of the Alamo. One of my earliest strong sensations of mortality came when Fess Parker, portraying Crockett in the Disney picture, faced Santa Ana's firing squad and joined history, and "Be sure you're right, then go ahead" became the proverb of a ghost.

So disappointed was I in that outcome that I got my father to buy yet another version of the Crockett tale, this one an illustrated paperback from the Oxena News Stand, and then got him to read it aloud to me three times. Each time I listened intently with the wildest hopes that somehow it would all turn out differently for Davy, that somehow the Mexicans wouldn't overrun the Alamo or, if they still did, that this time they would see what a good fellow Davy was and let him go, retire him to his mountaintop in Tennessee.

A lot of the subjects of those blue-back biographies at Sawyer School were presidents, whose young lives in any event seemed remarkably like mine: they were pretty good boys, no worse than Tom or Huck, who grew up hearing stump speeches and hanging around court squares or newspaper offices and who just kind of fell into the president business early. It all seemed familiar and fun to me, as I was used to haunting my father's and other lawyers' quarters in the Carolina Building downtown, and going with him to roam the halls of Pasquotank County justice, calling in turn on the clerk, the sheriff, the register of

Perquimans River, October 1996

deeds. So I was thrilled the day Daddy came home and clapped his hand on my shoulder and said:

"I got you a job down at the courthouse."

All that year the sheriff would appear once a month at our school door, which opened straight onto what had been a cornfield not long before, to fetch me and carry me to work. He was a big, relaxed man in khaki with a service revolver on his hip, and his appearance set some of my pals off; the boy who was lousy at marbles and who never hit more than a single at softball got to go off riding with a lawman, a man with a gun, and not just with a deputy, but with the head man, the High Sheriff of Pasquotank County.

He drove us back downtown, then escorted me to the jury room, a chamber on the west side of the old courthouse where eight men, in light shirts and dark pants, few of them with ties, sat and created the large pool of prospective jurors. My job was to pull a strip of paper from a boxfull-jumble of shreds, one at a time, whenever the besuited and gargantuan man with the long fat green cigars, the chairman of this strange empaneling agency, called for one. On each slip—about one-fourth inch by five inches, like an articulated fortune-cookie prediction—was a man's name. For two hours, from midmorning till the men broke for lunch, I sat beclouded by the bilious smoke that came continuously from the chairman's cigars. It went like this:

"All right," the big man would say. "Let's have one."

I would thrust my hand in, let my fingers search around a few seconds, savoring, after all, this small drama that momentarily centered on me, pull one out, and hand it to the big man, who would then slowly read the name out loud:

"John Charles Sawyer. Anybody know him?"

If he were a well- or reasonably well-known citizen of our county, several voices would speak at once:

"Oh, yeah!"

"Sure, I been knowing him twelve, thirteen years, he's a good fellow."

"Unh hunh, Charlie Sawyer, works at the tire place, his boy's halfback on the Yellow Jackets."

"Oh, come on, Sam, you know Charlie, used to live down at Weeksville."

"Was he in the Coast Guard for a while?"

"Yeah, that's him."

"Now I know who you're talking about, he's a good old boy."

A few remarks like that, and the others, who didn't know or know of this man, took their colleagues' judgment to heart, and nodded comfortably, approvingly, toward the men who had spoken up, by those nods accepting the jury candidate as fine, all right, okay—if he's all right with you, he's all right with me.

Then the big man would check a list to see if Charlie had done jury duty anytime in the preceding five years. If he had, then the panel would let him off the hook and throw him back like an undersized fish. If he had not had the honor, the big man would put Charlie Sawyer's name onto the short list, the real jury pool for the next term of Superior Court.

If the man whose nameslip I pulled and heard called out for the panel's consideration were *not* someone known to them, the talk ran more like this:

"Thomas Earl Shannonhouse."

Silence, and head shaking, and then after a bit they'd start to cipher it out.

"Is that old Tom Shannonhouse, from out by Nixonton?"

"That had that big cabbage patch?"

"No, I know who you mean," the big man in charge would say. "That old fellow's name was Something Thompson Shannonhouse, and they just called him Tom."

"Could be his son?"

"No, he didn't have any children. Never married."

"Is he dead?"

"I don't think so. If he is, I hadn't heard."

"Damn. Must be a hundred, then."

"Well, I never heard of him," someone else would say, "or this Thomas Earl neither one."

"Look him up there, Joe," the big man would direct, and the plain Pasquotank man named Joe would leaf through some sort of directory compiled by whom I don't know, the Chamber of Commerce, perhaps. If they couldn't find Thomas Earl Shannonhouse in this black loose-leaf book, couldn't find out what his business was or where he lived (and therefore to whom he might be related or known), the panel would reject him simply on the grounds that he was an unknown quantity. There were lots of Shannonhouses: this one might not even live here anymore, hell, he might be dead. If no one knew him, or anything about him, he did not make the jury pool. It was that simple.

And because it was just that simple, I understood it. You had to be Somebody to get this honor, the selection of which I was a key part. I could see, too, that it was just fine to be a farmer or a tire grinder—after all, this was the town where the fall harvest festival, the Potato Parade, was bigger than Christmas, so we all knew the source of our wealth and well-being—so long as someone on the panel knew you and would speak up for you during these jury-picking sessions and give the rest of the panel the key information:

"Now, I know *he's* alive. I saw him and his whole family eating fried chicken just last Sunday over at the Virginia Dare Hotel after church. He's all right."

"Needs to push himself away from the table now and then, am I talking about the right guy?"

"That's the one. But his wife is one more good-looking woman."

"Tell me about it."

"Let's move on, now, boys," the big man would say.

"Why you reckon she married *him*?"

"All right, son"—the big man, turning to me, plowing forward—"pull me another name."

I was not supposed to look at the spaghetti of paperstrips in the box before me. After all, I was employed there by the county not only as an operative of the panel but as an emblem of innocence. Of course in the process of thrusting my hand and arm into the citizenry I glimpsed the tiny typescripts, and occasionally a first or last name obtruded itself upon my mind. No offense there, though—they might have blindfolded me, had they been out to make the system failsafe. I just wasn't to sit there staring at the papers, or sorting through them, either one or both.

One morning while the discussion was proceeding apace I glanced into the box and saw one of the most familiar names in my little universe:

Charles Jarvis.

So familiar was the name of the man who, with his father, ran the small, white-shack neighborhood grocery in our corner of town that the heavens having let the *Charles Jarvis* slip land atop the shredded heap—rightside up—and present itself to me so boldly like that constituted some form of entrapment.

Into the web I felt myself falling—perhaps I was dizzy, victim of the big man's cigar smoke.

Charles Jarvis—the white slip might well have been a glowing neon, an alluring orange the color of COLD BEER signs in the windows of country stores.

This was a moral dilemma. I was never supposed to see anything in the great box, and now that I had, I wanted to ensure Mister Jarvis the honor of Juryman by going ahead and, to the blissful ignorance of the panel, plucking his nameslip and giving it to the big man.

"All right, son," he now said, turning my way. The men on the panel watched me with no more or less interest than they ever did, but I felt as though the most casual look from the least of them peered right in on the great debate under way just now in my soul. "Son?"

Be sure you're right, Davy Crockett had said, then go ahead.

I pulled Charles Jarvis's name.

My heart was pounding as the big man read it aloud:

"Charles Jarvis—you all know Charles, don't you?"

A chorus of "Oh, yeah" and "He's all right" rang out in the chamber. My candidate was one of the most popular of the day; their quick and cheerful comments certified him. In two shakes—or chop-chop, as my daddy always put it—Charles Jarvis was at the head of the new jury class. It would be years before I heard the expression "The end justifies the means," but I was its slave that day, as if it were emblazoned upon my heart.

Soon the session was over, and the sheriff was driving me in the squad car back to school. He bade me farewell till next month and gave me my pay—one dollar, a silver certificate—which I pocketed and was glad of, though it paled beside the far more valuable asset I had garnered:

A secret.

Murder will out, they say, and so, too, will jury tampering—even the before-the-fact, pony-league variety I had been guilty of, though there was only one way for my crime to be found out: for me to confess it—or, more accurate, to brag about it.

That evening I contrived a reason—"I think we're almost out of bread, Mama"—to ride my bicycle down to Jarvis's Store, a 16-by-24-foot white clapboard building hard by the upper reaches of Gaither's Lagoon, the sort of store that in South Carolina used to be called a *grab* and that for the most part has been sundered and plowed under by the Starvin' Marvins of the world. They were redolent of cheeses and luncheon meats, of grape and orange smells from the empty soda bottles in wooden crates, always of candy: Bonomo's Turkish Taffy and a whole colorwheel of sweetwaters in finger-sized wax bottles being far and away the pacesetters of Pasquotank, 1957.

I was bursting with pride as I knocked the kickstand down and propped my fat-tired red bicycle near the store's stairs, and went on in. Mister Jarvis put the loaf of bread into a paper sack, marked it down on our account there, and went back to sweeping up the absorptive green cleaning particles that lay salted all over the store's dark wooden floor. I watched him, put my hands on the edge of the drink box and pushed myself up on it, there to sit like any old idler at Will Varner's store in Frenchman's Bend in Faulkner's *Hamlet*, like a million before me, and a million yet to come. Well, this sort of behavior was understood, expected even, in men, but not in sprouts like me. Only a couple minutes passed before Charles Jarvis, a rangy fellow about five-eleven with black, Vitalis-sleek hair, stopped sweeping and looked over at me and said:

"Was it something else you wanted, boy?"

"No, sir," I said. "Just the loaf of Nolde's."

"Well," he said, still wondering, "don't you need to be getting on home?"

"Yes, sir, Mister Jarvis. But there was something I wanted to tell you first."

"Something you wanted to tell me?" he repeated, half laughing now. "Something like what?"

Now was my moment, and I was fired up and ready for it. I blurted it all out—about my job at the courthouse and the men on the panel and the dollar-a-day and pulling the slips—and I ended up with the remark:

"So this morning I saw your name at the top of the pile and I picked you!"

"You *what*!?"

"Picked you. For the *jury*!"

"You're kidding me—you did *what now*?"

I could not grasp what it was that *he* didn't understand about what I was telling him. He flipped the broom against some narrow shelving behind the counter, leaned on the end of the counter, looming over me, and asked me several exasperated questions. Charles Jarvis, future juror, was red-faced and fuming, and I was astounded at how badly this was going. Not what I had expected at all, and somehow I knew better than to say something about the honor of the position. But what would Davy have done?

"God-*damn*-it!" Mister Jarvis yelled and slammed his right hand down on the counter. "You know what this means? I'll have to lock this store up, to go be on a goddamn jury. And all because of *you*! Why, I ought to tan your hide, you little sonofabitch! Go on, get the hell out of here! Right *now*!"

Nothing like this had ever happened in those blue-bound biographies I loved so, and I was astonished and hurt, pretty much afraid for a good while thereafter even to go back into Jarvis's. He knew nothing of my motives, my thoughts about Jefferson and Lincoln, but what did *I* know about his trying to make ends meet off of a grocery the size of a garage? I reckon it was as good and clear a civics lesson as I ever learned, but there was another lesson beyond that, about the human heart and voice, one that transcended the Pasquotank and all the Sound Country:

There are times aplenty when a boy should keep his mouth shut and say nothing; times, too, when a man should stop and do likewise.

A better day it was when, one bright autumn afternoon, my father took me along with him to the forest of massive pines at Flatty Creek, with its gum and cypress sloughs, my first big woods.

Daddy drove us southerly down through Pasquotank, past the two hulking twenty-story blimp hangars, the round-ended one with the clamshell doors and the square-ender that burned down in the summer of 1995 in less than four hours between eleven at night and three in the morning, its giant metal cables and grids now hanging from the concrete that remains and clanging in the coastal winds. Past Toxey's old gas-pop-and-beer stand, past Little Flatty Creek and the cotton gin on the banks of Newbegun, to a right turn at the Quonset hut at Weeksville, then through the broad, open cabbage-and-potato lands to a crossroads called Four Forks. He pulled his maroon humpback '52 Dodge over to the side of Leigh Farm Road, threw the gear up into reverse, popped open the glove compartment, and produced a small flask about the size of a vanilla extract bottle, but clear with a clear fluid inside. With no explanation Daddy said,

"Put some of this on your socks and legs, son."

He had already opened it, and now I held it and smelled of it, felt around the tiny opening. It was medicine, or turpentine, I thought.

"No," I said. "It's greasy."

"Go on, put some on you."

"How come?"

"It'll keep the redbugs off you."

"The what?"

"Redbugs—some people call em chiggers."

"I don't want to," I said again. In our low-lying town, Elizabeth City, we had none of *these* bugs. We had mosquitoes, and a truck pulling a DDT smoke–spewing contraption that we loved and called "the fog machine" (and that we crazily ran along behind, appearing mysteriously to each other in the hazy air before it dissipated) kept the skeeters down. Still my father insisted, but I was stubborn, and we had only a scant three hours of light left. So he quit, took the little bottle back, only saying,

"Well, I really wish you would, but maybe they won't be too bad."

There were three of us that first time; our other companion was a Coinjock insurance man named Paul Spry. We strode along this year's corn furrows—it

Water lilies

would be fourteen years yet before Daddy would put the road in down to the creek—and I scrambled to keep up with the men. I thought we were only going to the far side of the field, there to inspect some trees, then turn around and go back. My legs were tired by the time we reached the edge, but that was only the first quarter of the way. There, at this grand and formal demarcation, my father turned and said,

"Now we're going into the woods."

We were there to look at the timber, and I well remember walking and curving round and doubling and trebling back in the cool October afternoon shade beneath the hundred-foot pines with their breast-height diameters of two and three feet. This four hundred acres has been family timberland for more than eighty years now, since 1915, and my father had been prowling these woods since *his* boyhood. One of the neighbors, a Sanders, recalled seeing him come stalking out of the wet winter late-day woods in the 1930s, Daddy drenched to the skin coming along the mule-drawn wooden railway that my grandfather was bringing logs out on back then.

"Who are *you*?" the farmer said.

"I'm Martin Simpson," he said, "and I'm just out here seeing to my swamp."

I remember how the land got spongier the deeper into the forest we went. I remember Daddy's giving me for the first time the lesson of moss-on-the-north-side. And I remember my first sight of a big water appearing through a woods, a silver mirror lain over in the wilderness, and how thrilling it all was.

Big Flatty Creek is really a river, easily a quarter mile wide where it rounds the point of our land. Two branches, Woodduck Creek (christened by my father) and Muddy Gut, run easterly out of our tract into the larger water. On maps, Big Flatty appears as a cleft in the south central shore of Pasquotank County, emptying at a shanties-at-pier-ends fish camp named Frog Island into the great Albemarle Sound. I wouldn't be at all surprised if Ralph Lane and his tiny fleet looked in on Flatty Creek when they were exploring the Albemarle for Sir Walter Ralegh in early 1586, sailing westerly and visiting Indian villages along the sound's north shore before turning up the Chowan River.

Back home in town that evening after my own first exploration, I was astonished that I was the innocent meeting place for a hundred or more redbugs, and that my father was now, with my howling encouragement, applying both calamine *and* turpentine, along with every other lotion, cream, and solvent he could find, emptying both the medicine chest and the paint locker in the garage hoping for his new pioneer-son's salvation. But it was all to no avail, because, failing the preventative 6-12 I should have used (and never refused again), the only true cure now was time.

So I learned just how much he knew what he was talking about, and I took him at his word that somehow, someday, I would come to know those woods, that I would need to know them. But I could still be surprised.

On a blistering August afternoon in the late 1960s, a plain old railroadman named Keppy Ferrell drove me out to Flatty Creek to see the new road my father had cut into the big woods. This sandy lane, thirty feet wide and a ditch on either side, ran through the cornfield for a half a mile, turned at the woods' edge, then bore on for another mile till it hit the creek at the point. It was to serve a small second-home development that, despite the spanking new road, was still in a nascent stage.

"Million dollar pro-jeck!" Keppy kept saying as we passed the blimp hangars, Newbegun, the Quonset hut. On the broad dark green steps of a south Pasquotank country store where we stopped, migrants sprawled—a dozen or more on a break—and drained Pepsis and Sundrops. Second homes were at two homes' remove for these exhausted people who lived out of school buses and ponyshed quarters—they seemed as oblivious to the old man's talk when we pulled back out as they had when we'd arrived, and they simply stared after us through a heat as thick as the dust hanging over the store's bottlecap parking lot.

"Who's going to *buy* all these lots?" I finally asked the touter, a former state legislator, who first looked stricken, then gave one of the main answers to so many Southern questions since 1865:

"Why, rich *Yankees!*"

In spite of the railroadman's enthusiasm and his devotion to my father, the market for such ventures soured, and the tall pines seeded the forty acres of cleared ground—*and* the new road. By the time my father died on another August day four years later, there were young pines from six inches to two or three feet tall growing in the road, young gums on the ditchbanks.

On the beach at Kitty Hawk one day along about that same time, an experienced timberman named Fred Markham stopped me and said:

"If you ever want me to go take a look at your woods with you, just call me up."

So in the fall of '73, three of us in our twenties—Bill Parsons, Eddie Farbuck, and I—met Mister Markham, a small spry man in his middle eighties, at the big woods and stomped on in. Immediately he was out in front of us by ten or fifteen feet, talking back over his shoulder about trees and old times in south Pasquotank, once stopping, turning, and laughing as he asked,

"I'm not going too fast for you boys, now, am I?"

When we reached the nondevelopment, he shook his head and said, "This land out here is just about perfect for growing pines—you don't have to do a thing." We all of us had a ball, jumping the big ditch, skirting the sloughs, and we hated to head back a couple of hours later. But the old man who so loved the woods needed to see about some timber of his own on the other side of the neck. Mister Markham had something of a cane, a stripped sapling, that he used more as a pointer than a steadier. Once he wheeled about, stayed me with his left hand while he aimed the cane groundward with his right, and we all focused on a three-inch seedling and he said,

"Watch it, now—you bout stepped on a *pine tree.*"

A couple of years later, in a tippy wooden canoe I glided along the creek shore here, noting the increase in the understory, the forest's steady return. For twenty minutes at dusk I watched a great blue heron stalk the shallows, and then I came back out later that evening and cruised the creek in a bright dark, entranced by the October magic of a very heavy midnight mist and the full Hunter's Moon that made it glow.

There were river otters here, and a woods full of owls, hawks, rabbits, muskrats. Once in July I stood in a slough off Woodduck Creek, wondering who had discarded an old tire way back in there and then watching the tire uncoil and turn into a cottonmouth with a girth as big as my upper arm. Another time, when I was out with a timber cruiser, a woman from Weyerhaeuser, I practically walked into a baby raccoon that quickly scuttled from eye level on up a slender pine and then hung on, shivering, till we moved along.

Next time out with the same cruiser, we were leaving the woods when three pickups worth of deer hunters stopped out on the main road and someone fired from a high-platform, truckbed seat at a deer their dogs had chased out of another piece of woods across the field. The deer dove into a drainage ditch and disappeared, but was moving our way as it did, and I shouted and halloed at the men still half a mile distant—to no response from them.

When the deer reemerged from the ditch, wounded and not forty yards away and now nearly in a direct line between us and the hunters, I hollered again and we hit the deck. The deer ran into a pine thicket on the other side of my father's lane, and there was no further fire. We stood and walked the rest of the way out.

"Why didn't you answer?" I fairly shouted at the men as we approached. "Why didn't you call back?"

"Oh, we saw you all right," an older fellow answered, adding, "We weren't gon shoot you." I am sure he told the truth, but I was filled with fear and fury, shivering like that raccoon up the tree, and as I pointed back up the lane toward where we'd been, all I could say in this rage was also the truth:

"Well, how the hell did *I* know that?"

Once in the dead of winter I was out with neighbor Sanders, a farmer whose deed showed his family holding several acres on our side of a lead drainage ditch, and our family with a like amount on his side. When we went into the woods to walk what would become the new line after a swap, I saw there a wondrous sight I have since seen only twice, in the Great Dismal and down east in Carteret County, and only after many more years had passed:

Snow in the Spanish moss.

Near this same spot, in the springtime, my old friend Jake Mills and his boy Mark and I marveled at bed after swaying bed of wild blue irises in the marshy upper reaches of Muddy Gut, where we turned our jonboat around and headed back out to Big Flatty and up to our fish camp on the point. The Mills boys and I made that camp for a couple of years before we moved north and tried out Lake Drummond in the Dismal. Should have stayed put—our luck was much better on Big Flatty.

"This is old-time *river* fishing," Jake said over and over again, as we crept along the undercut banks and mortally pulled in the big bream. One evening we set a trot line with milk-jug floats, but all we found the next morning was an angry and thrashing snapping turtle we'd scarcely snagged—we emancipated him for the good of all.

We went way up each of Big Flatty's three tributaries trailing the big yellow cats and the old-time bream, stopping up one of these streams late on a Sunday morning to admire a clutch of cottonmouths sunning on the deck of a twenty-six-foot derelict. One of my comrades—he with an immense south Georgia diamondback rattler on his Piedmont office wall—all of a sudden had a trophy in mind and a .22 tacklebox pistol in hand, but I had my hand on the throttle of our 3-horse Evinrude, and that was all the power I needed.

Not three minutes later, during our daring downstream getaway, something heavy and wet slapped my throttle hand behind me, and I let go the motor with a curdleblood scream that may still echo down in south Pasquotank. Now we knew the horror of every flatwater boatman's worst dream: the snake in the boat there with you.

I had moved forward and the boat was out of control—the creature was thrashing about in the well behind the rear seat. Jake handed me the paddle—this trophy was mine. I leaned back to get my first good look at the enemy, and what I saw and reported has the Mills boys laughing to this day:

It was a herring. A big one, though.

Time and time again I have gone back to Big Flatty, wandered and roamed the great forest that long ago ceased to seem strange and endless to me, and if I have found some small purchase on the way of the wilderness, it began there when I was still a small boy. On an early November day, my wife Ann and I once set out down the lane, driving to the edge of the woods where the rusting hulk of an ancient log skidder has sat for a generation. It was the first time I walked these woods with her, this bright, balmy blue-sky day, and I smiled, hearing in my mind my father's old suggestion as we rubbed a little Cutter's on our arms and necks, on our legs beneath our socks. Now the pines in the road have grown up, twenty years and thirty feet tall, and we strode far more easily than I ever did when they were breast height and bushy. The lane was clear, a carpet of pine needles all the way out to the quarter acre of reeds at the road's end, where Jake and Mark and I had hacked out our fish camps more than a decade before.

It is a mixed woods, and we like it that way. Where the last cutting was heaviest, the pines and young gums were coming on strong, and I thought of the surety in old man Markham's voice that fall day in '73, and even more of the great whispering pines I had first seen here thirty-five years ago. Now I was the one, the man other men would see coming out of the forest in all weathers; and now we were the ones, Ann and I, walking down the lane hands clasped and talking about what we, and our children, might do and find and learn together in this place.

A few days later, back in the red-clay hill country, Jake listened patiently as I told him of the changes in the woods, and what it felt like to be there yet again, and this time with Ann, till finally he said,

"Yeah, but what I really want to know is: Did you all get yourselves any *chiggers*?"

One July day in the early '70s, the same day I saw the giant cottonmouth in the slough, I came back into Elizabeth City after a long outing at Big Flatty and went to spend the evening with my father, who was in the Albemarle Hospital north of town, out between U.S. 17 and the Pasquotank River. In this same hospital my paternal grandmother had once surprised me with the greeting "Well, hey there, Al Hirt!" when I showed up bearded and she was recovering from a stroke. This July evening, though I came expecting to tell my father in some detail what I'd seen and heard in the big woods that day, I got a different surprise: the inside dope on one of my father's—and Elizabeth City's—odder, and ultimately zanier, entrepreneurial adventures.

"Your daddy ever tell you bout the time we all got caught up in that silver mine way down in Mexico?" Big old Zee Rochelle said this raspily and laughed. Zee ran the dry cleaner's where Main hit Water Street right by the Pasquotank, and now he lay in a four-man ward, in for emphysema, next to my father's bed.

"I've heard of it," I said. Already my father, quite ill and unable to talk, had started shaking with laughter.

"Now that was a hell of a mess," Zee said. "Back about nineteen-sixty—like to never got out of that one alive."

And so he began to tell it, how he and my daddy and several other would-be silver barons down in Pasquotank County waited patiently for six or eight months after plunking their money down and then, not seeing shipload after shipload of ingots pulling up at the old oyster-house wharves as they had pretty much been promised, got anxious and started laying siege to their amiable precious-metals man down in—where was it? Durango? Oaxaca? Veracruz? Discreet inquiries led to threatening letters, but nothing did any good, so far as getting the eastern Carolinians hard facts about their distant mines. All that ever came back to them were very occasional, and very brief, messages that featured the word:

"Soon."

Well, Zee said, soon they got to where they could interpret their Mexican miner pretty well out of English and into honesty. They saw that what "soon" meant was "mañana," and after a year or more of vain waiting for the silver bells to ring, they decided to make their move. They were not going to be like those breathless, ineffectual pilgrims at the Central Station in Conrad's *Heart of Dark-*

ness, forever hanging around desperately hoping for a whiff of the word "ivory." These men would act.

They would go to Mexico.

It was twenty-two hundred miles from Elizabeth City, North Carolina, to Oaxaca, Mexico, and I wondered as Zee wheezed out the tale, and my own daddy laughed continuously, about the part Zee had skipped over in order to get to the righteous indignation, the rage of the investors, the great raid these magnificent seven would now make on Veracruz, on to Oaxaca, pistols blazing and fortune following the flag!

I wondered what had made these Sound Country men miners to begin with.

"Your daddy called me about eleven o'clock one morning," Jack Jennette, a lawyer like my father, told me another time. "Said, 'Jack, you've got to get on over here to the Virginia Dare Hotel—we're on to something now. Room 910.'"

Mister Jennette was a white-haired man with great generosity and patience in his deep, watery voice. "Naturally," he said to me, "I wanted to know what your daddy was talking about, and I asked him, 'Martin, what is it? What's going on?' but all he would say was,

"'You've got to hear it for yourself, Jack. This is a good deal, you ought to get in on it, so come on over just as quick as you can.'

"Well," Mister Jennette went on, "it was getting on towards lunchtime, and my office was only a block from the hotel, so I decided to go on and check it out. Walked over, took the elevator up to the ninth floor, knocked on the door, and your daddy opened it and said, 'Jack, I sure am glad you came.'

"I went in, looked around the room, and there sat five or six of the best businessmen, shrewd investors, you know, that we had here in Elizabeth City, and pamphlets and maps and photographs all spread out on the bed. And standing up by a board with some other maps and diagrams, answering questions as they came up, was this tall, well-dressed—I think he had a string tie—man, Mexican, I guess, well-spoken. They'd all been there for some good little while, and you could see they were all sold on this fellow who, I don't know, controlled a certain amount of land down there—or said he did—that had silver in it.

"Seemed like a right nice fellow, and it was all real entertaining—I'm glad I went—so I stayed awhile, till I'd learned all I needed to know right then about how much it took to capitalize a small silver mine in southern Mexico, and then I stood up and said,

"'Well, boys, I'm supposed to meet a man for lunch, so I'd better be getting on.' And I said goodbye all around and walked out of the room.

"Standing there waiting for the elevator, and your daddy came busting out of that room, closed the door behind him, and came over just all fired up, just about begging me, 'Jack, don't miss out on this. Chance to make a lot of money here. Come on, get in on it with us.' I said,

"'Martin, you fellows are smart, all of you. Can't you see what this is?'

"'What're you talking about?'

"'I'm telling you, this guy here doesn't have any more silver mines to sell you than I do.'

"'Why, Jack, you heard him.'

"'Yes, I did.'

"'You saw all those pictures and maps and all.'

"'That's right.'

"'Well, what's wrong, then?'

"'Martin,' I said, '*Texas* is between Mexico and Elizabeth City. And there's a whole lot more money in Texas than there is *here*. And if he couldn't of gotten what he needed in Texas, well, then, there's four or five more states before he gets to ours. Why has he come all the way up here into the very farthest corner of North Carolina—thirty more miles and he's in the Atlantic Ocean—to get himself some money to run his silver mine? Because he *had* to! I wouldn't give him a dime.'

"Your daddy looked kind of dejected. He really wanted me in on it. But I couldn't shake him. They all of them had silver fever or something, and they were bound and determined to have a stake in these Mexican silver mines." Just then the elevator came, and as I got on he shook his head at me and said,

"'Well, all right, then. But I think you're crazy.'"

In the hospital that evening, big Zee rasped on about getting the passports and everybody getting organized and then flying down to Lord knows where and then putting up in a small-town hotel, an articulated adobe hacienda, and waiting for their Mexican contact to show up and come clean. A day or two later, he came around, and the Southerners told him they were there because they wanted results. He apparently was somewhat less optimistic than he had been that day in room 910 of the Virginia Dare Hotel, but . . . if they wanted to see silver, he would take them to the mines.

Good, they said. Can't wait. Now we're getting somewhere.

Next morning the Mexican called for them with two jeeps, and most of that day they spent rattling over jeep trails, coyote paths, and dry stream beds, till they at last reached a village where they could rent donkeys and ride on in next day to the rough country where the mines were.

"We could just about taste it," Zee said. "Had us some serapes—we were beginning to look like we belonged there. Everybody got up early, ready to go, and we saddled up those donkeys and off we went, and went, and went. Sometimes our man would stop and ask somebody something, directions I guess, but none of us spoke Spanish so we never knew what he was up to. We just kept riding. Camped out at some little village, and he promised us that the *next* day we'd reach the mines."

None of the Pasquotankers exactly leapt onto their mounts the next morning, and it was sometime in the afternoon before the saddle-weary men finally found their quarry, some scrapings, minor diggings, and several shafts—"more like holes," Zee said—half or better filled with water.

"Trouble with the pumps," the Mexican said stoically. There were no buildings, no superstructures anywhere to be seen, certainly no pumps. Somewhere in the same general neighborhood were other shafts, other parts of the operation, if the gentlemen would like to see them, too.

"By then we were begging for mercy," Zee said, up on his elbow in the hospital bed by now. "We just wanted a decent place to sleep. We'd finally seen our mines, and now we knew just what we had, and just what a big bunch of fools we'd all been. That old boy'd just rode us around and wore us out, and whether that was our mine or some other lucky bunch's, we didn't know, or care."

It was an odd and affecting scene, two sick middle-aged men in a ward high above the old swamp river of their youth, both with tears of laughter still streaming down their faces over their folly, their Mexican misstep, their own treasure of the Sierra Madre, that sent them home red-faced and humbled and with nothing but a few sombreros, pesos, and tales to tell, no silver outside of several trinkets and a bucking-bronco tie clasp for my father's only son.

On the way to school when I was a boy, my daddy used to sing "South of the Border," where the mission bells told the singer he couldn't stay, south of the border, down *Mejico* way. As I apprehended it, Mexico was a country of romance, not commerce, a place where Spanish was the loving tongue, as another song said, "light as music, soft as spray." Someday Ann and I may go there—not for silver, but for the music of the Great Dismal Swamp songbirds wintering in the Yucatan, for the mysteries of the Mayans. And if we do, as we traverse the southern shores somewhere along the Gulf of Campeche, I will salute the shades of those who sought their prize too far from home, remembering Zee's last words on the affair:

"Aw, we asked for it. Us big-time silver miners from Elizabeth City, North Carolina."

I'd like to believe I knew how rich we were, right then and there in Betsy. For if ever anyone loved the hometown of his youth, I am he.

All the places and stuff of our home on the river were endlessly fascinating: Mr. Wright's Coal and Ice place right there at Dog Corner where Charles Creek met the Pasquotank; the Gaiety moviehouse—for blacks only back then—half a block away; chalk-white Twiddy's Grocery Store that wasn't much bigger than most Fast Fares today but seemed to me a sizable emporium; the John Deere store with the bright green toy tractors on glass shelves in the window; Froggy's side-street sporting goods store that was a step up from Froggy's grab, another source of our Turkish taffy, out near the J. C. Sawyer School; the *Daily Advance*, called *AD-vance*, between the bus station and the river; and the tiny oblong Crank's Fishmarket my mother would send me to on my bicycle ("What'll you have?" Mister Crank always asked, if you didn't speak up right away and call the name of a fish, "Pabst Blue Ribbon?" and then go off into loony laughter), right on Tiber Creek across the street from where the boats that had gone down the sound would tie up. And City Bicycle, and Buck Daniels Seed and Feed—all these Water Street wonders that are gone or transmogrified now, except for the stunning Victorian metalfront of the City Cut-Rate Shop, with its columns, rosettes, and foliation, on down toward the drawbridge that carries folks over to the causeway to Camden and Belcross, Currituck and Kitty Hawk, and the big red-brick Weatherly Candy building at the corner of Water and U.S. 158 that more recently housed the best-named business in town: Tidewater Liquidators.

There was a Boy's Club downtown where we played with a heavy leather basketball that scarcely bounced, and where little Linda Miller and I went—she as a gypsy to my pirate—to the third-grade Halloween dance and she tried briefly to get me to jitterbug. The real jumping joint, where my family went out to eat T-bone steaks when times were jaunty and flush, was the Circle, a curved-front restaurant set where Ehringhaus and Hughes Boulevards converged on the west side of town. When back at home I would lie in my bunk and listen—first on an Oatmeal box crystal set, then on a one-tube battery transistor radio—to the "Night Train" radio show broadcast from the second-story cockpit of the Circle, signing on and off with James Brown's mythic song of East Coast steel-rail ramble, where the radio named the boys and girls who with whom and who in whose car, and the whole ballet of 1950s dudes and dolls and dates and heavy-chrome cars went on, I could *see* it because I'd just been there four hours before eating steak with the popular lawyer everybody knew and his good-looking wife everybody wanted to know. And I knew something of what Sam Cooke was singing about not by inference or imagination but by a pretty brunette named Leslie having taken me aside during a game of night tag in a bramble over near the marine railways on Riverside Avenue and saying "I really want to *kiss you!*" and just plain doing it, not once but thrice. The Circle in time moved on down the street a half a mile, and we moved upstate to the red-clay country, but on a brief drive-by visit when I was seventeen, damned if I didn't meet back up with Linda Miller, my gypsy princess from the Boy's Club Halloween Ball ten years before, now standing tall as a new queen of the "Night Train," right there in the Circle's bottlecap lot.

The biggest pleasure of that younger time, though, was just hanging around my father's law office across Main Street, on the fourth floor of the enormous commercial Carolina Building, its mass an entire city block just three blocks away from the Pasquotank. His rooms were replete with captain's chairs and glass-front oak bookshelves for the red and olive leather-bound law books, a banjo-clock with Washington and Mount Vernon painted on its pendulum glass in the anteroom, and an oil portrait of my late grandfather above the huge iron Victory safe in the big office that overlooked Main Street. I bore the name of both men, and a familial lawyerly succession here in the lowlands was intended to go on, but when my father called Chapel Hill one winter night in 1967 and said the Carolina Building was burning and he could see the fire in the sky from his house way out on the Hertford Highway, out past the Museum of the Albemarle and the cottage-style Whispering Pines Motel, *miles* from the Pasquotank and downtown, my heart went cold, and I knew *then* that I would never practice law.

For my interest in the law was not intrinsic. It was tied to that sunlit fourth-floor room from whose big windows we had watched so many harvest-celebratory Potato Parades, their huge and goofily grotesque Macy's-size balloon critters bumping and navigating unsteadily down Main Street below. It was tied to the stairway with the heavy gray painted banister that I glided my racing hand over as I took the steps both up and down at full gallop, and to the little elevator with a wheel to drive it and an accordion steel gate, and to all the other lawyers, the men far more than their pursuit—Frank Aycock and Killian Barwick, Herbert Mullins and Herbert Small, John Small and Jack Jennette—who were there then. It wasn't the law at all that had me. It was my love of that building near the dark river and the sense of order and way-it-was-supposed-to-be that I got from spending time up there learning to type on the secretary's old Royal and learning, too, to intone little dramas into my father's dictaphone with its red plastic recording bands and going with him on weekdays over to the county courthouse and watching him as district attorney administer justice to the miscreants and talk shop with the sheriff and the deputies and the state troopers and all the clerks, women and men, in the various registries on the ground floor, and all of them smiling to see him coming and never seeming to mind that he'd brought his boy.

Sundays after church school we'd often stop in at Hill's Confectionery just beyond the county courthouse, a stuccoed soda and sundry shop that began its life as an antebellum bank with an eyecatching triple-Gothic-arched parapet in front. Or maybe we'd go by the far more modern formicaed and stainless-steeled Oxena News Stand on Martin Street, a shop now extinct that was tucked away into the west side of the Carolina Building, where they had fountain drinks, newspapers, and magazines from all over and a lot more than Hill's in the way of toys. Here I bought legions of miniature men in armor on mailed horses going off on Crusades, cowboys and Indians, of course, World War Two army men, bazookas and jeeps, and Disney cartoon characters; and in years to come my yet-to-be wife Ann would drive to Betsy, up from her work in the Nags Head Woods, and come here for breakfast and a Sunday paper.

When you entered the Carolina Building off Main out in front, you walked up the gray, polished, sloping marble floor of an arcade, one and a half stories tall—the truly grand thing about this great World War One–era commercial wonder, a promenade that led directly to the front doors of the Carolina Theater. Robbie the Robot from *Forbidden Planet* took our tickets here once, and another time the skeleton from Vincent Price's *House on Haunted Hill* flew out of the stage left wings, a full-size probably radium-infused glowing plastic skeleton that mimicked in the theater the one on screen that Price was hoisting forth from an acid vat and that scared the hell out of every soul in the house. The Carolina supplied endless exotica—cowboy, jungle and war movies (Second World War *and* Civil, like Fess Parker's *Great Locomotive Chase*—after we'd followed Fess to the Alamo when he was Davy Crockett, we were prepared for any sort of adventure with him). Once I saw William Holden and Sophia Loren in a steamy movie called *The Key*, wherein one man passed this woman along to the next by giving away the key to the Italian port-town apartment where she lived—at least, I know *now* that is what was going on, but at the time it seemed like the slowest-moving and least-affecting piece of filmic stagecraft this young fan of Hopalong and Ramar of the Jungle and all the rest had ever seen. I couldn't then and still can't tell what the fuss was about Elvis Presley in *Love Me Tender*, but the Civil War was the big story in that picture, and there was some gunplay at the end and Elvis got shot, so even with faults this beat out *The Key* hands down.

After the Carolina Building or the courthouse or the Oxena or the movie, by bicycle or shank's mare, the way home was along the river. My buddies and I roamed and ran rampant all over the riverside, ran throughout the ruin of the old Tara-like Fearing mansion where Beautiful Nell Cropsey of mysterious misfortune and fate had first stayed in this town back in 1898, when her family moved south from Brooklyn to truck-farm here. Across the street from the Fearing place lived a millionaire oilman whose sleek yacht lay up in a slip beside his Normanesque fortress of a brick house and who outfitted the high school band, the Yellow Jackets, and I knew that those were his oil tanks out there in the Pasquotank River near the tawny burned-out shell of the old Dare Lumber Company and that it was his doing that we had Texaco Beach over the Causeway near

Camden and Shiloh, where my folks would take us to swim in the river and pic-nic, with fried chicken and RC Cola in a cylindrical Scotch-plaid cooler.

But for all my run of Betsy Town at the ripe old age of eight or nine, for all I saw and knew, there was so much more—phantoms of architecture, of his-tory—I knew nothing of. Like the old Academy of Music theater now molder-ing away downtown behind Chesson's ladies ready-to-wear department that had built itself into the hall and cut into the orchestra seating, so that if you walked through what appeared to be a dressing-room door you walked straight back into the late nineteenth century with vaudeville's nascence on stage—I didn't know about that back then. Nor did I know how the lawyers' offices that were now all clustered in the Carolina Building had once been *there*, in a row be-neath a ballroom off to the side of the theater's balcony, and that among them was the office of E. F. Aydlett, who had defended Jim Wilcox against the charge of murdering Nell Cropsey, and that another lawyer there a generation after *State of North Carolina v. James Wilcox* was M. B. Simpson Sr., my grandfather, who partnered with Aydlett for a brief spell before going on his own and be-coming one of northeastern North Carolina's best and best-known defense lawyers of his day.

Nor did I know then about the *James Adams Floating Theater*, which had wintered here and spring-and-summered all over the Sound Country and served as source for Edna Ferber's novel *Show Boat*. Nor that on the dark Pas-quotank an American president, James Monroe, had once sailed, though from my great-aunt Jennie I *did* know that Union gunboats chasing Southern boys off Roanoke Island and up the Outer Banks kept on chasing and ran them up the Pasquotank, sank several ships, and shelled our town, leaving a Yankee cannon-ball lodged in my great-aunt Jennie's upstairs bedroom wall—*her* grandfather Tom Bland dug it out, put a chain on it, and employed it for years to come as a hitching weight for horses.

The Pasquotank was *my* river, but it was the also the river of the Yeopim In-dians; the river of Moses Grandy, the heroic black waterman who plied the Al-bemarle in the 1800s and bought his own freedom three times before it stuck; of Tamsen Donner, who taught school here before finding her strange sad way west and into American history as a member of the Donner Party; and of the suicidal young poet Robert Frost who, having decided *not* to throw himself away in the Great Dismal Swamp, paid a dollar to come aboard a southbound boat at Northwest Lock on the canal and floated down toward the Albemarle, where, as he much later wrote in "Kitty Hawk," he was joined by

> Some kind of committee
> From Elizabeth City,

Each and every one
Loaded with a gun
Or a demijohn.

A century ago Frost was a pilgrim here, accepting fried chicken if not a drink from one of the duck hunters, a man who introduced himself to the poet as "Ed Dozier, owner of the bes' goddamn bar in Elizabeth City," no small claim in a booming port town with thirteen saloons. So was Wilbur Wright, who just six years later passed through the town, hiring Israel Perry and Perry's scarcely worthy schooner *Curlicue* and sailing on through two days of heavy weather, foresail and mainsail both ripped loose, before straggling half drowned and half starved into Kitty Hawk. Franklin D. Roosevelt, too, was a Pasquotank peregrine, riding down Main Street in the late 1930s in an open car en route to Dare County—and there passing the somber, gray Kill Devil Hilltop shaft that celebrated the Wrights' first flight in their 1903 stick-built biplane—on his way to attend and dedicate Paul Green's outdoor drama, *The Lost Colony*.

How often I wandered downtown and tarried both coming *and* going by that broad black river, never knowing that I, too, was a pilgrim in Pasquotank. A thousand times I stalked without success the dull green-black turtles on the logs and timbers of Charles Creek and just as often picked my way along the shoreline down by the point where the old domed and temple-like Elizabeth City Hospital was, where both my sisters were born, and lifted the faded red fragments of brick, relics of a brickworks that predated the hospital, and sent them spinning out into the river soundward so many, many times and knew the sound of the small waves that river made on the sandy beaches and old bricks and cypress knees and boathouse pilings, knew it all like breathing and touching, but like touching and breathing took it all for granted, and never once for a moment thought that my folks would soon say farewell each to each or that I would ever have to leave it, any of it.

But I did, Betsy, I did.

Going back to Betsy-land thirty years later, Ann and I one winter night drove not to Elizabeth City itself, but to Edenton forty miles west, to the antique town that reigned over the northern Sound Country till the coming of the Dismal Swamp Canal, which engendered my first homeport back in the 1790s. Set upon the broad Edenton Bay, a six-square-mile cove on the Albemarle's north shore, Edenton was a place deeply steeped in its own historicity. This was Governor Eden's town, his dwelling place on the west bank of the Chowan and he being the colonial governor who was forced by Blackbeard himself to entertain (and possibly collude with) the irascible and violent pirate down in Bath.

President Franklin Delano Roosevelt's motorcade passes the Carolina Building, Elizabeth City, August 1937

"You all going to see the Cupola House while you're here in Edenton?" asked Ruth Shackleford, the innkeeper's wife, after breakfast. With her husband, Shack Shackleford, she ran the Governor Eden Inn, a large but unprepossessing two-story bed-and-breakfast with a more pretentious neighbor, the Lords Proprietors Inn.

"No," I said. "We're going out on the water."

"There you go!" she said enthusiastically. She was an honestly happy person, eager that those she met simply be *happy*. Part of her effort to ensure this was to

Motorcar crossing Albemarle Sound railroad bridge, longest in the world over navigable water at the time, about 1910

fill her guests up with massive omelets, pancakes, sidemeats, juices, milk, coffee, prior to their touring the town, suggesting to all — and justly so — such wonders as the two-story framed Jacobean home known across the state and region for the octagonal cupola that peaks its roof. A second part was to encourage and agree, usually with this exhortatory cheer: "There you go!" as if she were a coach sending you into a ballgame.

When we booked into the Governor Eden the night before, the Shacklefords had showed me the two available upstairs bedrooms. As in most such places, these rooms were furnished with generic antiques and differed only in that the one on the south side had a shower, while the one on the north had upon an elevated platform a huge purple bathtub.

"Most of your men don't prefer *this* one," said Shack of the purple-tubbed room.

"Even so," I said, "I think we'll take it — my wife'll like it."

"There you go!" said Ruth.

And there we went, till next morning, after that huge flatboatman's breakfast, out onto the winter water we did go, putting the jonboat down into the dark cold January waters of Pembroke Creek, whose mouth really forms Edenton Bay, just upstream of the Old 17 bridge near the fish hatchery (and not too far from where a ten-year-old boy once chased me around, when I'd stopped at his father's vegetable stand, with a bonafide hog's head, shouting merrily, "*Head*

James Adams Floating Theater, docked in Edenton, about 1928

cheese! *Head* cheese!"), after paying our dollar into the rusty honor-system marina box on a pole.

Pembroke Creek is one of the mossiest places in eastern North Carolina—right up there with Merchants Millpond just north in even swampier Gates County, Brock's Millpond at Trenton on N.C. 58, and Greenfield Gardens in Wilmington—its cypress margins downright and absolutely shaggy with the stuff. In and among all the graybearded forest we found this midwinter congress of birds: cedar waxwings in flocks, a downy woodpecker, flickers, a white-headed nuthatch, kingfishers, a little grebe, mallards, cardinals, herring gulls, four great blue herons at once. Following Pembroke to its headwaters in Pollock Swamp, we went two bridges past the U.S. 17 Bypass bridge, past well-worn river cottages and far enough so that our old Ted Williams outboard would only churn mud and cavitate.

Then we spun downstream, out into the broad, still cove, onto the shining waters where the Albemarle Sound meets Edenton just a mile or two east of the mouth of the Chowan River. From the water the ancient town seemed to be floating before us, the old Georgian courthouse at the head of its green, the fixed cannon aimed out over the water, the double-piazzaed homestead, some sort of colonial dream made manifest. Those old French cannon at the harborside—

dredged up from out of the bay—might never fire again, but what a thunderclap over the cove they could make. Now the port welcomed sailors no more threatening than the middle-aged Connecticut cruising couple I met here another time, fresh back from a year's stint of white-collar panhandling in the Carribean (he preached to native populations, apparently from the deck of the boat, while his wife passed a collection plate amongst them, the both of them also doing sail repairs for pay and alleging they never worried about money running out because "the Lord'll figure it out").

Ann and I circled the harbor several times on this gray mistless morning and made it our own. Two great blue herons—one in the shallows, one atop a cypress—that we had passed on the way down into Edenton Bay were still in place when we cruised back upstream for the landing, and we slowed to watch them in all their statued grace.

We took them with us, and have them yet.

There you go.

Like Jove's locks awry,
Long Muscadines
Rich-wreathe the spacious
foreheads of great pines,
And breathe ambrosial
passion from their vines.
—Sidney Lanier, "Corn," 1874

Scuppernong

Around the Albemarle

"I love eastern Carolina," the architectural historian Catherine Bishir once exclaimed to me, adding, "There's just so much *blood* in the dirt."

Yes, there is, I thought, and in Tyrrell County, along the Scuppernong and Alligator Rivers where Spruills and Midyetts have long lived, commingled, and begat, no small sum of it is mine.

A few latter-day Spruills were still quite alive and well there when I was small, and at least one is yet—my cousin Virginia, who carried me to a freshwater crab-boil one blithe warm April day not too long ago out at Fort Landing, where Alligator Creek meets Alligator River and both meet the Albemarle Sound. On the way we searched the piney woods for the old grave slabs of my six-greats grandfather Hezekiah, who raised the Revolutionary regiment for Tyrrell and went off to be a colonel for George Washington, and his wife Rodah, who stayed home and raised the family. Not finding their dust and clay in an old field now thick with eighty-year-old pines, Virginia and I pressed on to the water, where we would find them in spirit and commune with them one and all—Spruills, Moores, Yerbys, Midyetts—at Willy and Feather Phillips's Fort Landing deck, all of us banging open and picking Willy's catch of Alligator River freshwater crabs, like a flight of gulls feeding over a gull-rock, the dark juniper water frothing from the springtime breeze in the two-mile bay just beyond us.

From the early 1950s I dimly recall the two old bachelor brothers, my great-uncles Paul and Phil Spruill. Uncle Phil was in the timber trade, a cruiser who came home when he was going blind in the 1930s and who ran a popcorn and peanut shop in the lobby of the Columbia Theatre for twenty years. Uncle Paul looked after him, helping him with the little shop, and it was Paul, a handicrafter of sorts, who made for me one of the gems of my boyhood: a small wooden wheelbarrow painted as deep a green as the coastal Bermuda pasture grass that grows so thick in the down-east fields.

The real live wire of the Scuppernong Spruills, though, was their expansive and plain-spoken sister, our great-aunt Catherine, an excellent cook who at the family table peddled her wares happily, unself-consciously:

"Have you had a biscuit? Good, then have another one—my, they *are* delicious!"

Years later, as my aging grandfather grew increasingly preoccupied with religion, Aunt Catherine once asked rhetorically of a roomful of family: "Since when did Jule get so *be-Jesus* on us?" It was Catherine who had gone grave-traipsing with an uncle of mine a generation before cousin Virginia and I went on the same exploit, Catherine who had actually rediscovered the lost last resting place of Rodah and the colonel.

And it was Catherine's son Thomas—future sheriff of the swampy county of Tyrrell (he would be the fourth Tyrrell sheriff the family has produced) and a direct descendant of the man who built the first bridge across the Scuppernong—who had in his mother's forthright manner so clearly upheld his and his community's cheerful isolationism when he declared with no shortage of sound-side brogue, "Oi don't care if they burn the bridge over Scuppernong River and tear it down, just so long as Oi'm on *this* soide!" As a small boy, Thomas once showed up at the hardware store with his pant's fly unbuttoned and his small pendant exposed. One of the men there advised him, "You bout to lose something, Thomas." Recalling this for his mother and father and sister Virginia later that day, when they asked him what he had done, Thomas declared with a grave dignity: "Oi put moi hands ahoind me and oi not say a word."

Well I remember being put upstairs to nap during visits there, and getting down upon the bedroom floor, lying on the rug with my ear cocked by an open iron floor register that gave me a purchase on the older family in the living room below. Theirs was the old tribal entertainment, the telling and tireless retelling of family incident and moment, the endless sifting of ash and bone. I could hear them, and what they said to the boy at the heat grate above was this:

We were Godfrey Spruill's people, children of the swamps and sounds, all of us sprung from the west Scot surgeon who made his way after the Restoration first to Tidewater Virginia, then in the 1690s to Bull Bay and the Scuppernong jungle where the black river met the Sea of Roanoke, the broad Albemarle Sound. Heart's Delight, he called this country, and he set his family up on a plantation named the Round About. Whether or not he was the colony's first physician, Godfrey Spruill was certainly on constant call over a wide waterine route. He made it through the vicious Tuscarora Wars of the 1710s and lived to commiserate with the survivors at Fort Landing who lamented the twenty Alligator River colonists killed or carried off by the Mattamuskeets and the Coree Indians. Doctor Spruill left progeny to build the bridge over the Scuppernong that still bears the family's name, to sheriff the county (in the 1770s, 1830s, and 1960s), to raise that regiment for Tyrrell in the Revolution. One April session of North Carolina's Provincial Congress in Halifax specifically directed my great-great-great-great-great-great grandfather Hezekiah to procure and purchase firearms, to maintain and repair all swords, dirks, and pistols in consideration of the "defenceless state of the sea coast of this province."

Before the Revolution was even fully accomplished, though, Colonel Hezekiah sold out his share of the Round About in 1781 and moved across the county to the north shore of Little Alligator Creek, where a branch of family would stay for a century; here the colonel's granddaughter would marry his grand-nephew, uniting cousinry in marriage, and produce the last of the antebellum Spruills. The family of Benjamin and Nancy Midyett Spruill somehow controverted the fate of their failed rebel nation and did better *after* the Civil War than before, their split juniper-rail fence still intact, their black labor force staying on in the same quarter houses as before but now cropping on shares, and their holdings on the ground increased in 1873 by a thousand acres of farm under the name:

Free and Easy.

This was the same year lumberman Moore came to the South from Maryland, to Tyrrell in the employ of the entrepreneurial Elizabeth City engineer Harry Greenleaf (he who built the railroad across the Albemarle and Pamlico peninsula and who resurveyed William Byrd's Virginia and Carolina boundary line and who later, in '01, led the outraged citizenry during the vigilante search for Pasquotank's Beautiful Nell Cropsey), Greenleaf having an interest in Alligator timber. And it was Moore's wife Priscilla who asked the abiding familial question—though she doubtless from that first asking and Lord knows how many more never got the answer she wanted, or needed, for she up and moved the Moores out of Alligator and Fort Landing and north to Edenton, to *town*, after only five years in Tyrrell; for even though the Spruills had taken an empathetic pity on the Moore family living down in the Old Cove slab camp and had built them a two-story clapboard home that, though abandoned, still stands which claim cannot be made of any other Spruill dwelling place in eastern Tyrrell, if any free-and-easy life existed there, Priscilla Moore did not find it and so goes down in the ledgers asking of Sound Country Carolina:

What sort of place?

Askúponong.

The sort of place, said this Southern Algonquian word, where the sweet bay, or bay laurel, or swamp laurel, grew. The beautiful black winding river of my ancient cousins and great-greats got its name from a word that like a stream shifted over the years: Cascoponung in 1733, Cuscopang in 1788, till it was Scuppernong at last. Once, in this variant vein, there was a spot on the frontier here called Scogalong, where an Anglican circuit-rider, or more probably a circuit-sailor, found fault with profligate parishioners who brought their rum jugs to church. Now there are Scuppernong townships in the two counties—Washington and Tyrrell—that adjoin along the river, a community called Scuppernong no bigger than a blink on u.s. 64, and a great Scuppernong Lake (Lake Phelps since 1775) several miles to the south, the lake that overwinters thousands of Tundra swans and that has yielded from its shallow depths Indian cypress dugout canoes many hundreds of years old. But it was yet another scuppernong that once made the word one of the best known in the whole American language, and this was the scuppernong that graced all these riverine, estuarine plains, the one I had known since before memory could remember, the sweet and tough-hulled bronzy-green grape that grew vining and twining all through the coastal plain and that drew me back twenty-odd years ago, deep into and all over the Carolina east, and confirmed me forever as a son of the Sound Country.

One summer day in 1973, on the way back up to town from the log woods at Big Flatty Creek in south Pasquotank, I stopped and looked in on the Hollowells at Bay Side. Frank Hollowell, a retired Navy commander, was grandson of the man who in the 1870s imported the *soja*, or soy, bean, not only to this Pasquotank River plantation but to this part of the world as well. Now most of Bay Side took the form of airstrips and hangars for the Elizabeth City Coast Guard Air Station, from which emanate all air-rescue efforts for ships foundering or lost in middle Atlantic waters. But the old plantation house still stood in good order, toward the front of a twenty-acre triangle of pines the Hollowells had held onto when they sold the farm to the federal government. In years to come, the Las Vegas singer Wayne Newton would buy the place from the commander, rip down the bramble of honeysuckle and crêpe myrtle that shielded house from road, and install ordinary brick pillars and a graceless iron gate in place of the curtain of green, then eventually sell out himself to a trucker also from Vegas.

Scuppernongs, Perquimans County, October 1996

This day in '73, though, was well before Wayne. The commander, a big, ready man, was afield across the highway from Bay Side, moving creosote poles around with a tractor. When I walked his way and hailed him and asked what he was about, he said:

"Putting in scuppernongs!"

"Scuppernongs?"

"Yes sir, scuppernong grapes—we're going to have a vineyard here—it's a coming thing."

Just then, though, the Hollowell vineyard was merely poles on the ground, and he explained to me how the grapes would grow, in long parallel lines with now a vine, now a pole supporting the strands of wire the grapes were trained up to, then another vine, then pole—so that it was vine or pole every ten feet.

"Who's gonna *pick* all these scuppernongs?" I asked.

"Machine," said the commander. "Oh, no, you'd never get enough manpower nowadays to deal with all this. There're some equipment builders over outside of Edenton who're gonna build a harvester, one that'll straddle these lines and shake the grapes off. You oughta go see them."

And so I did. The Woods, several brothers who as DARF (Dairymen Agriculturalists Ranchers Farmers) normally manufactured hayrakes with red frames and bright yellow spiked wheels, had hatched a plan to mass-produce grape harvesters. They had scuppernongs themselves, even had a winery in mind, and, with the only commercial harvester then available running thirty thousand dollars and still dropping a quart of grapes on the ground every time it moved past a vine or pole, they thought they could do better.

"We got a prototype," Ben Wood told me at the Chowan DARF shed, and bragged on it. I looked around and, not seeing anything like what he had just described there on the grounds, I asked,

"Where? Can I see it?"

"Oh, sure, but it's not *here*," said Wood. "It's down with the man who designed it, Harry Sell, down in Brunswick County, just outside Southport. He's got forty acres of scuppernongs—you oughta go see *him*."

So I did that, too.

With me again was New Hampshireman John Foley, my hale, sandy-haired fellow-traveler who September the year before had come along and braved a week at Lake Drummond in the Great Dismal, who had shaken scuppernongs off canal-bank vines into our swamp canoe. With a hound named Jake we roared off into the east for a warm October week of viticulture and visitation.

We found Harry Sell, an energetic, bespectacled man of sixty-two, out running his harvester—a tobacco highboy customized for the grape trade with two auto transmissions in series so low-low speeds were possible—up and down the lines, straddling the strands of grapes and steel rods vibrating the vines. The table, what the grapes fell on, was the key to the machine, with a plastic sheet lying above a set of nylon bristles that could negotiate the alternating poles and vines without any grapes being lost.

"On first harvest," Sell said, once he stopped long enough to talk, "we couldn't get any nylon so we bought out Wilmington's broom stock. Every several rows we had to change thirty brooms. But we had no choice—once those grapes are ripe, you've *got* to pick."

Now, after liming and 14-0-14'ing and, in sandy soil, 3-9-18'ing his grape lands to get the 5.5 to 6 pH the vines demand, Sell and his son were bringing in not sheaves but boxes of scuppernongs at the rate of five tons an acre (with some of their nine-year-old vines putting out ten tons in an acre and a half), selling them for $325 a ton. What if the old Mother Vineyard winery had bolted Carolina, moved on to Richmond, and that was where their grapes were bound?

What if most all these grapes that broke dry and clean from the vines wound up as quick-ferment alcohol in a host of fortified wines? That was the market for our grand old native grape in 1973.

If Sell were a grape farmer now, he had not always been; his life's work was as an electrical engineer, and he most recently had kept the VHF radios up for the menhaden fleet's spotter planes. I recalled other Southportians who had worked the pogyboats—Robert Ruark's grandfather, the "Old Man," was a captain, and Ruark himself had been a spotter in the old crow's-nest days. That was Sell's arena, too, before he retired into vineyard mastering.

"*Retired!*" he said. "Never worked so hard in my life. There aren't enough hours in the day or days in the year to give scuppernongs the attention they need."

After half a day walking the lanes and studying and getting up close to the highboy as it rocked and trudged along, Foley and I were ready to leave Sell's loamy place, but I remembered to ask him: "Are you setting up a winery, like the Woods, to go along with all this?"

"Oh, I can make up to two hundred gallons a year, under the head-of-household law that lets you do that, not for sale but for your own use, the use of your family," Harry Sell said. "But a winery? No, I don't think so. I'll teach my son how to make good scuppernong wine, and if he wants a winery, then he can build one." Then the old pogy-spotter Harry Sell said,

"You boys stop by sometime after Christmas, I'll have some good dry scuppernong wine finished by then—I'll give you a bottle."

Twenty years later I found a scuppernong plantation in my own Spruill family, when one sunny April morning up in Perquimans County, the Indians' *land of beautiful women*, my eighty-odd-year-old distant cousin Jesse Perry and I went riding out into the Center Hill section of Perquimans, near the Suffolk Scarp as it comes on down from the Dismal Swamp. Everything was in bloom, once again the profuse fecundity of the coastal plain: phlox, azalea, buttercup, mustard, dogwood. . . . We passed a nursing calf on Chinquapin Road, a brown and white Hereford beside the road.

"This section in here," Jesse said slyly, "it was nicknamed Bootleg Alley."

We were bound for his blueberry and scuppernong plantation, his old grape arbors at the edge of Goodwin Mill Pond, a tupelo gum and cypress reserve. Once we reached it, Jesse drove through the old blueberries, some of them exploded out to twelve or fifteen feet in width and height, and the much smaller, younger bushes, driving us first to the experimental pine stand that he called his "conifer arboretum."

Jesse Perry had spent much of his life working in agriculture and forestry for a foundation all over Mexico and Central America, and now, at the edge of his berry and grape farm, he was also growing all sorts of conifers, some bright green, some dull, many of them from more equatorial climes than our own. Here was *Pinus tecunamanii*, named in honor of the last Indian king of Guatemala, who died in battle. "A pretty rare pine," Jesse said, allowing that his hundred-foot-long row of yard-tall trees was the only population in the United States. He had grown them from seed, but pine shoot weevils and pine tip moths got after them, and the tree that grows to a hundred feet in Guatemala was surely stunted here.

Another exotic tree was the meta-sequoia ("an ancient, ancient tree, before the sequoyahs, from China . . . closely related to the cypress"). The meta-sequoia was about fifteen feet tall, branched all out in a Christmas tree shape. Like those Jurassic pines in Australia, these trees were hidden, in China, way back inland, and till recently no one thought about them or even knew they were still alive. And he had a *Pinus ayacahuite*, one of the biggest trees Mexico, a tall, mountain model that throve just above the frost line, just barely surviving in Perquimans County. There was an Arizona cypress, grown out from a Christmas-tree cone, and a droopy, short-needle fir called Leyland cypress, whose seed Jesse had collected from one growing on the courthouse square in Hertford.

Beyond these trees, and beyond the black walnuts, Japanese oaks, and Chinese chestnuts, the lord of the manor was a native: an eighty-foot-tall, double-trunked yellow poplar that had split nicely about fifteen feet off the ground and made of itself a gigantic tuning fork. We ambled on by it, along the marge of the swamp, whose natural levee keeps all these old scuppernongs from getting their feet too wet. Jesse Perry was in the habit, increasingly, he implied, of taking his work breaks over here beside the swamp and just plain staring into it.

He said he had watched fish mate, then spawn in the swamp right here a couple days earlier, some ponderous, slow-moving fish. "Sitting right here, kept seeing this swirl in the water . . . I really think there's a sort of fantastic . . . you see lots of little tiny things that all add up . . . here's a real genuine coastal wetland here, occasionally'll dry up, but that's about the way it looks most of the time . . . a foot of water, course the mud'll go down two or three feet . . . I think there's so much life going on in that kind of stuff there, I don't think you can even conceive of all the things that happen there. Minute little microscopic animal life right on up to that great big fish spawning. Then there's the otter come to get the fish. Beaver, muskrat. Every now and then I come in, the pond's muddy, there's only one answer, somebody's burrowing up under that hollow bank over there. Sure—there's no flow of water in there, it's seeps. Owls hunt the muskrats. And there's a family of hawks. Every year big red-tail hawks raise a brood. I think of this whole area as kind of my little preserve, and the boys have that feeling, too, Jesse, Robert, they love it."

"The place has that feel," I agreed.

"Does it?"

"Yeah, oh, yeah."

"Well, it ought to show, after a while."

And it has been a while, nearly a half a century, that the Perrys have been at it out here. "I spect this is one of the oldest commercial scuppernong vineyards in North Carolina now, that is, planted for commercial business," Jesse Perry said. "The state's full of old, old vines, but I don't know of an older one than this. . . . These are old, still got a few of the old scuppernong male vines I had to plant in there to pollinate the female vines, of course, and they're a rambunctious plant, just grows wild, and all it does is bear pollen. But these things here are all self-fertile.

"I haven't looked into the history of the scuppernong commercial vineyards, but I think this is probably one of the oldest . . . '48, '49, and what are we, '93? I don't know of anything any older, tell you the truth. There's about two acres of these really older ones. And then three acres over here, good five acres here. And I planted em all."

It was and always had been a job of work, and, though he loved it, his decision to plant this particular vine was not the least bit sentimental. "Scuppernong grapes—I planted em cause they're native to the area. They were here a hundred thousand years ago, whenever they began to evolve, on the coastal plain of North Carolina. They've had to survive, that's why they're here right now. They built in that genetic resistance to diseases, to fungi, to insects, to anything you can name, or they wouldn't be here. So I thought, 'Perry, plant em, you don't have to be there to spray em, they're gonna survive, you give em minimum care, nothin's gonna kill em off, and that's the way it's worked since 1948, '49. Let's go over there, I can show you some of the old scuppernong vines. Look, there's one," he said, pointing at a vine nearly a half a foot in diameter.

"Concord grapes—be gone five, ten years," said the organic vineyard keeper. "Less you spray em."

There were bumblebees everywhere, flying drunkenly around the blueberries after nosing into the flowers with their long proboscises to drink; honeybees, with their shorter, smaller rigs, had to drill through the base of the berry flowers to get nectar, doing the fruit no harm in the process, I learned.

What else did my cousin have strewn and grown about his grounds? The hind-end of a Sealtest cooler truck, cherry and pear trees, hollies, a few broken-down beehives—"bears tore em up," Jesse said. "Came down out of the Great Dismal Swamp and got em." Several palmettos of a variety cold-resistant enough to grow this far north. A '77 pickup that had trucked to Mexico and back. A red-blossomed tree that turned out to be an Ohio buckeye.

Jesse Perry's scuppernong vineyard, Perquimans County, October 1996

Yellow jasmine was everywhere, too, its light lemon scent easy on the spring air. We crossed the gravel road to another patch of Perry's ground, and he told me of yet another Jesse Perry, his "way-back" ancestor who had a pre-Revolutionary gristmill and pond above Goodwin Mill Pond called Perry's Millpond, such being the poverty of our nomenclature, as Thoreau complained famously when he attacked Flint's Pond in *Walden*. It was fine with me, though, and with the cousins Jesse. He said that when the state fixed the road and put in a bridge, the workers dug out timbers from the old Perry mill, big hunks of strut and support for the ancient and long-collapsed structure, put together, as Jesse said, "with great big old wooden pins." Then, somehow, without blasting the mucky land into unrecognizable form or oblivion as it moved two centuries of debris, the dozer uncovered some low sites, depressions. Jesse Perry, the current one, declared energetically: "Sure as we're sitting here it's an old Indian site—they were coming here for this clay." Though he has never come across a complete piece, since that excavation he has found handfuls of potsherds and bowl fragments.

We jumped a deer as we turned up a little lane. A bit into the woods there was a hundred-yard-long pond and a lovely line of pines alongside it, where Perry regularly sees more deer, quail, fox, occasionally beaver. This was Perry's "Bobby Chappell land," some more nomenclatural specificity to spite Thoreau. In buying it, Jesse Perry had made a promise about an old family graveyard with wooden crosses in these woods to Mrs. Chappell.

"'Mister Perry,'" she said, "'you're not gonna clear up the cemetery, are you?'

"I said, 'No, Missus Chappell, I wouldn't bother it.'

"And she said, 'Oh, that's fine, please don't touch it, just leave it there.' And I did."

We parked Jesse's truck and walked, and I saw on one of the white-oak posts supporting an old utility shed two small heads: one was the rubber head of a child's doll baby, the other a concrete lion's head.

"Weird totem pole," I said.

"Yeah," Jesse Perry said proudly. "The lion's head came from, of all places, Lake Como, in Italy. I found it in a old abandoned building there, part of the Villa Servalone that the Rockefeller Foundation inherited, and I was sent over there to kind of get the thing in shape. Spent about three months there.

"I found that thing, kind of smuggled it away . . . cause I thought it was fascinating."

"How bout the doll-baby head?" I asked.

"Oh, the doll-baby head, I don't know where I got that. I thought, I'm gon put it up there, cause the eyes would open and close and make it look like sort of a voodoo post, maybe it'd keep some of the boys from out of here—you know, they'd get kind of scared, or superstitious, no foolin! And a number of times I'd come back, somebody'd shot two, three bullet holes through the lion's head . . . but they haven't shot the doll's head yet."

"Scared to," I said.

"I kinda think so."

"Might put the evil eye on em."

"That's what I put it back here for—you see, one day it's closed, the other it's open," Jesse Perry said, then laughed. "Why not, why not?"

The old man really did have a fine tie into the real voodoo, the sweet mysteries of the universe, whether they involved the literal sugar of his scuppernongs (he had last season climbed atop a small tin-roof shed near his Sealtest cooler and picked thirty pounds of grapes in an hour or so, saying it would have gone more quickly if he hadn't been eating them just as eagerly as the raccoons that came in all the time from the Goodwin Mill Pond swamp and raided his vines) and blueberries or the procreative attractions that for other species, like those slow-moving fish he'd recently watched mating in the swamp pond itself, musked and scented the waters and made them sloughs of sex and survival of species. He had an appreciative eye for vitality, to which the jungled profusion of his plantation and wooded compound was ready, abundant evidence.

As we ambled about the Bobby Chappell land, cousin Jesse suddenly stopped, bent his back a bit, and pointed at an inch-tall shoot at the side of the pine-straw road. "Looka that little scuppernong grape," he said. "Looka there—idn't that marvelous!"

"Oh," I said, bending down to it, touching it. "It's coming off a vine."

"I didn't see that either—*hah!*"

"Yeah, here's the vine," I said, brushing pine straw away from it.

"That's what I was talking about, back out there in the vineyard," he said. "This is survival, man! Everybody drives on it, walks on it—but *whoo-hoo!*"

"Hundred thousand years," I said, repeating my elderly cousin's salute to the muscadine sport.

"Or more," said Jesse Perry, "or more."

A bottle of good scuppernong—Harry Sell's promise to Foley and me way back in Brunswick County in the early seventies—was no mean offer in our part of the world. We have, after all, been vinting the best for well over two centuries.

John Brickell, the Irish doctor who borrowed liberally from John Lawson's work and further popularized Lawson's ebullient claims about North Carolina, in 1737 wrote of our vineyards that "I have seen a small one at Bath-Town and another at *Neus*, of the White Grape. . . . I have drank the wine it produced, which was exceeding good." Other immigrants to Carolina took notice— Samuel Huntington Perkins, a Yale graduate on his way to tutor the young plantation misses at Lake Landing on the southeastern shore of Lake Mattamuskeet, arrived at Roanoke Island on the last Sunday in October of 1817: "Landed on the small & barren island of Rhoanoke," he wrote in his diary. Two days later his opinion of the island had improved: "I spend my time here more agreeably than could be expected. The Island is 10 miles long, & 2 broad. It abounds in Deer, Racoons, & Possum. The fig & grape here arrive to perfection. The inhabitants supply themselves with good wine, but manufacture little or none for exportation." Thirty years later another tutor, the Northern novelist George Higby Throop, in his book *Nag's Head* also praised a Roanoke scuppernong "'grapery,' underneath which you can stand and pluck the most delicious clusters until your appetite is cloyed with them."

Word got out, and, according to scholar Clarence Gohdes, so profusely did the hog's-eye-sized grape—long known as the Roanoke because it grew well on the oft-visited Lost Colony island and as the Big White Grape—grow around Scuppernong River that by 1810 it had taken the name of both river and region and, so named, gone forward into the world. Thomas Jefferson got wind of the scuppernong bouquet and in June of 1823 ordered through a Plymouth factor named Cox a thirty-gallon barrel of "the pure juice of the grape." By 1840, North Carolina was the premier wine-making state in America, and the largest vineyard here was Preacher Sidney Weller's six-acre farm at Brinkleyville in Halifax County. Weller, who had earlier been a mulberry tree seller during the silk-hope bubble of the late 1830s and early 1840s, got anywhere from $1 to $4 a gallon for his 1848 scuppernong.

An Edgecombe County family named Garrett bought the Weller vineyards just after the Civil War, recasting the operation as the Ringwood Wine Company, and the U.S. Department of Agriculture reported in 1871 that Ringwood Wine had 8,000 scuppernong vines. At least one member of this tribe wanted more—Paul Garrett, an unrivaled salesman for the family, later lit out on his own after an internecine dispute, set up a competing business, and eventually bought the rival family firm. He operated his plant at Chockoyotte, near Weldon, the rail and canal town at the rapids of the middle Roanoke River, and once in a drive for more raw material created a poor-boy boom down around Vineland (now Whiteville) when he offered through a local vintner to buy anyone's scuppernongs at fifty cents a bushel.

"I am swamped," the vintner telegraphed Garrett, telling him how the narrow lane into his Vineland farm was jammed by carts and wagons, each hauling one to three bushels.

Garrett, a man of prodigious energy and viticultural skill, won a prize in Paris for scuppernong wine; in 1904, a sparkling scuppernong called Paul Garrett's Special Champagne took top honors at St. Louis's Louisiana Purchase Exposition. Within a few years, wrote Gohdes, Garrett's sweet white Virginia Dare wine was "the most popular vinous drink of the United States." Garrett also produced a dry scuppernong wine called Minnehaha and a red Virginia Dare named Pocahontas, and the man whose operation at the time of Prohibition included seventeen plants from coast to coast, with a total ten-million-gallon capacity, was not shy about providing his customers this brute concoction of his wares, sort of a Sound Country sangria:

ROANOKE PUNCH
Juice of 10 strained lemons and 8 strained oranges
A pineapple, cut into pieces
2 qts Garrett's First Families of Virginia claret
2 qts Virginia Dare

Polish farm buyers with agent at St. Helena Vineyard, Pender County, 1914

2 qts Pocahontas
1 gal cold tea

along with this modest, simple advice: "Let stand on ice 4 hrs."

I have never made Roanoke Punch, not yet anyhow, but I did go back to Harry Sell's early in 1974 with John Foley, as Sell had bidden us. We were on a daytrip to Bald Head Island, once a haven for wild-hog legions and just then being opened up for second-home development by a group that had an antique colonizing and profiteering name about itself—Carolina Cape Fear—and that soon went bankrupt, leaving the exclusivity-appealing and profit-reaping to someone else. But before we caught the runabout to cross the broad bay from Southport to the back creek landing, we ate a middle-of-the-day dinner at the Sells' house.

Scuppernong wine, dry, was among the main courses, along with greens, roasted chicken, and corn bread. Harry Sell talked on about how there was always something to do around a vineyard, told us that they'd been pruning till just after Christmas. Sell said he and his son Harry Jr. and their first mate Elmer Sellers used to prune with hand equipment. "We did as much work in two hours before lunch as we did in four hours after. We could only work in forty-five-degree or better weather because you couldn't work with gloves on. I finally worked it out on the scales, and I figured we were using two-foot tons of energy per hour working those hand pruners. Damn right, we were shot at 5:00 P.M."

He had once thought he could beat the arthritic seizing-up that attended long days of work with those hand loppers, by designing a hand-held electric pruner whose cutting edge was a diminutive skill-saw blade, a two- or three-inch blade spinning at 2,400 rpm.

"That first day we had our new pruner going," Sell said, "we thought we'd changed the world! Went through those vines like Sherman through Georgia . . . effortless. Just knew we had it made then. We got back to the house that evening, started itching, like to drove us crazy, skin all red, welts, you know."

"What was it?" I said.

"Tannic acid," he said. "That little disc of a saw blade on the pruner was all the time throwing off this real fine powder and mist as it cut through those vines, and they're full of tannic acid. Never occurred to us that might happen, so all day long we were just soaking it up. Thought I'd die. One day's all we ever used *that* device. Now what engineer would have ever seen that on the drawing board? We're using a 125-pound-pressure pneumatic pruner now, and that's a great improvement. Come on, let me show you my wine cellar."

Out in the garage, the Sells had a gang of boxes full of green, unlabeled wine bottles. He gave us one apiece, wished us well, and told us that the *next* time we dropped by he hoped to have a collection of scuppernong champagne, and said he looked forward to sharing some of that batch with us. I brought the Brunswick County bottle back to Chapel Hill, saved it and saved it for months awaiting just the right moment to uncork and decant it, but before that time arrived, a visiting musician staying at my home, whom I never saw during his stay, went searching for a nightcap and, finding nothing in the cabinet but the scuppernong wine, opened it (without a corkscrew, too, so that when I came back home I found the half-drunk bottle sitting in my refrigerator, its cork broken off and punched down into it, floating in the literal drink along with a fragment of the pencil he had used to batter-ram it in) and left it flatter than the coastal plain.

There is another bottle in the Sound Country of eastern Carolina somewhere still, and I am still on a grand tour in search of it and the note or scroll or elixir within it that answers the cry *What sort of place?*, in unending search of mythical Mother Vineyard and True Vine too, the old vines that twine and my family's old times, whether woven and worn into or cast off and lost somewhere in this broad tabled land, this vast stretch of sandy, loamy, blue-marled earth, the endless farmsteads and forests and wetlands and the many waters that drain them. Nor should it ever have surprised me to have been pulled back down to these old familiar grounds, and by a vine.

In my great-aunt Jennie's backyard in Elizabeth City, below the chimney that the cannonball pierced when Yankees shelled our town from the Pasquotank River, there was a small scuppernong arbor and in its delicious dimness a swing where we children first began to inscribe our small arcs on the world. And over the river and down the sound, I remember the only elevated point on the mile-wide desert plain between Kitty Hawk's sea beach and its sound-side woods was a sand mound, perhaps twenty feet tall, forty feet long, and twenty or thirty feet thick—in season it was absolutely green with honeysuckle and Virginia creeper and wild grapevine, and stood out like an emerald against a carpet of bright sand. This was our summer land in the 1950s and '60s, and my Lamborn cousins and I climbed and clambered all over the wild-vine hill, drank the lilliputian servings of honeysuckle, and in Indian Summer ate our fill of scuppernongs and had us a prize place that we believed was all our own.

How I used to lie in my bunk bed on the western end of our small white cottage at Kitty Hawk watching the grapevine hill show up in faraway silhouette as heat lightning lit the night sky, knowing somehow though never forming the thought that I was among Sir Walter Ralegh's latter-day colonists, and that the ruby and silver and gold he sought but never found had been here all along and were here yet, presenting themselves each fall in wild vineyards all across the realm and hanging from lianas that long ago tied me with a touch to the wild and wondrous Sound Country earth.

Past the barnacled carcass of an oyster boat

The water opens a smooth new sheet.

We pick up speed on a dead reckon across the bay

Red nuns nodding astern.

—Peter Makuck, "Phantoms at Swan Quarter," 1987

Hulls

· ·

In a 1585 watercolor, artist and future Carolina governor John White painted our coastal Indians in what he called "The manner of their fishing." White's artwork features a fine line of fish-net-stakes running out into the wide water from a pound net, making it all look quite like Core Sound near Atlantic today. A snail and a horseshoe crab are caught forever in the lower part of the painting, and in the shallows of the distance, Indian men are at work trying to gig flounder or some hammerhead something. In the foreground are four Indians in "A Cannow," a dugout, one of them paddling or poling, another sweeping the shallow bottom with what must be a clam rake, and two of them huddled at the craft's center just fore and aft of a live fire.

It was an aboriginal sight White captured more than four hundred summers ago, as well he must have imagined and as we know well today. From the mucky, murky bottom of Lake Phelps, near the headwaters of the Scuppernong River, in very recent years have been raised the oldest hulls in the history of our state, the storied Lake Phelps canoes, cypress dugouts ranging in age from two hundred to two thousand years old. These old Indian boats from Scuppernong Lake, as Lake Phelps was once known, tell a Sound Country secret, albeit an open one, to wit:

No craft is so suited to the thousands upon thousands of our shallow-water acres as the canoe—whether dugout or molded—or the flat-bottomed skiff or the sailboat of scant draft and perhaps with no keel, or perhaps with a dagger-board that one can pull up, a centerboard that one can crank. Round-sterned sharpies, brought into our waters by Rhode Islander George Ives in 1875; dead-rise Carolina spritsail skiffs; Roanoke Island shad boats with their high-flying topsails, built by men named Creef and Dough—these were the shallow-draft boats our fishermen once sailed to set the nets, check the crab pots, tong and dredge the oysters, rake the clams, and haul in fish and shellfish by the half-ton to three-ton load.

So it is that all over the Carolina east there are olive-drab jonboats, some with sides high enough to take substantial chop near an inlet or from a sudden blow such as our rough open waters often offer, and old skiffs with sharp, pointed prows and snub-nosed fiberglass bateaus. In down-east Carteret County, the vast pine-scrub savannas and marshy marineland east of Punchy's Corner and the North River bridge on u.s. 70, there is hardly a yard that doesn't have a sixteen- to twenty-foot flat-bottomed skiff, or several, set out in it. Our near-year-round-barefoot friend David Hill from Atlantic just a few seasons ago built seventy or eighty flat-bottomed fiberglass craft with motors set up to jet-propel them over the top—Core Sound Skimmers, he called them. Honoring the same principle and hull design, though with far less propulsion, Ann's brother Tad once took to the waters of Nelson's Bay, off Core Sound at Sea Level, in a six-foot concrete-mixing tray—Pat Kindell looked out the window and saw her neo–native American son, a sailor of fairly tender years, floating all too merrily out on the Drum Inlet tide.

The Scuppernong dugouts tell one piece of a haunting, mysterious, and mul-tifaceted tale, a story told too by the *Scuppernong*, a schooner built in the mid-nineteenth century in Elizabeth City which, while carrying live oak timbers for a Confederate shipyard at Deep Creek, Virginia, was in 1862 burned and sunk by Union troops at Indiantown Creek in Currituck, and by the ancient Trent River ferry-flat raised a few years ago near New Bern. It is a story shared by the un-raised sunken ships *Three Friends* (1900) and *Anne Comber* (1908) and *Mary J. Haynie* (1921), which all went down in Pamlico Sound inside Ocracoke Inlet, and by the *Forrest*, the *Black Warrior*, the *Sea Bird*, and the *Fanny*, all of them Confederate, all of them dead in the black Pasquotank waters and sunk under federal fire when Elizabeth City fell in early 1862, and by the *Appomattox*, just thereafter burned by the Rebels at South Mills when they found it two inches too large for the Dismal Swamp Canal locks. Shared too by the *Lulu M. Quillin* (1917), which went down in Pamlico Sound near Avon, and by the *Tamarack* (1921), which sank within the Pea Island National Wildlife Refuge between Oregon Inlet and Rodanthe. And these are but a few of the *named* boats and ships—

there are far more whose owners, histories, registries are writ only upon the Sound Country waters 'neath which they rest, and rare is the reach of water here that is not marked on navigational charts by the symbol for wreck, an oval-bordered, stitched skeletal expression, flat and noncommittal but appearing with a chilling near-regularity nonetheless.

Here lies a vast and varied phantom fleet, a great navy of the night that we shall see arisen, whole and afloat, only at that Day of Judgment when all the waters, the inland seas, and the deep and mighty oceans alike give up their dead: the women and the men and the children, and too the valuables and treasures the world has gone on just fine without for lo these decades or centuries since the crafts that once carried them all sank and settled absolutely here in our creeks, our rivers, and our sounds.

Who awaits that day? Who seeks to hurry it? And what is the manner of *their* fishing?

It was late afternoon in early February, and there was a light midday snow hanging in the Spanish moss of the Sound Country. The wind was up to thirty miles an hour when I drove over the Wright Brothers Bridge, and the whitecaps were ripping swiftly where the Currituck meets the Albemarle. The frothing waters and the concrete bridge rail and the sound-side beaches miles to the north were all that was light in this world, for the deep gray-green of the sounds melded with the dark gray woods and leaden sky above and beyond. A few miles south, I parked my station wagon at a pine thicket across from the closed-up amusement park (Dowdy's, where in the long-gone summers my Lamborn cousins and I once enjoyed the stationary roll and low heights of a diminutive Ferris wheel and learned our first driving on Dowdy's go-carts) and roamed some high sandhills just seaward of the Nags Head Woods for an hour. The hills were not long ones like Jockey's Ridge a mile south, but fat, squat teapot dunes. I didn't realize how fast the land was rising till I made a ridge about a half a mile back off the road, U.S. 158. Then I turned and gazed down on the pine thicket and felt the gale wind blowing out of the Northeast at the end of this gray day. Beyond the thicket and the bunches of stick buildings, the ocean was gray-green, with whitecaps breaking all over it in a fury. For the first time in many years Nags Head did not look overbuilt and new to me; it was an old place, sagging into the sea, and I stood and saw it that way but only for a moment before I went racing back down the field of dunes to get out of the cold, bitter wind.

Just before dark as a winter rain came on, I drove over the great plains of Roanoke Island marsh south of Manteo and called on a couple in Wanchese, the Silvers, who took me in like the eastern pilgrim I was. She was Nancy Wood Foreman (of the Elizabeth City Foremans descended from Clay Foreman of Pike

County, Illinois, one of the Yankees who like others named Kramer, or Roper, came down south after the Civil War and cut lowland timber and ran mills and made lumber and fortunes and families to pass it along to), and down here they called her Salt Marsh Wood because that was where she liked to spend her time. The table she set that night was a groaning Outer Banks board: squash, tomatoes, beans, all of it that Nancy Wood had put up from last summer's garden, an enormous loaf of homemade bread, a stew-pot full of sea bass from her husband's most recent ocean-fishing outing (thirty-six hours out, a $720 share for him plus whatever odd fish he wanted to take home), potatoes, salad, all in all a roaring coastal dinner.

These are the nights we really remember: not the quiet, stormless, and still nights of July or August when heat lightning is distant and even desultory, but the ones when the elements are at the door and in the timbers, when the low-soughing, joist-creaking winds say with certainty that the warmth of home and hearth is a grace and not a guarantee. Before Nancy Wood and her husband Winston (called Winky) sent me to bed in an unheated second-story room, where four quilts and a retriever named Jambo atop them kept me warm as a haystack, we sat in their front den with three hounds lying up against a gas heater, talking for hours of old hulls and where they lay hid from all but God and ingenious man.

There was the *Central America*, sunk somewhere off the Carolinas just before the Civil War with sixty million dollars worth of gold in her hold. "Some guys from Florida came to town," said Winky, a big bearded fellow of about thirty. "Hired my boat—I was one of the two crew—and we went out looking for this old sunken treasure instead of fishing. They had bottom plotters, all sorts of electronics, but then they ran out of money and we were searching on shares. I was gonna get one percent, but, hell, that was six hundred thousand for me if we found it!

"And we *did* find it! That radar printed out a hull shape and size, matched it perfectly and we went wild, all of us popping beers and talking about, well, I'm gonna spend mine on this and so on, till somebody called us ship to shore and something about that incoming radio signal jammed our bottom plotter and it all disappeared. Boy, you've never seen such a bunch of long-faced guys—because we'd drifted a mile or more by then, and the *coordinates* were on the screen with the hull and it was *all* gone—and nobody'd bothered to take a five-cent pencil and write em down on the cabin wall. We'd had gold fever, but we gave up after that and went back to fishing. But for about twenty minutes I knew what it was like to be worth six hundred grand!"

It was a grand tale—and the fact that the *Central America* turned up twelve years later, not somewhere off our very own and nearby Bodie Island but off

South Carolina's Sullivan's Island instead, hasn't tarnished that moment or story at all. Better, though, was Winky Silver's report of a more modest hull hunt.

"We went up Alligator River not long ago, up some creek, me and my buddy and this old man, looking for an old schooner, big one, two hundred feet, he'd worked on back in the thirties. Four-masted schooner that they'd taken out of trade in 1935 and sunk up in fresh juniper water where the worms wouldn't eat it till they could afford to raise her and put her into some kind of service again. And that old man swore he could go right to her, even after forty years. So we went huntin it and finally he says, 'Here! It's here!' and we stopped and ran an oar down—nothin. Moved all around, soundin—nothin. 'Well, maybe it's on up a little more,' he said. So we went on a bit more. Now this was shallow, and there wadn't supposed to be but maybe a couple feet of water over the deck—old cypress ship, or cedar, never rot, be good as new if we could just find it and raise it.

"A few minutes later he got excited again, said, 'Run your oar down about now!' and by now we just knew we weren't gonna find it—too much changes along a shoreline, the way trees grow out and all, and his memory, after forty years, just no way. But we stopped, moved over by the shore, and he said, 'Try it here' and after two or three thrusts of the oar,

"*Thunk!* We hit the deck of that old ship, and that old fellow rolled his pants up, went over the side of our boat, walked up one side of the deck and down the other, soundin *thunk, thunk, thunk* with that oar as he did. Couldn't believe it— forty years and he'd never been back there since the day they sank it.

"So now we got us a schooner to raise."

"How're you gonna do it?" I asked.

In the small Wanchese den we could not have been warmer or more comfortable. With all the shifts and swirls of the northeast winds off the Atlantic, it felt in that old frame house as if we might really be out on the water ourselves, old salts in some socked-in out-on-the-sound pilothouse between Wanchese and Wade Point. "They built this house backwards," Winky Silver looked around and remarked. "Walls first, then floors, out of old ship's timbers.

"Raise that schooner? Not sure—we know we got to pump it out, cause it's filled with silt after all that time. But then how you float a waterlogged hull, I don't know, I mean, in some way we can *afford* to. We've thought about all kinds of flotation—you won't believe our latest idea."

"What is it?"

"Ping-pong balls," Silver said.

"You're not kidding," I said.

"No, no. Thing is, it'd take an awful lot of em, don't you reckon?"

I reckoned it would, and as it was late and that was enough speculation, we turned in—Silver to his wife Nancy, whose ancestors like mine sought and found a living in the big deep woods that thrive near all these wide waters, me to the crisp, cold room and the bed the dog would warm.

Next day was bright and brilliantly sunny, and I awoke, sat up, and looked out on the working waterfront and sun sparkling on Wanchese harbor, bejeweling it. Out in the yard was a billy goat as big as a cow, with its horns a faded blue from some Carolina fans' paint job a couple years earlier (Winky was an N.C. State man). On one side of the house was a Quonset hut that Winky had bought after the man who lived in it died; Winky put a couple of axles under it and hired a pair of winos to sit on top of the thing with sticks and poke the power and phone lines up out of the way as he hauled it from Manteo to Wanchese with a pickup truck. Behind the house was a large, caulked cinder-block tank with two thousand diamondback turtles in it that he'd caught out in the sound; there wouldn't be that many in the tank, he said, but it was a Chinese holiday in New York and they were all on a fast and since he sold the turtles to Chinese restaurants up there Winky had to hold them till the fasting was done. Lying all around were crab pots, crates, pallets, and boilers (which could be converted, he said, into gas tanks on workboats).

Then Winky Silver, the dogs, and I rode over Roanoke Sound and down over Oregon Inlet to Pea Island, where he had a boat tied up in the marge of Pamlico Sound and wanted to pump the rainwater out. Riding down N.C. 12, the thin, oft-flooded roadstrand on Hatteras Island, he said, "Keep your eyes on the roadside and maybe you'll see a pheasant." A minute later up one hopped, flapped its wings, then dropped back down into a brush pile. We stopped and waited to see if it would reappear, but down it stayed.

After walking and splooshing out in hip waders to his drowned skiff, Winky proceeded to bail it with a snazzy hand pump that looked like two different caliber bazookas, one inside the other, with an angled drain off the outer sleeve. I stood on the shore watching him work, watching as well some Canada geese swimming and feeding in the shallows, and I thought about the Alligator River schooner he'd found and about a distant mirror of that boat, another time and another schooner similarly secreted away.

On the day secessionist-agrarian Edmund Ruffin pulled the cannon lanyard and fired on Fort Sumter across Charleston harbor and started the Civil War, an Ocracoke ship owner and captain named Horatio Williams slipped his schooner *Paragon*—against the orders of the harbor master in Charleston—out into the ocean homeward bound. With a crew of two he sailed her up into Ocracoke Inlet, but went past his homeport and crossed Pamlico Sound, then sailed west across Albemarle, passing Bull Bay and entering Roanoke River. A half a day's sail upriver, Captain Williams told his crew what he was about, answering their

queries: "Sure we're sinking her. Nobody'll use the *Paragon* till the war's over."
He went below, chopped a hole in her hull, and sent her under to the tips of her
masts, burying her sails in the woods nearby. A year and a half after Appomattox they raised her, pontooned her with barrels, and hand-pumped the water
out of her hold. The *Paragon* was made of heart-red cedar, and she went straight
back into the coastal shipping trade.

Maybe that four-master of Winky Silver's is back on top of the water, too, and
no longer in the muck and mud below. Maybe the old man who found her again
sounding an Alligator River creek lived to see her raised, restored, whole, and
making good headway running before the wind. Maybe against her dark green
or black hull, on her stern, are the letters N A N C Y, and she makes port now in
Wanchese, now in Beaufort, now in Barbados far to the south, as she must have
many times when she hauled lumber down and brought molasses or blockade
rum back up in the really old days that were only yesterdays for the man with
rolled trousers and an oar for a cane. Maybe she is shallow-draft enough to wander the sounds and then go up into the big estuarine rivers—Roanoke, Pamlico,
Neuse—and maybe children used to daysailers and runabouts come down to
river-port wharves in Williamston and Little Washington and New Bern to mar-
vel at a sky full of sail, as tall a ship as we get in our waters these days, shouting:
"There she is, that's the *Nancy*! Sat up underwater in Alligator River forty years
and now here she is!" And the old-timers, too: "I hadn't seen one of these since,
hell, way before I can remember. Wonder if I ever saw this one somewhere, cain't
never tell . . . might of even shipped out on her sometime or nother."

Maybe, but I don't know. That windy February night was nearly twenty years
ago, and I have heard nary a word about that sunken hull since. But I can see her,
going outside at Oregon Inlet in the morning, crossing the bar late that day at
Beaufort Inlet, four sails moving steadily up the channel past Bird Shoal. A hungry eye can see a long way.

In less than half an hour Winky floated his skiff. The wind had shifted around
to the southwest, and under the bluest of Carolina skies the boat's prow now
looked into the breeze, the craft itself bobbing easily, cheerfully even, as if it were
unsinkable. When Winky came wading in, I asked him where a man could buy
a pump like that, and he said he didn't know, he had made this one himself out
of some pipes he had lying around. It figured. On the short walk back up to the
car, Winky Silver spotted a diamondback turtle in the reeds and picked it up,
laughing loudly as he exclaimed,

"One more for the Chinese, if they ever start eating again!"

Prowling the dark and ghostly dimension wherein dwell scores of perma-
nently decomissioned schooners and thousands of waterlogged skiffs is as fasci-

nating as staring with wonder into the volcanic remains of Pompeii and Hercu-laneum. In our realm we now study nautical archaeology at the state university in Greenville, on the Tar River, and we have a formal Underwater Archaeology Unit on this case down at Fort Fisher. Occasionally a purposeful cadre of diver-detectives, the mud puppies of Little Washington, helps the cause—their ex-ploits in the murky Pamlico, led by longtime dark-water diver Eddie Congleton, a few years ago found a 176-foot federal gunboat, the USS *Underwriter*, burned and sunk by Confederates in February 1864, and prize antique artifacts that in-cluded the first and only naval cannon carriage—an 1,800-pounder—ever found in North Carolina.

Late last year, in November 1996, salvagers up from Florida working in twenty feet of water on the old outer bar off Beaufort Inlet laid hands on what one of them, Mike Daniel, called "an encrusted ball of cannon, with coral growing on the top layers, and sea life, octopus, all around." Two large anchors, a 24-pound cannonball, and a foot-tall bronze bell with 1709 inscribed upon it convinced the salvagers they had discovered the shipwreck they had sought for eight years: a 200-ton, 40-gun vessel that foundered and fell into the Graveyard of the At-lantic in June 1718, the pirate Blackbeard's *Queen Anne's Revenge*.

Even so, the real story is of boats afloat, of boats and those who build them.

In the Green Swamp of Brunswick County, at least two craftsmen, Tommy Spivey and Dodo Clewis, in very recent memory were still hacking dugouts out of cypress logs, a solid tie to the first watercraft John White saw and drew here in the 1580s, sixteenth-century cousins of those two-thousand-year-old Scup-pernong Lake dugouts that were the hulls of the native Americans. On Bruns-wick's coast, near Bald Head where the Cape Fear River empties into the At-lantic, Allyon's 1526 Spanish colony built the first ship made by Europeans in America. Historian Hugh Lefler said that coastal Carolina shipbuilding was "ex-tensive in the early days," our forests providing white-oak frames and flooring, pines and cedars for masts and spars and yards, our live oak reputedly the source of the best ship trunnels in the world. For smaller craft, our two-masted "periaugers" were famous riverboats, and we put flatboat lighters to work mov-ing shingles out of the eastern swamps as well as getting cargo on and off ocean-going vessels in such places as the vanished port of Shell Castle Island, just in-side Ocracoke Inlet.

There is an old shipyard spot on North Landing River in upper Currituck called the Launch, another way down on Lockwood's Folly River where the name of the boat builders and that of their tiny town are one and the same: Var-num. A long stretch of coast lies between the two, and we have built in this Sound Country everything from the log canoe to the 400-ton steamer at Sty-ron's Shipyard in Little Washington a century ago, and on up to the great concrete ships—follies, almost—that my grandfather Page worked on in Wilmington on the Cape Fear during World War I, boats so top-heavy that when they knocked the chocks out from under the first, the boat heeled so far over to port she not only slid all her dignitaries down across decks to the port rails, she did so with such alacrity and then was so slow to right herself that she alarmed all hands with the real possibility of a simultaneous launching and sinking.

Nor are we any strangers to odder vessels. Paddler-chronicler Nathaniel Bishop voyaged across Sound Country waters—part of a 2,500-mile quest—in his fourteen-foot, fifty-eight-pound, shellacked paper canoe *Maria Theresa* in 1874–75. Though successful, he was nonetheless treated to constant adverse comment about his craft. On the Albemarle and Chesapeake Canal, "The old lockmaster urged me to give up the journey at once, as I never could 'get through the Sounds with that little boat.'" Along Currituck Sound, an old man at Dew's Quarter Island judged: "Sich a boat as that aren't fit for these here waters." A pipe-smoking woman of Ocracoke told him: "I reckon I wouldn't risk my life acrossing a creek in her," even though Bishop had just made a remarkable crossing of Hatteras Inlet, with dolphins swimming alongside him, uncomfortably close. Carolinians marveled at the paper canoe, scratching at it with their fingernails, poking it with pocket knives, and passing more judgment: "That feller will make a coffin for hisself out of that yere gimcrack of an eggshell." Undaunted and undeterred, Bishop went "down the little sound called Bogue," suffered the cold rain of Swansboro, and stood down the Stand-Back, where tides of the two inlets Bogue and Bear met and where Bishop said "sharp raccoon oysters . . . scraped the keel."

Larger, though no less unusual, was the *James Adams Floating Theater*, a thespian barge that trolled our coastal towns for theatrical trade during the first third or so of this century. This 122-foot lumber hauler was refashioned by a Little Washington shipyard into a melodramatist's dream, and it modeled for novelist Edna Ferber's *Show Boat*. Jerome Kern's enduring ballad "Ol' Man River," from the stage musical production of her book, may be a hymn to the Mississippi, but the river on which Miss Ferber spent several days showboating with the *James Adams* was our very own Pamlico, and she had her own piquant lyric for it:

"Bath, North Carolina," she wrote, "turned out to be a lovely decayed hamlet on the broad Pamlico River." Awaiting the showboat in an old brick hotel there and informed that this had been a governor's home in pre-Revolutionary times, she was nonetheless disinclined to her diet: "Breakfast was a grisly meal. A slab of indefinable blue meat floating in a platter of greenish grease." Once the *James Adams Floating Theater* came and carried her off, though, she declared, "New York was another planet," adding: "The supine South lay green along the Pamlico shores. No sign of commerce marred the scene; no smoking factories; sometimes for hours no glimpse of habitation."

The *James Adams* later sank, twice, in the upper Pasquotank and in the Dismal Swamp Canal, along whose canal-bank highway so many northeastern Carolina working men and women now trek daily on their ways to Virginia's enormous Newport News Shipbuilding Company, where its 500-acre shipyard awaits them. Though our state has nothing like it, the North Carolina Shipbuilding Company in Wilmington in the 1940s was a large war-effort yard, and we still do all right; for everywhere in the Sound Country are boatworks and marine railways and one-keel shops no larger than garages. Some, like Barbour of New Bern, Parker of Beaufort, Albemarle of Edenton, and Grady White of Greenville, have built powercraft that cruise one end of the Inland Waterway to the other. Equal in quality and downright legendary for distinctiveness of line are the tapered-gunwale, flare-bow boats of Harker's Island in down-east Carteret County, and across the Straits behind Harker's, Bryan Blake of Gloucester (who is also an energetic Cajun button-accordionist after the fashion of *les Balfa frères*) can turn out a sharpie about as nice as anyone ever saw a century ago.

It has been both a privilege and a pleasure for me to have watched the keel for a sixteen-footer being laid in a small shop there on Harker's Island, to have seen a dory skiff awaiting its finishing coat at mossy Gause Landing in coastal Brunswick County between Ocean Isle and Sunset Beach, as it still is to look in regularly on whatever's being crafted at the Maritime Museum's wooden-boat shed on Taylor's Creek in Beaufort: long slender rowing boats; ship tenders named *A. E. Martin* and *C. F. McMillan*, now manned and womanned by the recreational group the Beaufort Oars; spritsail skiffs; juniper skiffs—every bit of it a thrill and a wonder to behold, the fabrication of worthy craft, whatever the hull style, length, and beam. And no small part of that thrill is knowing that these traditional boats—as well as the extremely popular flat-bottomed Carolina, Shark Island, and Jones Brothers skiffs that are all made in and around Morehead City—are being crafted for our waters and waters like them, that they can slide themselves in and through all sorts of shallows, that they are the most useful of any boats here, that they are truly *of* this place.

"What happens with a lot of folks nowadays," Todd Miller of the Coastal Federation (himself the owner and operator of a small trawler and a man given to the enjoyment of a slow-rolling Bogue Sound shrimp-run by night) once said to me, noting more recent maritime trends, "is they get too much boat, draw too much, to get the most use out of them in our waters." Ann's mother Pat Kindell, who trades property in Beaufort, concurred with Todd Miller's observation, saying: "Folks're always asking for 'deep water, deep water'—but there's just not that much."

Boatbuilder Bryan Blake, Gloucester, November 1996

Close to the South Carolina line, you can walk across Mad Inlet to Bird Island at low tide, and at or near dead low, a jeep can drive over the Swash and tidal flats to Portsmouth Island at Core Sound's north end. In waters like these, you want a boat that really *will* just about ride the dew. The plain old skiff—sharp prow or snub nose, flat bottom or dead rise—is that boat, and out on the many waters of the Sound Country, whether to sail or motor or paddle or pole about the tidal flats and creeks, it is and always has been worth far more than its weight or displacement in the best coin of our realm.

For centuries the Carolina sounds have by turns smiled upon and smitten many an acre of unfurled sail. My own first moment before the mast came one bright autumn afternoon on Pasquotank River, not in one of our native and diminutive moth boats, but in Doctor Frank Weeks's 33-foot sloop docked out

Boatyard, Marshallberg, August 1996

behind their waterside Winslow Acres home downriver of Elizabeth City. No one had ever told me that when a sailboat cut through a chop you got wet from the spray, but I learned it one afternoon just a little ways into my ninth year. Cold water it was, too, but I had a big time in the land of the moth boat, coursing the wide, black river from four till almost dark with the elder Weekses and their sons Frank Jr. and Harry, who was one of my best friends. In his small sloop, Cap'n Michael Sharp sailed me into a thick and gorgeous Pamlico River fog one October Sunday afternoon long ago, and just a few summers ago Cap'n Jim Rumfelt introduced my twins Hunter and Susannah and me to acrobatic sailing, trapezing off his sixteen-foot catamaran over a light chop just inside Beaufort Inlet.

But this brief history is light fare compared to eighteenth-century Spruill family sailing, when they were out on the water constantly not for sport but for transport, and when the men tied their women to the masts in heavy weather to keep them from being lost to the storm-tossed Albemarle, where, in a blow, closely spaced four- and five-foot waves pile in upon the Durant's Island shores. "I've fished off Frying Pan Shoals during the winter," Fort Landing crabber Willy Phillips once said to me, "and crossed Carolina Beach Inlet in a gale and fog—but that water off Durant's during a storm will beat you to humility." I stand in appreciative awe of those who have met the Albemarle with respect and success, for its reputation is one of squall, ferocity, and ruin with little warning. And I am amazed at the sea-level, close-to-the-bone exploits of one of the more adventurous sailors my family has ever produced—my elderly, scuppernong-growing cousin Jesse Perry.

When this ancient mariner told his tale to me, we were driving slowly south through Perquimans County, through the old Quaker settlement of Belvidere with its towered, Queen Anne homes. He allowed as how the kinswoman through whom we were related—distant to both of us by generations—had been named by her father after his boat, the *Buena Vista*, and this oblique maritime memory of Buena Vista Spruill prompted the recollection of his own favorite craft.

"Somewhere in the thirties," said Jesse Perry, "I had bought a small, double-ended sailboat, lovely hull design, I just loved it. Saved up my money in California, worked in the canning plants out there, Palo Alto . . . came back east, found this little hull, wanted to get a sailboat, found this sort of open hull at a boatyard up at Whitestone Landing, suburb of New York. So I bought it for about $900—had an open framework and a canvas cover for a cabin . . . two masts, though, two good masts. Fixed it up a little, got a stove, up at the Whitestone Landing. On Thanksgiving Day, sailed out of New York, snowing that day, down the East River, right on down, bitter cold, didn't get very far . . . tide took me on down East River—tied up at some coal piers at the lower bay, as you come into New York Harbor."

"How big a boat was this?" I asked.

"Twenty-eight feet," he said, "almost twenty-nine. Finally ended up, came down the Inland Waterway, down to the Delaware Bay, and out around Delaware Bay, all under sail. Some bitter times, I'll tell you—some tricky times, too, crossing some of those inlets. Under sail, you never knew. Got into Chesapeake Bay and hit some good cold weather, northwest wind, *really* breezed down the bay. I'll tell you. On into Dismal Swamp Canal, on to Elizabeth City, and finally up to Hertford, on the day before Christmas. Sailed up back of the house. Boat had a little keel on it, drew about two feet of water, and I couldn't come on in to the shore, to the pier back of the house, so I threw over the anchor back there in water bout four, five feet deep.

"And took off my clothes, got naked, slid overboard, waded ashore, put on my clothes, this is about five o'clock in the morning . . . banged on the back door, Mother came down, '*Aha!*' She liked to had a fit, home for Christmas, I tell you, I was *lean*! Had exactly five cents, when I got there, that's a fact. Just made it."

A tractor hauling a hopper of chicken manure passed us by. It was April,

Jesse Perry aboard the *Sea Jay*, 1930s

planting time in Perquimans, and everywhere there was plowing, disking, seed-drilling, agriculture in the air. I remembered another April, when John Foley and I were down painting the deck and trim of my grandmother's cottage at Nag's Head, a 1930s elaborated shack just north of where the *Huron* came a cropper back in 1878. An AM radio station from Hertford was trumpeting "Planting time in Perquimans!" and bragging that *if* you came down to Hertford Hardware and *if* Catfish Hunter, the fabled baseball pitcher who hailed from Hertford, was in town and *if* he came down to the hardware at the same time *you* did, then you *might* see him! It was hard to be here in the big broad East in April and not be happy with the world. Jesse Perry drove on down through the country and carried on about his best boat:

"Tied it up back there and kinda got myself back together again. Got a job, one thing and another, to begin to work on it. My thought was to rebuild it, take it over, make a real sea-going boat. Cause I was gonna go on down the Inland Waterway, and cruise around the Bahamas, just like these rich people."

He laughed heartily at himself as soon as he conjured up this Depression-era image, remembering the lone nickel he had upon his return to Hertford: "No money! Anyhow, I rebuilt it, jacked it up on some big stumps, right back of the house, back of the bulkhead, so I could get to it quickly. Jacked it up well up out of the water and begin to rebuild it, finally got it the way I wanted it, all decked over, nice cabin, ketch rig, jib, little mizzen, mains'l, *lovely*! And put it back in the water, had it all caulked and painted, did it all myself.

"By then I was out of money again of course, so I was gonna go trappin. A little late in the season, but I sailed on outa the river. Trappin wadn't that good in the Perquimans River, cause most of the land's tilled around the edge of the river, cultivated farms. So I headed around to a place I thought might be pretty wild, and that was Big Flatty Creek, down on the Albemarle. Sailed on down there with provisions for about a week. And round the mouth of Perquimans River, cross the Little River, and on over to Big Flatty.

"I'd never been in there before, but I had the charts and it showed a pretty shallow bar coming into the creek. On the chart it showed at least three feet, that was low water. But I didn't know whether the water was low or high when I was there. I didn't want to run aground. I drew then almost six feet of water, cause I'd added a keel to it. Blowin a bitter gale right out of the northwest. So I took a long run out into the sound, came back in on the tack, ran right steady abeam, right hard abeam, so I could lay the boat way down and tilt the keel way up, as I came into the creek. That's just what I did, slid right on in, never touched bottom. Over in the creek, it's a little deeper, four, five feet deep inside, which was deep enough. Pulled up to a pier, long pier ran way out in the creek."

"Coming out of the east side of the creek, to the right as you went in?" I asked, thinking of the old Carolina fish camps at Frog Island, long rickety piers and shanties on stilts out over the water that are there yet.

"Unh hunh. Pulled up to this pier, and tied up. Cold, Lord, it was cold. Walked to shore, one-story house, building there, people living there, some folks, nets and so forth round the house. Man came out of the door as I walked up there, held out his hand, big smile, said his name was Midgette, and I told him my name was Jesse Perry from Hertford, and that's all we ever knew about each other. Said, 'Come in, Mister Perry, what're you doin way down here in that boat?' Called himself Cap'n. So I went on in, cause I was cold.

"Sat down, they had a big fire going. Big family, wife, bout three or four girls, right pretty. One of em bright red headed. Really all just as friendly and nice as they could be. We just talked and talked and talked. Got to talking bout some of my travels, some of the things I'd seen—they hadn't seen some of those things, we talked a lot about that. We talked about what he was doin—he built boats and sold em, and fished and raised a family, and that was about it.

"And I stayed down there, trapped in Big Flatty Creek for about as I remember two weeks. Had a kayak that I made, that I towed with me, so I used that to paddle up the Big Flatty Creek, upper creeks, estuaries, put out my traps, caught muskrats, few gray fox, and course some coon, but not very many—I think people'd already been trappin em there.

"So I spread out along, put my line of traps out along Albemarle Sound, pretty swampy country, low, pines and sweet gums, pretty wild sort of stuff along the Albemarle Sound. But I caught quite a few mink back in there, that was sort of an answer for me, and I got a couple hundred dollars, I guess, which was a lot of money then."

"What'd a mink bring?" I asked.

"About twelve dollars for a hide. I remember I had ten at one time, sold em for a hundred twenty dollars. I thought I was a wealthy man then."

"Where'd you do the trading?"

"Elizabeth City—Glover."

"Duck Glover?" I said, recalling that the old Dismal Swamper Reggie Gregory took his hides to the same broker, who in turn carried what he'd gathered from the Albemarle trappers up to New York to sell.

"Yeah—I didn't know his first name. All I knew was Glover's Furs and Hides."

On the domestic side of his Big Flatty adventure, Jesse Perry said that family at Frog Island had a piano and played music nightly. "Yes, yes . . . they had it in the living room, big room, big wood stove, warm, oh, it was wonderful! Had an upright piano, and his wife played, all church music—no dancing music—church hymns, so forth, and we would *sing*! Hymns, we would all rally round there, Cap'n Midgette, myself, and his wife and the three girls, sing church hymns for a half an hour or so, after supper . . . just sort of a form of entertainment, you know. I thought it was kind of strange—I was never one much for singing church hymns, but I sang *there* and I was *happy* about it, too, I'll tell you! Really nice, so hospitable.

"They did a really interesting thing, I thought, and still do. They didn't know anything about Jesse Perry, and I didn't know anything about Cap'n Midgette—the whole thing was based on mutual respect, trust, so basic. There wasn't any cussing or swearing, wasn't any impropriety, any bad manners, just nice, relaxed—friendly, hospitable. I was no more or less than what I demonstrated to them, by the way I acted, and that's the way they were to me, too. Real relaxed situation. But if you're a nice guy, that's the way it's gon turn out—if you're an S.O.B., that's the way it's gonna turn out, too!"

It all recalled the hospitality shown me by the Silvers in Wanchese that wintry night, and other humble hearths hereabouts, too, where sojourners in various times have been made welcome. Boatman Bishop in his paper canoe pleasurably camped and cabined his way through the Sound Country during the Christmastide of 1874, even got invited to a Hunting Quarters wedding. Outdoorsman and naturalist H. H. Brimley spent his first spell of Currituck time in 1884 at Ned Midyette's place on Church's Island, agreeable Uncle Ned being the owner of four shooting batteries in the sound. Closer to the turn of the century, pioneer bird-protector T. Gilbert Pearson also found comfort and cover from men whose occupation—market-hunting the Carolina sounds—was anathema to an Audubonner, as well as from fishermen and life-saving crews.

On a log lying aslant in the dark Perquimans River was a good-sized turtle, a slider sunning itself in the early afternoon. Jesse chuckled and gave it a nod: "Been there a thousand years." And on the sandy-colored *S*-shaped bridge over the river, a fellow in a tan uniform was fishing with three rods and reels, his lines out and wet, if not yet tight.

"But anyhow, coming back to Perquimans River, again, northwest wind blowin. So I was tacking a lot, trying to, coming up the sound. Had to run out to the sound on a long reach, no motor of course, on a long reach, and head back in—rougher than Billy Hell out there, when you get out there to the lee of the shore, way out in the sound . . . and I was towing the kayak, way out in the sound, trying to come around—what is that big point that comes down? *Reed* Point! Goes wild, big bar, you get in there, and it's all solid breakers. Anyhow, I was trying to get around Reed Point, heeled way over, tacking, really close haul, rough weather and the kayak got swamped back of the boat, filled with water, course it's like a dragnet, just like an anchor hanging on there . . . and my boat couldn't run with the wind, you know, and slide along, with the waves over this big thing hung on the back . . . I could see what was going to happen, man, it was cold . . . water was freezing on the deck and on me, too, I'll tell you . . . I said, we not gonna make it, me and the kayak . . . I just took a knife and cut the knot and let 'er go . . . oh, it went down the Albemarle Sound, last time I saw it, and we just took off, then the boat, she could move! You follow, she was just laying there with the wind just pushing her down, going too far down and I could see what was going to happen, and it was rough, too. We took on off then and came on into the river.

"You've had those experiences, where you know right away what you got to do. There idn't but one answer. And you've got to know what that is right quick, too, and *do* it! Can't say, well, I hope I can do this, or I hope I can do that. That was the last of my kayak, I hated to see it go."

"Did you do any more trapping?"

"No, I could see I wasn't going to get enough money ahead by trapping to go down to the Bahamas and cruise. No, that wasn't working, that part of it. The boat was working fine, but I wasn't making any money."

"Hard way to serve the Lord," I said, as we pulled back up to Jesse and Sarah's big Front Street home on the river.

For some mystical reason of light and enchantment the sunrise at vernal equinox comes in the upstairs sun-porch window, throws a thin beam through that room's hall-door keyhole, and strikes a glint off a brass doorknob at the far end of the hall, like some inexplicable calculation that the long-gone and far-away Mayans had made a gift to this Sound Country son and his family, forecasting it by centuries toward the one who would as forester-physician care for their pines in Mexico and who would give a few of their seeds a place of honor in his Perquimans County swamp.

"Yeah," he said, laughing, as he was much given to, about the glorious folly of trying to strike it rich in the Depression by sailing the craft he called *Sea Jay* down from New York in the holiday cold and trapping Big Flatty Creek. "Sure was."

One early autumn afternoon in the mid-1950s, my friends and I were down on a Pasquotank River beach, right at Cottage Point near where an old brickworks had been and where to this day there are brickbats and red rocks water-worn from them. We were there watching the celebrated hydroplane races of the Elizabeth City Yacht Club's colorful International Cup Regatta. The river-port town that had given the world the beautiful and useful little sailing dory, the moth boat, now gloried in the time trials of a boat good for nothing else but speed. Still, it was magnificent seeing one plane at around a hundred, throwing up the most fabulous geyser of a wake, the rooster tail.

All day long we had heard them from the S. L. Sheep schoolyard a half mile from the river, like a riled-up hornets' nest sounding out over the low-lying town, and we couldn't wait to get down to the Pasquotank and join the admiring throng along its banks. This particular day, though, we were to get more of an eyeful than we could, or would, have ever wished.

One of the boats, one of the best of them that year, was on its last and fastest downriver run, when at that highest of riverine speeds the sleek shellacked craft and the young Canadian man at its wheel flew all to pieces—wood, lacquer, steel, blood, and bone in one fantastic moment blew apart and, as the last of that rooster-tail water plume fell, melted down into the river itself.

How often over the forty years since then I have thought of that single stunning instant and the fatal disintegration before my eyes that showed so clearly, fiercely even, our tenuous grasp upon existence. Never before had I been in a boating accident, or even come close. What was it, some pin, some bit of integument or glue, some small weak point that betrayed the mission of this astonishingly fast watercraft and tore it apart and lost the life of its pilot? By how little a thing *are* we lost or saved? I wondered.

One March afternoon a couple of years ago, Ann and I had taken our little daughter Cary and our big retriever on a jonboat outing up the Newport River. Seeing a dock built out into a wide chute up behind a pine island, I went toward it and promptly ran us aground at the small and unambitious speed of about five knots on a broad, unmarked oyster reef.

Old trawler near Bonaparte's Landing, Brunswick County, August 1996

That inauspicious act broke the shearpin on our old Ted Williams 7½-horse outboard, and I had brought none to replace it. So Ann and I paddled a quarter mile downstream into the narrow opening of a bulkheaded marina, a convocation of hundred-thousand-dollar cruisers and sailing craft from whose supply officer I intended to buy the part.

"A *what?*" said the beefy, good-natured thirty-year-old fellow at the marina's clubhouse. Not only did they not have one, the man I needed it from had never even heard of a shearpin.

"How bout a nail, then?" I said.

Together we searched through the jumble of a toolshed till at last we turned up a bent nail I thought would do for diameter, then got a hammer to straighten it, a bolt cutter for length, and made a jury-rigged pin to get us home. Twenty or thirty million dollars worth of boats nearby and not a shearpin amongst them. The nail, once straightened and cut and installed in the Ted Williams's lower unit, got us all the way back down the Newport by sunset, the high-piled cumulus clouds beyond the Newport bridge gone gold and the sky the aquablue of a songbird's eggshell. We went farther down and then through Gallants Channel to where we always beached the boat that year, at the little net-house cottage in Beaufort on the point across from Piver's Island.

Heaven be thanked, even for small favors. So what if our Desoto Buddy Boat *were* a modest fourteen-footer running on a chopped nail? It was also flagship of our family fleet, this flat-bottomed snub-nosed skiff, several times swamped, yes, but never yet sunk (a point of no small pride in a land where thousands of vessels good to grand, including the very USS *Underwriter* itself, lie on the bottoms of creeks and rivers or, in what must be an indignity to old boats, *half* sunk, sunk to the waterline and now just sunning places for cottonmouths), and in this boat, this widened aluminum articulation of the Indian dugouts John White saw so long ago, we made it back to Beaufort roads, back to safe harbor and homeport yet again in our humble once and future hull.

Sunny Side

. . . .

The Roanoke Valley

Late one afternoon in November 1989, I stopped alongside N.C. 561 between Caledonia and Rich Square, and, Lord, it was as snowy an evening as Frost ever showed his horse—the river-bottom floodplain on the western side of the Roanoke was all cotton, blooming and blowing to the far gazes. What an atavistic shift!

Thirty years earlier, when cotton was playing out in eastern Carolina, its last stand to my eye was that little three-acre patch directly across the street from J. C. Sawyer School in Elizabeth City, a living agrarian antique plot that someone was tending and picking by hand and an eleven-foot sack. Then in the late '70s, a few isolated stands of cotton started showing up, and its gray lint hung dripping from the stalks in the picked fields, the lint dotting the roadsides where some of it had spilt from the wagons and trucks bearing it to gins that had sat idle for the better part of twenty years. The return of cotton in the east has been swift and enormous, from a hundred thousand acres in 1989 to eight times that by the end of 1995. My old friend Jake Mills—who hunts the brambled ridges that run along between the basins of the upper Tar and Roanoke Rivers, scaring up birds, rabbits, and deer for the last fifteen years—said of '95 cotton that "lint-land" had gotten so extensive it was cutting into the bird habitat, a matter of no small import to a man who always has Flicker Wilkes's falling-off-the-bone quail recipe in mind for the back end of the hunt.

King Cotton's reemergence notwithstanding, Jake and company still go diligently after birds in this country, and when they do they are afield on foot for hours, making rounds just like a trapper checking his line in a certain order time after time. One of their coveys is called the Eleven O'Clock Covey because they always strike it in late morning; another is the Blue Shutters Covey, another the Mailbox Covey, the names taken from the places these colonial birds live, reliably and perennially.

When deer is the quarry, the hunters range much wider and farther afield, and frequently go by pickup from one section to another, since both the open grounds and the forests are vast and the chase can go on for miles and hours— though one sees no shortage of still-hunt tree stands at the edges of big fields. Jake reckons that, though the reported take in eastern Carolina is enormous, the real kill may be ten times the official numbers, and that, even so, the deer population is exploding. It is all but impossible to drive the coastal plains at night and *not* see deer in the headlights, abject fortunes of them grazing in soybean fields; I once saw more than twenty in bean-field stubble at Corner High, just a few feet off U.S. 158, at three o'clock in the afternoon, idling and as at home as if they were Gates County taxpayers and voted regularly at the Ruritan hall up the lane.

Over in the Roanoke valley at the Community Hunt Club, a big pole barn with helices of antlers around its rafters and top trim boards, the upper Halifax air is rank with blood when the hunters come in at the day's end and a dozen deer or more are hung, bled, and butchered. Several men do nothing but sharpen knives for others who dress meat for two hours. Boys throw handfuls of guts to deer dogs thrilled at the ruck and gore of the workday's reward, and men and women, white and black, stop by to see if there is any extra meat—there always is. A meld of congeniality and predictability and fatalism runs through it all; no doubt this is what you do of a cool fall Saturday, nor that you will leave the club with deer meat whether you got off a shot or not, nor that your dogs will be fed there in the pole barn cold and dark, though not everyone's hounds are so lucky.

Jake recalled once seeing a boy with a rifle over his shoulder dutifully walking a rope-leashed dog down a dirt road, the boy waving Jake's truck to stop and then asking:

"Y'all want a dog?"

"That one?" Jake's friend Ed Carlton asked.

"Un hunh," the boy said.

"You givin him away?"

"Un hunh."

"What's wrong with him?" Ed said.

"Won't hunt."

"Well," Ed said, "we got to get on," and they left the boy to his task. Later that afternoon, a mile or two from where they'd first encountered him, Jake and Ed saw the boy again, now with only the rope and the rifle. When Jake told a woman in the Piedmont about all this, she said, "Oh, that's sad."

"Not sad at all," Jake said. "That boy's not learning for the Research Triangle Park, he's learning for Halifax County—the deerhound that doesn't hunt, doesn't last."

Jake had also seen a dutiful—and genial—fatalism in the big cheerful hog farmer whose lands the hunt was coursing one weekend. When they found him to greet and thank him for the hunting grounds, Jake's party caught the farmer just finishing the operation of yanking eyeteeth out of his young pigs.

"How do you do that?" Jake asked, and the farmer reached a bloody hand into his back overalls pocket, then held out his implement, channel-locks, saying:

"Pair of plars."

"Doesn't that hurt?"

"Naw," said the farmer. "Not unless you pinch your finger."

Such are new times in the land of cotton, not forgotten any more than are the old. As the Flatwoods Hunt Club tells it, by bumper sticker and with similar humor:

GUN CONTROL IS HITTING YOUR TARGET.

The rapids and falls of the Roanoke River are not slight. They are between the towns of Weldon and Roanoke Rapids, a few miles above Halifax, our old colonial capital and Rebel stronghold where General William R. Davie and his uncle-in-law and political rival Willie Jones sponsored many a fine late-eighteenth-century horserace.

To Weldon once came Frederick Law Olmsted, who was powerfully hungry one afternoon in the 1850s and assured by the stagecoach driver that there was time during the stop to get a bite to eat. The journalist-architect went into an inn there at Weldon that advertised FRESH OYSTERS, but he was disappointed. "The only palatable viand within my reach was some cold sweet-potatoes; of these I made a slight repast, paid the landlord, who stood like a sentry in the doorway, half a dollar." It had scarcely been fifteen minutes since he'd gone in, having left his baggage with the stage driver, but the stage had taken off and left him stranded. "I am pretty good on the legs for a short man," Olmsted wrote, "and it didn't take me long, by the *pas gymnastique*, to overtake the coach."

Olmsted then reboarded his ride, which promptly overturned. In the ante-bellum complaint he lodged over the four hours it took to go fourteen miles, one sees that disdainful northern attitudes about our regional disregard for time and forward motion are nothing new. When the stage driver finally stopped on the banks of Roanoke River, Olmsted said dejectedly: "Where are we—not in Gaston?"

"Durned *nigh* it," said the coachman. "That ere's Gaston, over thar; and you just holler, and they'll come over arter you in the boat." Gaston, wrote Olmsted, was a mile above them, and on the other side of the river—he and his fellow travelers were indeed strangers in a strange country, at the edge of night, their next move a careless stage driver's casual suggestion that they "just holler."

Eventually the redoubtable Olmsted convinced some boatmen to come fetch the stage party over the Roanoke, and all was, if not well, at least tolerable. The little town he sought, Gaston, was the northeastern railhead for the Raleigh and Gaston Rail Road; it was the namesake of jurist and lyricist William Gaston, the man who heard a tribe of traveling Swiss bellringers chiming away outside his downtown Raleigh home one holiday evening and who then took their tune and applied to it his cheerful statriotic lyric: "Hurrah, hurrah, the Old North State forever—hurrah, hurrah, the Good Old North State!" Its bridge over the Roanoke burned at the close of the Civil War, and Gaston went down—nowadays it is downright submerged, immersed in the waters of the dammed and flooded upper Roanoke. Judge Gaston's town now sleeps beneath *Lake* Gaston, and back downriver near the old Weldon mill the rockfish spawn each spring, their great procreational "rock-fight" long noted by sportsmen and travelers alike, in the moiling boil of water below the falls.

I thought about all this energetic amatory spirit one morning in May, driving to Halifax past the Romance Disco and Lounge on u.s. 301 above the town, then stopping at the lower edge of Halifax town and parking by the old cotton gin not far from where I had first seen the crop coming back into this country. Doug Rader, the energetic, red-haired biologist who was with me down east to explore Occoneechee Neck, first wanted us to look in on Quankey Creek, which cut a sixty- or seventy-foot gorge through the great rock border of the Roanoke's western side on its way into the Roanoke itself.

On a fern and poison-ivy hill, where tulip, sycamore, and sweet gum trees on the slope below grew to fifty or sixty feet, I stood overlooking the gold and amber water of Quankey Creek far below. A railroad crew was working back near the gin, bees and mosquitoes busy at closer range, and a three-and-a-half-foot poplar hung against the hillside sky at a seventy-degree angle. Doug and I went down and found ourselves some Miocene fossils in the draw. Sparrows and wrens were at play on a sandbar, and when we climbed back up the high hill, atop which privet and honeysuckle were flowering all about, we were just about knocked down by the heavy air, redolent of spring in the east.

On just such a day, on May Day in 1841, the Burgwyns, planters hereabouts, had a little fish fry over the river at Garysburg, and Anna Greenough Burgwyn made note:

"The *muddle* it seems is a dish peculiar to Roanoke & is made of the rock fish, ham, & red pepper stewed together. The table was arranged under the trees. It was of rough boards uncovered with a cloth. . . . There were two barbecued pigs, two boiled hams; the muddle, served up in a bake kettle, that is, the kettle stood directly upon the table, a large sturgeon, served up in a bread trough, & dishes of fried fish. This was all."

A hundred and fifty years later, almost to the day, two hungry men stood in a wet road just behind the Roanoke River's natural levee, miles deep in the big bottom that is Occoneechee Neck, some of it still belonging to the family named Burgwyn. Besides the food cooler we had failed to haul in with us, *our* muddle was figuring out whether to make a sally on the next slough, or retreat through the one that moments before had nearly sunk our Volkswagen.

"I tell you what," said Doug, "this road is an interruption in the water, not the other way around. This is *wet land*."

"Well, if we got to get stuck, Doug," I said, anticipating the query from an as-yet-to-be-made acquaintance, some man with a tractor or a winch-rigged four-wheel who would ask us politely if we were ignorant or just plain stupid, "I want us to be in the *first* mudhole, not the second."

It was a bright blue-sky day, clouds billowing, and we were having a big time trying to find a breach in the river's natural levee, some sandy skid to slide the jonboat down into the Roanoke. From Garysburg, we had headed south on N.C. 1128, expecting to gas up the Ted Williams 7½ and find pimiento cheese and sardines at Mud Castle, and we thought the hummingbird hovering under a porch chair at the first turn was a good omen.

EAT MORE PEANUTS, said one sign at the only grocery down the way, and another implored us to GROW AND USE MORE COTTON. Fine, but the store was closed, had been for some time, so all the peanuts and cotton we would see this day were what was in the ground.

On our way back into the neck, there were buttercups, wild geraniums, lyre-leaved sage, an indigo bunting, a sandy road snaking along between a cotton field and a piney woods, past a hunt camp and kennel and a tiny pond where a great blue heron lifted up, a borrow-pit where turtles sunned and swallows nested in dark, round holes in the pit wall. Then we wound around through what was swamp forest till the 1980s, now a gum and tulip cutover with a lot of heart-rot stumps and deerstands in the trees every quarter mile or so. A second indigo bunting.

The Roanoke made this neck of land as it swung out, curving ever westward, till it met the strong and high-rock boundary that holds it in, on the *west* side. The river may have once made its main bed of Occoneechee Creek, which meanders southeastward from the upper part of the neck to empty into the Roanoke just upstream of Gumberry Swamp and Camassia Slopes. Far easier to read than the palm of one's hand is the record of Roanoke River's ever-increasing arc, writ clearly in the disposition of streams, sloughs, ponds, and contours of the floodplain neck on the Halifax quadrangle.

Doug and I studied the contours of our own situation, then engineered our way around and back out past the twenty-foot slough that had slowed us, but not before we walked about through the standing water and muck of the levee road. We saw a crawfish, a water boatman, a frog, tracks of deer and coon, we heard the tattoo of a pileated woodpecker, and we inadvertently interrupted the rites of spring by slogging in on a pair of mating black snakes—one went Doug's way, toward the river, the other slammed into my left boot in high dudgeon and with justifiable righteous indignation before disappearing into the bog. Doug pointed out a "monster" poison-ivy vine the better part of a foot in diameter. Near a wide-plank canal bridge, we jumped two young deer, and saw a third indigo bunting—as many in two hours as I had seen in my life.

As Anna Burgwyn said in another time of a different bounty, "This was all."

"Rode down thro the neck," wrote Henry King Burgwyn, Anna's husband, in his journal, June 20, 1840.

Burgwyn and his brothers had only the year before inherited the Roanoke bottomlands called Bull Hill, Occoneechee, and the Level, and Henry and Anna—Yankees both, from New York and Boston—had made their way to Northampton County and the neck in the spring of 1840. In mid-April, Anna wrote home:

"Henry drove me out to his plantation last Sunday, for the first time. . . . The situation for the house is beautiful. On a hill, at the foot of which there is a pretty little stream, & its sides are covered with trees enough to protect us from all sun or wind. . . . We saw wild turkies as we passed along the road, & the mill pond is the rendezvous for wild ducks, so that we can there procure food for the body as well as the mind."

For a time, Henry Burgwyn took an interest in fox hunting and horse racing, but after brother Collinson's death in 1842, the business of planting the neck absorbed him and brother Tom almost entirely. The Burgwyns studied agriculture, employing deep plowing, subsoiling, liming, and clover growing to make the neck produce; and to get that produce to market, they promoted Roanoke River navigation—in December of 1843, the schooner *Demarest* lay up at Occoneechee Neck, there to bring lime in and carry Burgwyn corn out and up to New York. In their first two decades in this country, the Burgwyns shifted their crop from cotton to corn and wheat, Henry bringing one of the first two McCormick reapers into the South (below Virginia) and estimating his nine-hundred acre wheatfields would yield twenty bushels to the acre, $50,000 in 1855.

These legendary planters tried hired Irish labor as an alternative to black slavery, but they gave up and became ardent defenders of the Southern order. In March 1856, agrarian editor and slavery advocate Edmund Ruffin visited the Burgwyns, and in August 1860, Henry Burgwyn joined Ruffin's Publication Society to speak up and write for the slave South in which he had prospered.

The Burgwyns would pay a high price for their South. Less than three years later, on the first day of Gettysburg, July 1, 1863, Henry Burgwyn Jr. fell with most of the Twenty-sixth North Carolina Regiment and died. Henry Jr. was, at twenty-two, one of the youngest officers of the ill-fated army, and history knows him as the "boy colonel of the Confederacy."

Mebane Holoman Burgwyn, the boy colonel's more recent kinswoman, has written of better fortunes in her Occoneechee Neck adventure novels. In *Hunters' Hideout* (1959), brothers Cal and Mike visited the Mud Castle Store, and the brothers—torn between studies and the glories of the swamp—explored cliffs, jungles, and undercut banks before capturing a shaky-handed jewel thief down by the river. And the Roanoke itself, "relentless red destroyer of crops as it flooded the Occoneechee Neck," was a major character in *River Treasure* (1947), restoring a branch rerouted by the great flood of 1877 long enough for twelve-year-old Guy to find a chest of Civil War silver and win for his drowned-out family the down payment on a new farm.

"Been looking for that treasure all my life," said William Johnston, the easygoing farmer whose flat to slightly rolling cotton and wheat lands at the heart of the neck include such former Burgwyn holdings as the Cypress, the Level, and Occoneechee Wigwam. With a smile, he admitted,

"Haven't found it yet."

As Johnston bade us welcome to do, we drove through the farm, through the long slender cypress ponds of his family's Occoneechee Hunting Preserve, then walked the jonboat through his hip-high wheat at the end of a long lane down to the river, and made our landing there where the bank was not sheer bluff, but a low drop and beach beside a willow.

It is a good thing to put one's boat in and onto river water where it has never been. I had crossed the Roanoke by car all my life—I could not remember a time when I did not know the sight of the big swamp through which the Williamston-to-Windsor causeway cuts; but never before had I set afloat below the dam, where it still is a *river*. There was a real thrill to it, something learned the moment we cast off, in the several seconds adrift before the motor fired and we were once again in partial charge of things. If your boat is a small craft, with a small engine, you really are *in* that water, *of* it, under no delusion about what constitutes the superior force. The motor winds faithfully along, a riverine landscape of ash and sugarberry, sweet gum and sycamore, unfolding before you, and the delight of the sun and slight breeze the boat's motion affords and the smell of the river, of mud and fish and May water warmer than not, all merge. And then the boat slows, or slides forward slightly faster than it should, or shifts course two or three or five degrees, none of it your doing, your hand steady and unvarying on the throttle, and you know you have *felt* the river, as one mass of water stalls another, or overcomes it, or twirls one within the other and turns you too as it eddies, as it rushes red, brown, or yellow depending upon whose turf it carries suspended along with it pell-mell to the Sea of Roanoke, the Albemarle Sound, then more slowly to the real sea herself.

We went with the big flow downstream, crossing to take a look at a muskrat's hole in the high bank opposite the neck, where shells of freshwater mussels the rat had been feeding on showered down like confetti into the mud below the nest. Small wonder that Occoneechee trapper Q. J. Stephenson sometimes baits his muskrat traps with mussels. There were two fishermen with cane poles a ways on, and a great blue heron that flew ahead, and then an osprey.

"The return of the osprey to the East is a big story," said Doug warmly. "A wonderful story." I would remember his remark, and how he said it, just a week later down on Great Lake in the Croatan when I climbed out of this same boat up into a cypress and peered into a low-built osprey nest, where three young pumped hard, lung and heart, against the mid-May heat. Right now, it was quite enough to see the one majestic bird gliding along the river at Occoneechee Neck.

Merrill Lynch, the Nature Conservancy's veteran Roanoke explorer who had given Doug the maps we were using and who hails from nearby Roanoke Rapids, salutes the neck: "Some of the richest birdlife we have is down there. The Mississippi kite, an insectivorous hawk that feeds in the air, is a Southern species from down along the Gulf—its northernmost range is along the Roanoke at Occoneechee Neck. The cerulean warbler, that occurs only in mature bottomland, it's there. In the mature floodplain forest sandwiched between the Burgwyns and Johnstons there's a heronry, full of great egrets and great blues. And the turkeys were never hunted out down there, so what's there in the neck are natives, native genes."

Up high-banked Occoneechee Creek we roamed a bit, cutting the motor and drifting, listening to a thrush, a dove, cattle lowing. Then we wound down-stream past Gumberry Swamp and, near three fishing women, tied up at the base of the great Camassia Slopes, got out, and climbed.

This is the Roanoke of relict plants the ice sheet sent our way, a steep land unique in North Carolina, with its flowering herbs spring beauty and toad-shade, wild blue phlox and the white buttercup false rue-anemone, and a poppy called Dutchman's breeches. And though we were too late to see the lavender bloom of the *Camassia*, the several hundred wild hyacinths that are here and virtually *only* here in North Carolina, Doug and I took full account and no small pleasure in what we did see: an eight-inch worm snake hiding beneath a piece of plywood, the resurrection fern adorning an enormous oak just up the slopes from a green tarpaper shack, buckeyes, Mayapples, Christmas ferns, sagittaria, arrowhead, jewelweed, a slope of chickweed and *Galium*, a skink, the lower half of a gasburner waffle-iron, a leggy beech tree, a sycamore four and a half feet in diameter, and a beautiful glade.

The glade was a flat pocket in the slopes, a terrace only eight paces wide, a little boggy bottom perhaps thirty feet above the level of the river, and at its river end stood a cypress nearly a hundred feet tall, knees formed up out of the wet ground all around. We mused upon the knurled figures before us, and upon the attitudes they might portray, of supplication, of embrace, till Doug remembered:

"My mother once made a nativity scene," he said, "all out of cypress knees."

"I can see it," I said, and I could, as he laughed not only to himself in appre-ciation of that memory. And I could see the tiny cottontail shivering in the blue-eyed grass in the road that comes down the slopes, the pink and red honeysuckle ambushing the small trees, the tiger beetle on the ground, the big coon prints in the soft flat mud beside the river where we soon untied our boat and moved out again.

More great blues rose croaking at our slow approach upriver, wood ducks in twos and threes skittering over the Roanoke, too, a single kingfisher sitting grandly atop a dead-white sapling spire at the mouth of Occoneechee Creek. In a little while Doug and I would pull the boat out, noting and wondering about the several deer skulls and vertebrae and other bones laid there in the river mud at our landing, then for a time traipsing one of Johnston's fields of emergent cot-ton looking for points, the same field where he had found an Indian grinding stone, and finally heading up toward Mud Castle and home.

Before we came up off the Roanoke, now lightly coated with cottonwood fluff, we stopped briefly beneath a huge raft of wild white roses cascading off the far bank. They were just out of reach, too high to pick, though their sweet and heady scent for these moments covered the river.

It is all too little a while, I thought. Trapper Stephenson and his daughter once found a mastodon's tooth in a creek bank near here, held in their hands that piece of the ancient elephant and gazed into the mouth of many thousands of years gone by. A steamboat captain was pleased one antebellum New Year's Eve that his twenty-horse *Pilot* had made Occoneechee Neck from Norfolk in fifty hours: no time at all. A boy who came of age in the neck died for a two-year-old nation that would itself be a memory less than two years later; this boy colonel lies atop an oak-tree hill in Raleigh, far from and unlike this waterland portion of our realm, though perhaps in nearer mud and clay lie those hands whose labors sent the colonel to school in Philadelphia before his state sent him to his end at Gettysburg. And the creatures that breed here, whether rare like the woodchuck and cerulean warbler or not, do so innocent of these affairs, as do the rockfish spawn, their eggs drifting downstream from the rapids at Weldon toward Palmyra and Hamilton to hatch, some of them someday bound for a cast-iron pot and someone's famous old-family-recipe fish muddle.

From this neck of land called Occoneechee and the rugged river that curved and curved and made it, a Roanoke rose for them all.

A Jamesville log truck with a load of oak passed Ann and me on U.S. 64, just east of the Texfi and Benneton plants at I-95 in Rocky Mount, showering dirt, splinters, and debris as it did. Farther east, the Tar River at Tarboro was in heavy, early-spring flood, the better part of a mile out of its banks to the east. Red tractors of the peanut farmers were out scuffing the earth, getting ready to plant. We drove by Madame Lurane, Palmist, on the right just east of Bethel, then the Woodmen of the World building across the road, and Ann glanced at the club next to that. "The Villa," she said blithely. "Looks like a good place to get killed."

We bounded along toward Williamston on the Roanoke, and I shook my head over the widening of 64 in Robersonville, work that had turned a boulevard of enormous, overarching oaks into a broad, naked street of slim character. And I showed Ann the shopping center where for a long time years ago stood Miss Camellia, the World's Largest Ceramic Guernsey Cow, replete with stout and seemingly active blood vessels painted on her pendant udders. The shotgun block building where the Acrostolic Church once met was now Flanagan's Funeral Home, and I spotted a fading RUFUS FOR GOVERNOR sign near the Smithfield Hog Buying Station just east of town. *Sic transit.*

But that night at the Sunny Side Oyster Bar, the well-rested and relaxed little frame building right near the corner of two great eastern Carolina highways, U.S. 17 and U.S. 64, it seemed as though nothing had changed in a generation, if not two. Thin orange and green neon tubing outlined the Sunny Side by night,

Barnhill Supply, Everetts, Martin County, March 1993

and inside there was rockabilly and rhythm and blues on the box, and on the wall fish-netting, a stuffed shark, and a tin ad for Remington Game Load showing a duck hunter in his boat with the quip, "Let 'er rain!"

That was the front room, though; it was the back room, the actual bar, that had drawn us here. It was a room purely and simply set up for feasting on bivalves and shrimp—its ceiling was green, its upper walls white and separated by a black stripe from green lower walls. On the parqueted counter you got paper placemats—no plates—and behind the counter black men in green aprons stood in sawdust, shucked and served, knocking the oyster shells away as they did. Down the bar sat a pair of men in their forties, one of them with a half gallon of vodka poking up out of a brown paper bag at his feet; he ordered a soda.

I remembered the first time I'd stopped in here, with Cumberland County's Libby "Let's go get us some *sliders*!" Seymour, and how one of our compadres, mountain boy Barry Mines from Virginia, when asked how many oysters he wanted, answered, "I don't know, two?" to an uproar from the staff and the rest of the clients there that night, till Robert Bonds came forth with a couple of pecks, proclaiming, "Okay, now—now I'm gon get you *right*!"

Not just how *many* do you want, the men asked, but how *long* do you want em steamed? A sign on the wall was intended to help you:

2 minutes=Rare

3 minutes=Medium

5 minutes=Well done

There being half-minute gradations, I believe Ann and I ordered ours medium rare that night, and got our sauce and butter mixed hot from separate teakettles just before the oysters came out. To make it easier on everyone, the preprinted bill read:

SUNNY SIDE OYSTER BAR
Williamston, N.C.
Finest Steamed Oysters and Shrimp
—ANYWHERE—
Peck Oysters
Half Pecks
Dozen Raw
Pounds Shrimp
Half Pounds
Coffee-Drinks
Beer
Other

Charles Roberson, the owner back then, was a genial, nerved-up gray-haired fellow in his late thirties, talkative and proud of his place, and firm, too, like some Judge Roy Bean of the Roanoke Valley: "You get outa hand, talk dirty, you're *outa* here! Don't be a bad boy in the Sunny Side Oyster Bar—it's the *sunny side*! Nothin bad's ever happened here!"

This season, he said, they'd run oysters from October 9, 1992, through April 10, 1993. Back in the 1950s, the Sunny Side steamed, shucked, and sold 150–200 pecks a night and stayed open till midnight, doing double the business after 9:00 P.M. over what it had done earlier. "Took its toll on us, I reckon," said Roberson.

Nowadays the Sunny Side only meets its public till 10:00 P.M. In the fall of '92, though, on the night after Thanksgiving, there were a hundred people waiting at 8:00 P.M., eighty-five at 9:00, still eighty-five at 10:00 as people kept showing up. "We served em all," he said. "If you're in here when we cut the lights off, you're *on* the list—and we *feed* you!" He recalled the power's having gone out once, but, as there was plenty of gas in the boiler and they therefore had plenty of steam, they went on and served by candlelight.

The black men who worked the Sunny Side had themselves something of a well-tenured fraternity, and they seemed bemused by their white clientele. Timothy Smith, whose charges we were this evening, had worked sixteen of his thirty-three years at the Sunny Side; James 'Skeet' Rodgers, Harvey Everett, and Darnell 'Geezer' Bonds all had fifteen years in here; and Robert Bonds was the junior member at nine. They also had other, full-time jobs—Smith worked at the West Point Pepperell plant at Hamilton, another was also in textiles, two worked for the town, and one was a contractor.

Out back beside the bar room, in a crude plywood steambox, the peck buckets were stacked, a pound of shrimp in a strainer off to the side. Whichever of the five men was cooking would flip the lid, pull a ready batch out, pop a raw batch in, all to the timekeeping of a big white-faced school-cafeteria clock on the shed wall. Steam went rising through openings in the cut and twisted corrugated tin, hot clouds up into the starry early-spring night.

Around and about the shed were piles of oyster shells, bushel bags of oysters, and nearly two dozen cats. One of them had its head skewed off to one side, nearly at a right angle to its body, and this strange misshapen cat was the men's favorite.

"Come here, Crookedneck!" they called, and he came. "See, that's his name, cause a car hit 'im and broke his neck, and he answers to it."

"You ask anybody," said Charles Roberson, back inside. "My daddy, Mister C. T. Roberson, he made this place what it is, nicest man that's ever been built, and now he's got Alzheimer's and don't hardly know me half the time—me, I was just *born* into this place. Been in here ever since I could walk, used to sleep on a sofa over there behind the counter. I'm just carrying on. . . ."

So were we, and shucker Timothy Smith, like Robert Bonds had four years earlier, got us *right*. On our way back to the nearby motel, sated and on foot, I glanced once more toward the smoking, steaming shed and saw Crookedneck eagerly lapping from a stream of the operation's offal, its *R*-month run-off, the cat's lower jaw positively slathered and drooling with oyster gurry.

We had driven through Williamston a little after breakfast, then left its big brick warehouses, its tobacco markets, its fish- and cab-stand combination, and walked down by the Roanoke where the Union Camp log barges lay up at a wharf downriver of Odis Whitaker's Highland Lumber Company and what was left of the once-enormous red wooden fertilizer plant. Buzzards were aloft in the sunshine on the cool eastern breezes, and we made for the land without care, Sans Souci. Now we were deep in the Roanoke delta, the 150,000-acre hardwood bottom where chutes like the Devil's Gut cut off the huge curling meanders of the river, and where eventually another stream—Middle River—carried the waters of the Roanoke and the Cashie back and forth down where it all poured out into Batchelor Bay and the western Albemarle.

On the road down to the Sans Souci ferryslip, past a field where several pigs

Robert "Kooles" Bonds at the steamer, Sunny Side Oyster Bar, Williamston, March 1993

and a goat held sway, we passed a parked blue pickup with a Peanut Pride plate on the front, waving at an old man nearby who raised his cane in reply.

It was high water in March on the bayou curve of the mossed, cypressed black-water Cashie River at Sans Souci the spring morning Ann and Cary and I spent there. The landing on the north side of the river was flooded, as was the road beyond it for an eighth-mile or more. Over some pound and gill nets just downriver from the ferryslip, ospreys were stooping, dropping, fishing for real. There were also an egret, several blue herons, and a good many crows. The ferryman was a burly and bearded fellow in his thirties named David Earley. Earley had been ferryboat pilot here for ten years, sharing a seven-on, seven-off schedule with one other man. On his days off from navigating the dark Cashie, he was a plumber by trade. Here at the river, when he wasn't shut down by high water, wind, or ice, Earley ferried people he called his regulars back and forth, farmers mostly, a few salespeople, a woman who lived on one side of the river and whose child went to private school on the other—"I carry her back and forth four times a day." He occupied himself fishing, visiting with pals that dropped by, and working with wood. This March morning he was busy in re-laxed fashion repairing a wood-strip and fiberglass skiff, and the boat's shellac

Sans Souci ferry, Cashie River, March 1993

shone golden in the morning sun. There was little midmorning call for the service of the two-car cable ferry, so we talked awhile as Ann walked Cary out on a pier than ran near the nets, where they could see the big birds at easy work.

"Sans Souci, well, Sans Souci is really, I believe is on that side of the river," David Earley began. "Everybody calls the whole area down here Sans Souci, but I think on the other side over there is where they mainly call Sans Souci.

"I don't know a whole lot about the history of this place, but I know they've had a ferry for over a hundred years.

"There used to be a wooden ferry here, when I was a young'un, my granddaddy used to bring me down here—there uz a old wooden ferry—and they had a like a pitcher pump, you know, you see out in country folks' yard, and that's how they pumped the water out of it, it would leak, and they'd have to pump it out every day. They used to pull that one cross, *I* don't remember when they pulled it cross by hand, but they *used* to pull it cross by hand. The cable run over that top rail, and they had a board with a notch cut in it, and they'd catch that cable in that notch and walk down the ferry and pull it across like.

"The cable went all the way across the river. They had a couple of pulleys on there, and it sort of fit in a groove in the pulley right there alongside the ferry and they'd just walk along with a board and they had a notch cut out in that board and they'd hook that around the cable and pull it, pull it cross by hand. Keep walking, walk forward, then back up, hook it again, walk forward till you get it cross."

"How'd you happen to come to run this ferry in the first place?" I asked him.

"Well," said David Earley, "the fellow that used to run it, he died, and the job was open and I knew one of the bosses and I talked to him about it and got the job. . . . Rest of the boys that worked for the state, they didn't want it, they didn't want to come down here. . . . I live right acrost the river over there, bout two miles . . . I built a house last year."

"Say you build a lot of stuff down here?"

"Yeah," he said. "Build boats, carve decoys. Just old wooden creek boats, flat-bottomed. Built about six or seven, I reckon."

"How much traffic you get?" I asked.

"Twenty-five, thirty a day in the summer. Winter slows up."

"Why does the state keep it going?" I wondered aloud, as more than a few do.

"Well, it's been one down here so long, it's sort of like a historical place down here. You know, it would cost so much money—lotta people ask 'Why don't they build a bridge acrost here?' but it would cost so much money to build a bridge acrost here—they've already got the ferry down here, the onliest thing, they pay my salary, and Harvey's salary and just the fuel that the ferry needs. But you have a lot of farmers using it, and salesmen, salespeople come through every week."

"Well," I reckoned, "you must like it."

"Yeah, I do. I enjoy it. I enjoy it. Gets a little boring in the wintertime, but I find something to do with myself."

"You got pals come down here, make sure you're okay?"

"Yeah, I got buddies come down here, we cook fish down here sometimes, stuff like that. Real pretty down here in the spring and summertime, when everything's green. Lot of cypress. When I first started down here I'd fish some while I was down here workin, but after while you know you get tired of catchin little ol' small bream and stuff. I fish right much when I'm off. My house is on highway 308, about two or three miles from here, it's not far from the water."

The Sans Souci ferry was an elemental rig, a flatbed scow with a little cabin to the side and a big two-cylinder Detroit diesel motoring the boat back and forth, winching it along a submerged cable that ran shore to shore. The diesel was a

David Earley, ferry operator, Cashie River, March 1993

noisy, leaking thing that the state mechanics were trying to fix, or perhaps replace with a John Deere engine—something, Earley said, that would run a little
smoother.

"You had the same hull the whole time?" I asked him.

"Un hunh," he said. "They've rearranged it. They took it down to Wanchese,
they come up here on a tug, pulled it to Wanchese, and they pulled it up and
scraped it and painted it, they changed the little pilothouse . . . they changed that
around. Used to, had a six-cylinder Chevrolet engine on there and it was right
inside the pilothouse with you and it had a radiator on it run *hot*, it would run
hot if you run the ferry very often, so they changed it, put that diesel on there.
Um, hmm, sitting right in the pilothouse with the motor. It was really quieter
than that diesel was. But it would run hot, with it being in there like that and
had the radiator on it, with the motor bein right in the room, and the heat from
the motor, it wadn't gettin any air, you know, it would run *hot!*"

Facing the river year-round with such a craft was elemental, too. Earley had a
cold wind blowing at him most every day in the wintertime, from the north
mostly, and it backed the water up. After a rain, he found, a strong east wind
would blow water up into the Cashie and raise the level.

"It'll change from day to day," Earley said. "You come down here and it'll be so high one day I can't operate the ferry, and then the next morning come down here and it's dropped back down to normal, when the wind dies down. It's just so cold, it's cold wind off the water down here."

"You don't ever have a still day?"

"Not very often," he said, "not very often."

What *did* happen with frequency was the ferry's breaking down. "Most time I'll pull it across, if it breaks down halfway across I can pull it. Sit on the end and grab the cable and pull it cross. Takes you a little while to get crossed but you can get crossed all right," he said, allowing that in ten years he had never once had to use the little Coast Guard–required lifeboat on board. Earley has had to employ the ferryboat's ramp as an icebreaker, though.

"Every oncet in a while the river'll freeze over and you got to close it down if the ice gets thick," Earley told me, though when I suggested that the ferryboat would probably break a pretty good bit of ice, he added:

"Yeah, I've broke ice probably a inch or so thick with it—you can take that ramp and keep beating it on the ice, you can work a path through there."

But now it was just about spring and getting good and green, and Cap'n Earley liked it down here on the Cashie in spring and summer, found it real pretty. We kept watching an osprey or two fish the pound nets, and Earley said he even saw an eagle from time to time. What about other wildlife? I asked. "See much bear?"

"See em occasionally. Most times in the fall, you know, when they had the peanuts out in the field, you see em down here right often then. Crowd come down here huntin em this year and they didn't kill any . . . I was *glad*. Hunters stayed in that cottage right there. I think bear season opened for a week, and they stayed the whole week and they didn't never kill a bear."

"Were they frustrated?"

"Yeah, I think they were a little bit. Woodard Hunting Club down here, they invite em every year and all of em get together and hunt down here. Woodard Gun Club. They open the season one week, and hadn't been any bears down here probably the last five or six years—you just started seein some bears, and they opened up the season. Won't be long fore they'll kill em all."

"Many in the Roanoke River bottom?"

"Yeah, there's right many bear in there—there's gettin to be right many bear."

"A lot in Dismal Swamp, Alligator River too," I said. Not too far east of here, my upstate neighbor James Bradshaw, while out fishing, has heard them rampaging the Alligator riverside near Gum Neck, and seen many a dead bear weighing down the back of a pickup truck.

"Un hunh," mused Earley. "I reckon they're finally working their way over this way."

"I hope so," I said, wishing for the increase of eastern bear.

"I do too," Earley said, "long as they don't kill em out. You take most of the

people that come round here bear huntin, they're from the mountains, you know, and they got good bear dogs and all, and they know a lot more about bear huntin than people around here, and it don't take long, you know, to kill em out."

"When you see em swim the river, where do they swim?"

"They swim right acrost that bay over there, and go to that point over there," he said, indicating the landing on the far shore. "I seen em come right acrost there. And deer, see a lot of deer swimmin the river. I've seen some bear probably up two hundred fifty, three hundred pounds—they killed one down here year fore last weighed five hundred eighty-some pounds."

"I know they kill lot of deer."

"There is a *lot* of deer."

"Other wildlife?"

"You see otters, ducks, geese, see some—like I say I saw a bald eagle bout three weeks ago, stayed down here about a week—just one, you don't see them very often down here, I think I've seen two since I've been down here."

"Beaver, nutria?"

"Mushrat, you see a beaver every once in a while. It's gotten where there's a lot of beavers up and down the rivers now. You don't see that many right here . . . but you go up the creeks, up Roanoke, up them creeks up there, you see right many beaver lodges and all beside the creeks."

"Is there much river traffic?" I said.

"Right much," he replied. "Bass boats, mostly bass boats. No commercial traffic. There's a little bit of commercial fishing done right down here, but it's not much—I think there's one fellow's got some pound nets down here but that's all the commercial fishing we got right here. Belongs to Scott Smithwick, he's the onliest one that commercial fishes this end of the river. He lives on the other side of the river over there, too."

"Where would he sell those fish?"

"He takes em over to Murray Nixon, I think, over in Edenton, over that way, sells em over there."

"Retail, not a cannery?"

"Retail fish market."

The eastern streams and bays and sounds once produced legendary hauls, and not all that long ago, as I recall the fishing boats and the strong piscatorial smell in the air along Water Street in Elizabeth City. When Porte Crayon wandered through the Chowan and Albemarle just before the Civil War, commercial fishing hereabouts was the main event, with "scarcely an estate bordering on the

Capehart Fishery, near Black Walnut Point, Albemarle Sound, 1880s

Sound furnishing a practicable beach where there is not a fishery established," Crayon wrote, visiting the operations at both Belvidere and Montpelier. "The surface of the water is dotted with boats of every description," he noted, "from the cypress canoe, paddled by a lonely and sallow-faced angler, to the ten-oared barges that carry out the cumbrous seines. White smoke curles up from groups of cottages on shore, where busy crowds, composed of whites, blacks, and mules, wage unceasing war upon the shad and herring." Nowadays the Perry-Wynns Company in nearby Colerain packs its cans of Chowan's Best with herring roe not from Chowan River or the Albemarle Sound, but from Canada far away.

Here at Sans Souci, some of Cap'n Earley's visitors were bass fishermen, some water-skiers, the occasional drunk. And he had one traveler who regularly looked in on him from above, from just atop the deck. "Big Navy airplane comes acrost here bout every week, and it flies real low, it's a big plane and I always wondered what it was. And the pilot come down here, about six months ago, I was talkin to him, he said, yeah, he flew, he's the one that flew it acrost here—they're flyin some kind of trainin missions or somethin. He told me next time he come acrost he'd wag his wings at me—I saw him yesterday, he come acrost and he waved . . . um, hmm, good gracious, thing's not much higher than the trees. It's a big plane, too. They use this as some kind of reference point, they'll come right over here.

"That's what he told me, said I'll *wag* my wings at you."

Along about this time, a blue pickup truck drove up slowly, and the small man who climbed out was the same old farmer who'd waved his cane at Ann and me earlier that morning. David Earley introduced him as Jackie Simmons, who came down to the slip regularly to keep the ferry operator company. Glancing again at his Peanut Pride license plate, I asked him:

"Are you a peanut farmer?"

"I ain't *nothin!*" he fairly shouted, laughing. "I'm one of those *has-beens*, and I wadn't much *then!*"

Our talk turned to logging, lumbering long being among the biggest of eastern Carolina pursuits. "They don't haul any of that down the river anymore, they used to. I remember when I was young and I lived in Windsor right there about a block from the river, and you'd see barges with logs and all—I hadn't seen no barge up here in years. Most of that's out on Roanoke, you know, going to Weyerhaeuser."

But both David Earley and Jackie Simmons had a few pithy words to say about the 200-gallon-an-hour helicopter logging that had been going on in the Roanoke and Cashie basin in the early 1990s.

"They logged down here last year, logged the river," Earley said. "Last week they were logging over there on Roanoke River . . . crowd outa Oregon. And they fly that helicopter in . . . they got a crew that comes in ahead of the helicopter, and they go in the woods and they cut down the trees, and then the helicopter comes in, they got a crew that goes into the woods and hooks the cables to the logs from the helicopter and he drags em out to the deck and drops em off and then he goes in and gets another load, comes out, hauls about three big logs at a time. He pulls the logs out to the deck with the helicopter and then they load em up on the trucks, but that's the onliest way you know they can get in them swamps to log cypress. Think they cut down some tupelo gum, mostly cypress."

"Logging on the Cashie above here or below?" I asked.

"They've logged *both* sides of it," said David Earley. "Down and up, too. Sure have. They can really move some logs, boy. Mostly cypress, and some tupelo gum, but they had great big piles of logs with that thing, it's a whole lot faster

Herring nets, near Edenton, May 1949

than you would think it is, whole lot faster than a regular logging operation, I'll
tell you that.

"They'll go in a place like that and it don't take em long. They'll fly them logs
out and they'll be gone. They parked in Jackie's back yard. That's where they kep
it at."

Jackie Simmons laughed shallowly. "Tried to get me to go to ride with em, I
said, 'Unh, unh.' I ain't gon ride on *nothin* I can't carry me a pocketful of
wrenches along with me to work on it if it breaks down. *That* thing, you don't
pull off on the shoulder and work on it a little bit. No sir, I don't go up there on
them things."

"They can really fly," said river-pilot David Earley, saluting the Vietnam vet
log-copter jockeys, though not their purpose. "I wish they were gone."

> Sweet vale of Avoca! how calm could I rest
> In thy bosom of shade, with the friends I love best,
> Where the storms that we feel in this cold world should cease,
> And our hearts, like thy waters, be mingled in peace.

Because the immensely popular Irish poet and melodist Thomas Moore visited the Great Dismal Swamp at the turn of the nineteenth century, we have a

poem of his called "The Lady of the Lake," which in celebrating the legend of a crazed lover chasing the will-o'-the-wisp ghost of his dead fiancée around the swamp ("Where all night long, by a firefly lamp,/ She paddles her white canoe") drew, nay, *spurred* thousands of visitors to the dire- and dreary-named place. And because he toured another spot of romance, the confluence of the rivers Avon and Avoca in county Wicklow in eastern Ireland, a "Sweet vale of Avoca," "in whose bosom the bright waters meet," we have his poem "The Meeting of the Waters." This melody of Moore's plays on in eastern Bertie County, and we, too, have an Avoca—formerly a plantation, now a settlement and a tobacco company's huge basil farm: a stout peninsula between where the Chowan River comes down and joins the flows of the Roanoke and the Cashie, which wind through the Purchase Islands, spread into Batchelor Bay, and open into Albemarle Sound.

One sunny September Sunday morning Ann and I stopped our car at the edge of the nowadays Avoca Farms, stepped out into a light breeze that was heady with the smell of basil, and walked in this remote openness to a grove of short pines, oaks, and magnolias where the Capehart family had long ago built and since kept up a little Gothic church, the Holy Innocents Episcopal Chapel. The chapel might hold sixty parishioners, about the number of those buried in the diminutive graveyard there. Many were children: a Capehart daughter who died at one, her brother born the year after her death who died at twelve; a twenty-year-old woman born in Trinidad nearly two centuries ago, now buried with her two children who both perished in infancy. About the longest lived of anyone here was not a landed Capehart and was scarcely *in* the cemetery at all— this was the slave Tom Robin who had stayed on after Freedom "to the end" at age seventy-nine, allowed his short curved-top marker, a good twenty yards off to the side from the rest. We spent a quiet hour or so in the shade of the grove, with its worn marbles and lichen-encrusted stones, before moving along down the old farm lane.

On the water below Avoca was another plantation, Scotch Hall, and here the literary relations became more direct. As "Cypress Shore," Scotch Hall was the setting for tutor George Higby Throop's 1851 *Bertie, or Life in the Old Field: A Humorous Novel.* "O! my home, Brave old Cypress Shore! Peace be within thy walls!" Throop exclaimed over the place.

Somewhat later, though in similar spirit, the noted Carolina gardener and horticultural writer Elizabeth Lawrence went back to Scotch Hall in October of 1960, and she wrote:

"In East Carolina time stands still. Scotch Hall revisited seemed to me unchanged since I saw it last, over twenty years ago. As I entered the house, the door to the piazza was open to let in the warm October sunlight, and looking down the long boxwood walk I could see the blue waters of Albemarle Sound.

Holy Innocents Episcopal Chapel, Avoca, Bertie County, September 1996

The walk between double rows of box, tree box without, dwarf box within, was just as I remembered it, but looking up I saw that the old trees that form an avenue from the house to the water had suffered from the hurricanes. . . . Unlike the brick that the wind blew off of the tall graceful chimneys of the house, the branches of the trees cannot be put back.

"The trees are pecans planted by George Washington Capehart soon after he built the house in 1838. His daughter planted the box, and his wife planted the Seven Sisters rose at the end of the piazza."

Confederate jessamine, a fragrant white flowering climbing vine, grew at the other end of the piazza. It was a plant, she said, that "seems to flourish in old gardens along the coast. This one came from Mrs. Slade's in Hamilton." She also noted that the flower garden was "a modern one, planted thirty years ago by Mrs. Capehart, the present mistress of Scotch Hall," and remarked upon its "intricate design of triangles around circles" and its "beds and walks." And something else caught her eye, an eccentricity, a floral atavism:

"Scotch Hall is on Bachelor's Bay, across from the mouth of the Roanoke River and not far from Windsor. The name was given to the place early in the eighteenth century and appears in a deed to James Lockhart in 1727. The Capeharts' house was built on the site of an older house, and every spring bulbs

Scotch Hall bluff overlooking Albemarle Sound, September 1996

planted in the old garden come up and bloom. They are out of line with the later plantings, but the Capeharts have always liked these small ghosts from the past, and have left them where they were planted so many years ago."

Avoca's basil is cut and pressed, and the oils of these herbs find their way into cosmetics confabulated well away from here. The old Scotch Hall holds onto its propitious prospect, up on the big bluff of Batchelor Bay, and the massive, towering boxwoods still bush and blow in the east wind that pushes and piles the waters of Albemarle Sound up this way.

Sunrise comes to Black Walnut Point, between Avoca and Scotch Hall and just a hair below the thirty-sixth parallel, in a long reach over three national wildlife refuges: coastal Pea Island where the pheasant and snowgeese haunt the roadsides of N.C. 12; Alligator River with its diminutive colony of red wolves and its stout crowd of bear, one of the three largest populations in the American East; and Pocosin Lakes, where ill-fated fields so recently torn from the pocosin jungle are now reverting to wilderness once more. And when the sun appears from up out of the Scuppernong River and Bull Neck Swamp, over Pea Ridge and Mackeys Ferry, up out of the Albemarle Sound itself and plates this broad, drowned notch in the world with light, it must seem yet as always to whosoever lingers here—fishing, writing, garden-admiring, in whatever occupation or *av-ocation*—almost like some wonder of the Mayans, or some gift, the way a slender beam of sunlight through a Perquimans County keyhole once seemed to cousin Jesse Perry.

Nothin bad's ever happened here! as the oyster-bar owner said. *It's the sunny side*!

Sitting by the river in the moon
light. sitting by the river with you
by my side. its wonderful with the
right one Sailing up the river
all a lone with you its so wonderful
sailing with the right one
singing songs to gather as we
sail a long. banjo strumming violin
playing. its wonderful what it
do to you. . . .
—Old manuscript page, found glued to the
   wall of the Fort Landing Store by Feather and
   Willy Phillips, Tyrrell County, Spring 1988

Ghost Pocosins

Between Albemarle and Pamlico

No lands in the coastal plain have changed as much, and as recently, as have the pocosins. In 1962 these naturally occurring, freshwater evergreen shrub-bogs still covered nearly 2.25 million acres in North Carolina—almost three-quarters of the pocosins in the United States—but by 1979 forestry and farming operations had totally or partially altered all but about 700,000 acres. Of the nation's many types of wetlands, the Environmental Protection Agency in 1985 described North Carolina's pocosins as one of the most critically endangered. These boggy embayments and stifled streams, these *swamp on a hill* formations so called by the Algonquian-tongued Indians, have proven far more accessible to tear down and drain than the Great Dismal, which first elicited the recommendation to destroy from the likes of William Byrd II in the eighteenth century.

Byrd's ill-fated contemporary John Lawson made a number of references to pocosins—variously spelled *poquosin, pequessen, poccoson,* and *percoarson,* this last being Lawson's choice—in his 1709 book, *A New Voyage to Carolina,* but ecologists, differentiating these often impenetrable ripshin thickets from river bottomlands, wooded swamps, and marshes, have labored well into the twentieth century to arrive at a good, broad definition.

According to Curtis Richardson, in his 1981 survey, *Pocosin Wetlands*, "Wells described them as . . . occurring in broad, shallow basins, in drainage basin heads, and on broad, flat uplands. These areas have long hydroperiods, temporary surface water, periodic burning, and soils of sandy humus, muck or peat (1928). . . . Woodwell also stressed that pocosins are a successional stage maintained by fires, composed of a combination of pocosin pine, a dense shrub layer and peat soil (1958). . . . Kologiski added that common synonyms for pocosin include bay, bayland, bayhead, xeric shrub bog and evergreen shrub bog (1977)." A few years later, in 1989, my fellow Occoneechee Neck explorer Doug Rader listed four "topographic situations" where pocosins occur: "isolated depressions (Carolina bays), swales separated by 'fossil' beach ridges, heads of coastal creeks, and broad flats between existing drainage ways."

The great Tar Heel naturalist B. W. Wells in the late 1960s mourned the loss of Pender County's Big Savannah, a 1,500-acre grass-sedge bog he had seen from a train-car window in 1920 and called "probably the most beautiful wild flower garden in the eastern United States." I felt a similar grief when I saw what was happening to the East Dismal Swamp twenty-odd years ago, when the late trucking magnate Malcolm McLean had an army tearing down the half-million-acre wilderness between the Albemarle and Pamlico Sounds, the first run of a superfarm that ultimately failed him and his people just as the torn-down Open Grounds pocosin in down-east Carteret County has failed its Italian owners, while fouling South River nearby.

Much of the great Albemarle-Pamlico neck has come back around into the commonweal, though, owing primarily to the interventions of the Nature Conservancy and the Conservation Fund, and the stewardship of the national Fish and Wildlife Service. Now the hands on the sluice-gate wheels of the thousand-mile drainage ditches keep them closed more often than not, and the water is rising where McLean's men were once running it off as fast as they could. No one knows yet if you can really back a pocosin up into its former jungled glory, but in the land of the Pocosin Lakes and the Alligator River, we are starting to find out.

For some strong reason—the old fierce pull of homeland on blood perhaps—Ann and I without a word having passed between us both wanted to go to this wetland and no other in the midwinter week after we were married, and so off we set on New Year's, off to where the ghosts of these great old endless scrubs brought them forth for us in the wet winter mists and for a few moments at Pungo, at Phelps and Mattamuskeet, we saw what was left of them, imagined them as they once had been, impenetrable hells of myrtle and titi, fetterbush and brier, that throve on fire—loved it even, whether set by Indian hand or

Train of poplar, pine, and tupelo logs, Roper Mill, Belhaven, 1907

through lightning by the hand of God—and defied everything on earth except the blade.

The River Forest Manor in Belhaven was our home of the moment, set right there on the Pungo River where it comes down to meet the Pamlico, a sailor's waystation, a big old flute-columned home on the river with too many bedrooms not to have become a guest house in these, its latter days. A poster here read:

Coil up Your Ropes
And Anchor Here
Till Better Weather
Doth Appear.

And so we did. From the closed-in second-story sun porch, one could wake up and survey the morning light on the many waters, and in the whale of a bathtub, at six feet long by three feet deep, something of an enamel dugout that they throw in with the room, one could luxuriate and wonder over what he, or she, had just witnessed at Mrs. Way's Museum, the odd hodgepodge of indiscriminate acquisition and collection that houses everything from pickled tumors and malformed critters to the Fleas' Wedding, visible only with the aid of a glass, with a bride-flea and groom-flea done up in micro-minuscule white dress and tails. Or one could contemplate historical issues of sovereignty, such as the propriety and legality of Virginia's assault on 1718 Ocracoke Island, haunt and hideout of Edward Teach, the colonial pirate Blackbeard, who lit punts and fuses in his beard and flouted all known constraints of man and God and law.

And one could wonder, was Blackbeard paying off Governor Eden or Eden's secretary Tobias Knight with stolen commodities to get them to look the other way and give tacit condonement to his *salvage* operation, or was he merely storing—secretly—casks of sugar in the secretary's barn in Bath? And did Blackbeard's headless body really circumnavigate by swimming Lieutenant Maynard's sloop thrice after Maynard separated the pirate's head from the rest of his bad self and threw that feared and famous torso to the sharks of Teach's Hole at the climax of the Battle of Ocracoke? (There are those who say the tide was falling at the time of that celebrated detachment and that there wasn't enough water around the battling boats for the headless horror to perform the feat, even if what remained of Teach had had the will and the strength for one last display of idiotic bravado.)

And did Blackbeard's skull really wind up back in some waterfront shebang in Bristol or Liverpool—or worse, in Charlottesville, Virginia—in use as a drinking mug? 'Twould have been a fit fling into futurity for the barbarian whose favorite libation was an admixture of ale, rum, gunpowder, and a lighted match. One could further ponder the unforgotten lore and remember that Blackbeard the Pirate, when whole, took numerous wives for short-lived conjugations and that one of them was the dark-haired Satchwell girl from a family of English immigrants whose descendants include Marie Cox of Bath and her son, my extraordinarily musical cohort Don Dixon.

Dixon grew up plying the same Pamlico waters as Blackbeard, but with far more success and longevity. His uncle Joe Ed Cox had a place on Pamlico River outside Little Washington and a few miles east, a cottage up on pilings on a little spit of land a hundred yards wide or so, dotted with tall pines. "He called it the Roost," Dixon once told me, "'cause he said 'that's where the chicks came.'"

"When I was about six or seven," Dixon said, "Joe Ed built this wooden speedboat, had a big ol' Evinrude on the back. And I don't think they could get skis to fit on my feet, but they wanted me to do *something*, so I'd just hold on to a tractor-tire inner tube, and he'd tow me along behind on that. You get pretty high up in the air—they *really* bounce. Till I got a little bit bigger and the skis could fit on my feet, *that* was my version of waterskiing. Get farther away from the jellyfish that way, and there were a *lot* of jellyfish down there. . . . We would go out to these little islands, in the middle of the river, and have picnics and stuff."

Better it was, I knew, to linger on the Pamlico exploits of the low-country soulsinger than on those of the depraved swashbuckler. In a tub as grand as the

River Forest Manor's, two could contemplate as easily as one, unhurriedly, and then, at a time of year when absolutely no one else was stirring thereabouts, make off alone together into the ghosts of the great Sound Country pocosins.

Cuckold's Creek flows under u.s. 264 northwest of Belhaven, but we rolled right over that divide and had us what can only be called a major fried-fish lunch at Mel's in tiny downtown Pantego. Then, as we drove north toward Wenona, we saw hundreds upon hundreds of blackbirds swarming in the trees along canal road 1626 before we left Beaufort County and crossed over into Washington.

Bearing east to Pungo Lake, we spotted seven swans in a slough, then thousands of snowgeese flying in *Vs* and forming clouds low and close to the horizon, looking east over cornfields from near the west side of the lake. Ann and I parked the car with the jonboat atop and walked half a mile, maybe three-quarters, down a grassy lane toward Pungo Lake. It was early afternoon, but it could have been anytime of day between eight and four, so gray and drizzly were the thick January mists. Our faces were wet, and our light ponchos seemed to direct rivulets of water down our necks, but we pressed on, hearts set upon seeing the big pond in winter. Years before, I had once made my way, on a moonlit February night, miles and miles across the drained forests to the south of Alligator Lake, east of where we now were. A herd of deer, several dozen of them, bolted before the headlights, ran up out of the big drainage canal and across the road out into a beanfield. At that road's end there was a small cabin set back in the cypress, and I turned the car off and left it long enough to walk past the cabin and into the lake's forested marge, listening and thinking as I moved in the moonlight from one small hummock to another that I was hearing a party in progress across the lake. The laughter was vivid, enormous, extreme—there was so much cacophonous cackling going on that by the time I could walk no farther without going into the drink I thought it quite grotesque, and then I realized the gathering to which I bore aural witness was nothing more than some major waterfowl take-down out on the lake. When I gave a barred owl *Who-cooks-for-you?* cry, all that honking and squonking got briefly louder as the avian entertainment moved to some farther pavilion a ways down the shore, but, despite the joyful noise of that company, the night was too cold for me to follow.

Now, with Ann, I hoped to see what I had only heard on that other of the pocosin lakes, and I wasn't disappointed. She and I made our way through taller grasses, switch cane, and gum out to the willows and a slender beach on Pungo's southwesterly side, and we stood listening to the lake's ambient squawking and regular splashing as birds came in to land or took off, their wings beating the surface as ducks or geese took flight. There was no shortage of feathers in the lakeshore's lonely shallows. When the mist clouds over the water shifted a bit, we could make out the lake's dim-gray far shore, and on the water itself more snowgeese, swans, and ducks, there too a raft of Canadas a couple hundred yards away. These birds weren't as noisy as the Alligator Lake crowd had been, but that had been a bell-clear night, where today all sound was muted and muffled by the closeness of the shroud. But for the black about their necks and heads, they were the color of the very day itself, the winter mists made flesh and feather, vivified puffs of fog. We were to them of no more import than the big willow bushes we stood by, and the pattern of the traffic that had brought them here was entirely different from our own, foreign even. We were two lovers for whom a gray-misted flatland lake in winter was the height of romance, and the company we were keeping on our own flight across the lowlands was for the moment a community, a whole town of geese on the move. They might move no farther south now that they and January had settled in, but they had certainly plucked themselves up whole-flock from the edge of Hudson's Bay or the Great Slave Lake or Baffin's Bay where the whale fishes blow, or from some sluice of a stream up in Nova Scotia or from some island marsh in St. Pierre or Miquelon that had afforded them summer comfort, and through whatever combination of breeze and instinct the gods yearly stir in them made their V-line way to this small eastern Carolina puddle called Pungo.

Chill inevitably finds the bone, though, so we retraced our steps and tracks, stopping for a short spell at an observation tower a mile east. Then we cruised slowly along a canal, spooking mallards two by two and four by four out of the canal, getting out for a quartet of otters that puffed and blew and snorted at us ridiculously, us leaning against the car laughing, trying to guess where their hairy heads would be popping up next. In one field bright green with winter cover were more thousands of snowgeese and, in nearby corn and soybean stubble, thousands of mallards. Cattle in a pasture were lowing as we headed on back into Belhaven, lowing deeply as an evening mist came on heavily and began settling itself down over the dark fields and settling over the golden ones as well.

One afternoon that week, we put the jonboat in at the U.S. 64 bridge over Pungo River, a few miles east of Belhaven. It was the first time we had been out boating together, just the two of us, and neither of us had ever been on this water. Something about this fact now makes me wonder if we weren't a little comical, like my friend Richard Vaughn's brother, who with his wife lives on a twenty-seven-foot sailboat berthed in Belhaven. Richard told me he drove his brother and his sister-in-law up to Mayo, Maryland, to buy the craft, and that he was astonished to watch his next-of-kin exchange money for boat title and then float off: "Sixty years old and hadn't been on a boat for thirty years, and we're there fifteen minutes and then there he goes puttering off towards Belhaven, me standing there on the dock watching. And they made it! Only ran aground twice." Our boat, I am glad to recall, didn't run aground at all, though I admit there was some serious cavitating when I really horsed the 7½ Ted Williams engine.

Under the bridge and up the Pungo we went, through golden midwinter marshes and around pine hammocks, our avian companions on this outing a marsh hawk, a few domestic ducks and mallards, and a great blue heron we spooked repeatedly as we wound our way up the narrowing river. We passed some old wharf pilings, a dead tree with eighteen skulking buzzards in it, a bleak jury and a half to happen upon, as if this breed of bird were so demoralized by its millions of years at the world's boneyards and charnel houses that its posture at rest was a hunched and hunkered stillness, a grim, cold, timeless judgment upon the warm and living: "You, too, will be mine in time."

Then we saw the others.

Hundreds and hundreds of buzzards were kettling up high above the Pungo marshes, in the vast thermal reaches of the blue and ceilingless sky, starting at sixty or eighty feet and continuing their cyclical, spiraling swarm out of the range of sight. Blackbirds in such grand quantities one expects, but I had never seen anything like it with buzzards. Given the grimness that jury had just invoked and imbued us with, we were now amazed and overcome by the dark lofty swirl of them all.

Later that evening we found the antidote—a fortune of swans floating like eastern cottontufts upon the broad waters of nearby Lake Mattamuskeet, as gay in all their laughter and high trumpeting as the buzzards had been dark and silent, such bright white and so much of it that not even the deepening oriental dusk could dim it.

Mata-mackya-t-wi, the Indians said of this place. *It is a moving swamp.* Hard to look out upon its forty thousand acres and believe that this largest of Carolina's natural lakes was itself a ghost for nearly twenty years. To drain Mattamuskeet for farming, the Southern Land Reclamation Company between 1909 and 1916 built an enormous pumping station on the lake's south side, with a 125-foot smokestack. Southern Land went under, though, selling out to North Carolina Farms in 1918, which firm in turn sold out to New Holland Corporation in 1923. Four enormous steam engines of nearly a thousand horsepower apiece, in league with attendant drainage canals, finally worked, and there were twelve thousand acres of Lake Mattamuskeet's bottom under cultivation—rice, wheat, rye, the biggest soybean crop on the globe—when Franklin Roosevelt was elected president. But the elements ruled here—rainfall, pestilence, and absolute mud—and the New Holland farmers threw in the towel; Mattamuskeet enacted a kind of revenge of the pocosins, taking little time to refill its shallow declivity and reclaim itself from its reclaimers. In 1934 the moving swamp became a wildlife refuge, and the Canada geese and tundra swans who whistled their ways hither were guests of the nation. And the pumping station? It ran along for four decades as Lake Mattamuskeet Hunting Lodge, though more recently it has served as a retreat for artists, academics, and even some wintertime snowgoose contra dancers.

Kestrels and kingfishers were with us on another day, frequenting the roadside wires as we headed from Belhaven back toward Mattamuskeet and N.C. 94's long causeway across it. Ann and I were now bound for Kilkenny, a small river landing on the upper Alligator, but first we stopped on the north side of the moving swamp for a big plate lunch at Harris' Steak and Seafood in tiny Fairfield—home of the Hyde-a-way Motel, where every room has a sign in the bathroom bidding hunters "Please don't clean your guns with towels and washcloths—we have plenty of gun-rags at the front desk."

The landing at Kilkenny was no more elaborate than a road's end; a fifteen-foot ditch there led a hundred feet out to the Alligator River. We cruised through pocosin and marsh a mile and a half or so upriver, then back down past the landing for a couple of miles, passing through a narrow forest of dead cypress along the riverbanks. It was a bright, brisk day, and everything was out feeding while the feeding was good: a red-tailed hawk, a pileated woodpecker, robins and flickers, four blue herons, endless flights of redwings, ducks and swans in small flocks flying overhead, a barred owl that we only heard, a kingfisher that flew along ahead of us, and a pair of orange-toothed nutria on a raft of reeds that they had snugged up against a bend in the serpentine river. Ann's brother once told me that the root-eating nutria were such a problem in places on Core Banks—tearing up sea oats and other dune grasses that helped hold that thin strand together—that one cadre of duck hunters during downtime would routinely cruise the coast with .22s, eliminating the exotics. Here in the Alligator barrens, though, one pair seemed harmless enough on this winter's day. And as for gators, we were near the northern limit of their range and certainly at the height of hibernation, but I remembered, too, that my fisherman friend Gilbert Turner, for whom Hyde and Tyrrell Counties were a second home, once came across a burned-over patch of marsh hereabouts, and found in its center the stark and bleaching skeleton of a four-foot alligator.

"I am *cold*," Ann said. The sun had fallen behind the forest wall, the dead trees and the living, and it was suddenly still and frigid in our little aluminum boat. So we came about and made for Kilkenny.

Ice was forming thin shelves in the shadows of the riverbanks, and, back at

Upper Alligator River, January 1989

the landing, Ann and I had a devil of a time tying the boat off on the car-roof with plastic rope that was painfully stiff and difficult to knot at twenty-six degrees. It was a clean-cold frosty dark by the time we left Kilkenny Landing, northbound now through the scrub-pine pocosins toward Columbia.

Former days, and ghosts of kin and other folks, crowded my mind as we turned through the little Scuppernong River port and drove for East Lake and Manteo: my grandmother's introduction to my grandfather in the Tyrrell jail, then under construction and now nearly a century old; my grandmother's mother schoonering into Alligator on the lumber-camp escapade a quarter-century before that, this family being befriended by grandmother's father's people, the planters of Free and Easy. In this lowland phantasmagoria there were darker moments, too.

From way up Alligator River where the stream narrows and the juniper woods crowd in, Nat Meekins, my first cousin twice removed, as an infant a century ago made the trip back down toward this place on a night of decidedly different humor. Nat's mother, a Spruill, had died and was encoffined, and his widowed father was bringing the infant and the dead woman back to her people around Alligator, one for burying and one for raising. The freight-boat, like some mournful marine caisson, slowly bore them north one frigid winter day, but when they pulled up to the landing that night well before midnight, no one was there to meet them. But the freight-boat's schedule, such as it was, must be kept, so the pilot and mate threw off the lines and plied for the Albemarle, leaving father Meekins and his infant son Nat huddled against the coldest cold, sitting atop the coffin of wife and mother like ice figures till someone named Spruill or in a Spruill's employ fetched up with a wagon at dawn to retrieve them, eight hours for that baby to try to survive while crying in the wilderness for the mother who was there but could never more do him any good and eight hours, too, for that father to clutch the child he could no more satisfy, knowing that the one likely promise of his lifetime in that unpopulous country lay dead beneath him as he stared bitterly out over the dark unlighted waters and strove to see the face of his God that he might ask Him the simplest of questions, beginning with:

What sort of place have You brought me to?

In the present of a cold January night, Ann and I crossed the long Alligator River bridge bound for East Lake, Mann's Harbor, Manteo, aids-to-navigation beacons flashing faintly to the north and south of us and no craft moving except the upside-down jonboat above our heads. The cold now freezing the river and its creeks to their very edges was hard, too, upon the brittle manuscript mounted on an old store wall at Fort Landing not three miles distant from us there on the bridge, a page unknown to us then and penned by an unknown hand but in a tongue not at all unknown the admirable proclamation:

Its wonderful with the right one.

Let the bear roam these wilds in greater numbers than anywhere in the American East except the Okefenokee far south of here and the Great Dismal just north, and let the red wolves roam and struggle and strive here in numbers barely attaining double ciphers. Let the pilgrims who pass over this bridge regard the great river and the boats that float it, the scows, schooners, sloops, cruisers, and skiffs, and let them know, too, of the ghost-boats that sleep beneath it, and let them each to each raise a glass to the wind that blows and the ship that goes and the lass that loves a sailor.

We will be back we will be back we will be back we will be back.

Tupelo, Sweetwater Creek, Martin County, September 1990

In late July of 1968, my mother and sisters were down at Kitty Hawk, and I had just returned to North Carolina from an eastern Montana wheat farm and cattle ranch where my friend Bruce Strauch and I had been working for a spell, painting octagonal granaries on a wheat ranch and stacking railroad ties cast off by the Northern Pacific that ran through the ranch. Wearing a slouch hat and light, summer clothes, I set out hitchhiking for the coast from Chapel Hill and made the timber-and-tobacco Roanoke River town of Williamston in good time.

The farmer who picked me up at the corner of u.s. 64 and u.s. 17 was small, wizened before his time, and I soon found out why. Between us on the front seat of the sedan lay a newspaper clipping with a photograph of a young soldier and a headline that said:

LOCAL MAN DIES IN VIETNAM

Out of the corner of his eye the driver saw me looking at the faded newsprint, let me keep looking, and held off saying anything for a few minutes. He had been right friendly when he invited me to ride with him, but now it seemed he was drawing in, letting a tension build. We went some miles before he spoke:

"That's my son there."

"Yes, sir," I said.

"Hundred and seventy-ninth man killed over yonder. What do you think about that?"

"I'm real sorry," I said.

"Thank you," he said. "But I mean, what do you think about the *war*?"

"Well . . ." I drawled, and said no more. I didn't want to get into an argument, I didn't want somehow to belittle his grief, and, selfishly of course, I didn't want to lose my ride. Though I was certain he was daring me to criticize the war and start something, when I looked over at him squarely I saw he was staring straight ahead at the two-lane road, both hands on the steering wheel and his lower lip quivering. Crossing the bridge at Gardners Creek, where out past a boat ramp there was a cabin in the cypress, a homemade diving platform and rope swing at the creek's edge, there he finally said:

"You want to know what I think? Well I'll tell you—I think that's the biggest goddamn mess this country's ever been in. Viet*nam*! Who the hell ever even *heard* of it?" He didn't cry, but his eyes were glassy and now his voice was fairly choked with rage and grief. Finally I ventured the timid comment I had withheld before:

"I think we're gonna be real sorry we ever went in over there."

"*Gonna* be?" he erupted bitterly. "*Gonna* be? I'm already sorry, son." He lay his hand down on the newspaper clipping and tapped it, and then I saw it for the

Gardners Creek, East Martin County, September 1990

sorrowful talisman it was. "There was just no damn need of it," he went on. "No damn need of it atall."

Somewhere east of Jamesville the farmer slowed, stopped, and let me out on the road shoulder, wished me luck, and turned down a sandy lane through some pastureland where the egrets and the cattle were about evenly paired. The dead soldier's birthright perhaps, or perhaps they were tenants. It had been cloudy all day, and now a light rain was falling. Two well-dressed, middle-aged black men picked me up, and talked enthusiastically about an upcoming event at the eastern Tyrrell County church where they were elders and where they were going to see about something in the sanctuary. When they reached their church, they apologized for leaving me off in the rain, though I had a poncho and a Montana slouch hat and resilience aplenty and made light of it all. I stood near a small hoglot and watched them through what was now a downpour as they pulled into the churchyard north of the highway, parked, and walked up the half dozen steps to the church door and disappeared within the sanctuary.

I pledged with the earnestness of my age and of that day and time that I would stop someday and go into that church and make an anonymous donation in honor of the two men; I haven't yet kept that pledge, but I will. In honor of them and also of the farmer who had to spend the rest of his life riding the coastal roads with his son set upon the seat beside him forever young and forever uniformed staring proudly up at him from out of an old and fading journal, forgiving the father his lack of belief in the war that took the son while simultaneously begging forgiveness of the father for the son's not coming home and taking charge of the farm like he had promised he would do. A few miles north of where I now stood, my own soldier lay somewhere in a pine flatwoods at Alligator, my ancestor Colonel Spruill who raised Tyrrell's regiment in the Revolution, and thereabouts, too, lay dozens more whose blood I now bore along u.s. 64.

The women, Homer wrote, wept at funerals first for the dead and then for the living, for themselves and their "own sorrows each." I stood beside a small-farm hoglot in eastern Tyrrell County, a lone figure not quite a man but moved by the men I had met that summer day, and tried to let my soul be still as the very rain itself wept over the vast and water-loving pocosins all around me that were not yet ghosts upon the land.

Croatan

. . . .

Valley of the Neuse

"I liked your noise," said the small man who joined me at the railing of the tour boat *Mystery*.

We had just started down Taylor's Creek toward the channel and Newport River, and I had less than an hour before finished giving a honky-tonk, piano-man concert in a small brick Beaufort warehouse called Fishtowne Alley. Now we were drinking cold beer.

"You what?" I said.

"Liked your *noise*," he said again. "Your *songs*."

"Thanks," I said. "Glad to hear it." I looked back out at the full moon welling up over the water, and listened to the boat's big diesels thrumming in the warm June night.

The fellow next to me was a wiry little man who rocked backed and forth slightly on his feet. He had the humorous and unthreatening shiftiness of a carney, and when he spoke it was through his teeth, like he was clenching one set of incisors:

"I'm Don Bailey," he said, putting forth his right hand to shake and jabbing at his chest as he added, "Bull riders do it all night, y'know what I mean?"

"I don't know," I said. "You a bull rider?"

"Well," said Don Bailey, "I didn't just get here fallin off no cabbage truck, y'know what I mean?"

Then Ann walked up and I introduced them, and, since I had used the word *wife*, he observed: "Y'all married, that's good. I mean I *guess* it is. Me, I got me a woman, most of the time she stays with me, my place up the river, but sometimes I don't know she just gets on my ass and I just got to get out and go get me a case or two of these ol' beers just to stay level and I don't know maybe she'll be there when I get back maybe she won't—bull riders do it all night, y'know what I mean?"

If I hadn't known at first, I was getting a quick, clear picture. Don Bailey kind of cocked himself on the rail of *Mystery* and sounded off about the Coastal Federation, for whom I had done the show—"Oh, they're all right, I reckon, I mean I ain't got nothin against em, *yet*!"—and about other conservers and preservers that he was even less sure of, like the Nature Conservancy.

"Oh, yeah, I know all about *them*. They're all the time after me to carry em out in the Croatan, cause now I know *that* place like the backa my hand, ain't *nobody* knows that damn place like Don Bailey, you ask anybody, they'll tell you. You ever been in there?"

"No," I said. "But I'm going."

"Well, you need *me* to carry you round in there. I *know* things about that place. That's some damn wild woods there, boy. Got Indian places, burial grounds and all, ain't nobody knows where they is but *me*. I ain't gon take *them*, no way—but I'll take *you*, you want to go. Hell, I'll carry you so far back in that Croatan woods, get you so turned around and lost, if I left you, you wouldn't *never* find your way out again, not without *me*! Come on, let's go anytime you're ready! Bull riders do it all night, y'know what I mean?!"

Though I haven't taken the old bull rider—a journeyman tugboat mechanic, I later learned, who has slept at least a few nights in his pickup truck parked in his friends' driveway on Turner Street in Beaufort—up on his invitation, I might. In the meantime, trusting my own ability to get turned around in the woods as well as the Forest Service's large-scale map, I have thrown myself into the Croatan with a vigor and have found there many of the same glories I once found in the Great Dismal, and a few new ones to boot.

In May of 1991 I went east, deep into the big Croatan forest. After stopping in at Wilber's of Goldsboro for some *real* barbeque, driving down u.s. 70 in the late afternoon was sublime, a dream of light and image come true and just there not even for the asking or taking, just there. The huge dark-brown fields ten miles west of Kinston were magenta-tinged in the late afternoon light, and, after

Big fields west of Kinston, 1991

a sally into the Neuse Sport Shop (that epicenter of easternness all full of crickets, rubber worms, and grubs, some of which were so sparkled up they looked
like metal-flake hot rods or new-age tuxedos; sodas, Trilene, rope, fishing and
camping gear, off-brand beer like Pearl from Texas at a discount for the good ol'
boys *and* girls whose jonboats and well-scuffed runabouts made an agreeable
maritime maze of the parking lot outside), I roared down the Avenue—that
long straight shot between Wyse Fork (where the Rebels in the spring of '65 tried
to hold the Blue Coats down in the Gum Swamp and, failing, backed on up
westerly to bloody Bentonville and ultimately to the Bennett farmstead near
Durham, where the Southern revolt and its counter-federation ended forever)
and New Bern—and reveled in a springtime splendor of lavender, pink, and yellow wildflowers, of red poppies and daisies, and some of the leggiest cypress
trees in the world.

There was a log truck beside the road at Tuscarora, and the May marshes at

Trent River were broad as ever and both golden and green as the new season came on. Two men in a small boat out on the Trent were fishing standing up, a right vision of tranquility and harmony that whether fiction or not still held in my mind well past the JESUS IS LORD OF NEW BERN billboard and the OBSESSIONS II ALL GIRL STAFF outfit next door, past the tawdry, colorful jangle of Havelock: the Movie Mates peek-show and Liberty Pawn and the tattoo joints and the trainer-jet on a stick marking Cherry Point Naval Air Station (the same way another plane, similarly held frozen mock-aloft a dozen feet over the down-east deck, marked the grass strip at Aulander a few counties to the north) and the Hyper Space family entertainment parlor, as if some marriage of institutions had occurred between the air corps and the county fair and their offspring were all the concerns of this military midway spread out here between the broad Neuse River and the lakes and pocosins of the Croatan National Forest.

Next afternoon I drove into the Croatan with my jonboat atop the little gray station wagon, west on Riverdale Road down below New Bern. There were exploded thistle and cattail tufts beside the road, young pine candles, the old dark water I favored once again greeting me, and this time it was at the small tar and timber bridge over upper Brice Creek.

Songbirds were *chee*ing, and a cardinal was flitting about like Adam in a union suit against the green of Eden. I turned again and drove through a tall and vigorous pineland that reminded me of the Francis Marion forest in South Carolina before Hugo swept through and broke the boughs of a million trees.

Alone at the Brice Creek landing I put the jonboat in amidst the wild grapevine and the mixed oak and pine. It was a shady place on what was now a hot day, a good place to be alone in a small boat, wild blue iris and mossy cypress at the narrow stream's edge. Two hummingbirds *scree*d by low to the dark water, and I cut the motor, sat drifting and watching a mother osprey setting her shaggy nest atop a dead and moss-shagged cypress. A hawk flew over, then the osprey's mate returned but flew off as I neared. Still the mother sat the nest, her tail fanned over its edge, and at last I could hear the cheeping cries of the chicks. Selfish but satisfied, I yanked the cord and headed on downstream.

Around past the airport was the old-time stuff: trailer camps with small docks, a few ducks and geese, here a ruined dock and there a brand new one with something like a pew to sit on and witness the riverine world. Denoting travelers of different sorts were fishing boats called *Philander* and *Gulliver II*. For a few minutes I puttered into a dark hidden lake through a little channel off Brice Creek and watched a muskrat glide warily by beneath myrtle bushes on caving banks.

Past a rusty tin boat shed and a Canada goose feeding in the shallows, after the first highway bridge, I slowed and read a sign near the dock that went with a fine suburban home:

SUBMERGED

DANGER

BARGE

I couldn't help but wonder once again about the vast, undiscovered underwater navy, the fleet of the drowned and dead ships of all sizes, hulls like the Trent River ferryboat flat from two centuries past that the Maritime Museum kept for a spell over in Beaufort. But that sort of meditation is better left for the docks and draughty taverns, I found, for shortly I was nearing Brice's confluence with the Trent and, entering the marshes, had to watch out for and keep skirting grass-rafts that I knew would surely foul the jonboat engine's prop, which they did.

Then down the Trent I went, under the U.S. 70 bridges, through the old harbor of New Bern where bright blue canvas dressed up the white boats. Big brick Tryon Palace, the tourist draw, sat across the way, a monument to the last days of British colonial grandeur. "A very genteel house built, the only one of brick, on the banks of the Trent," the peripatetic German doctor Johann David Schoepf wrote when he saw it just after the Revolution, during the winter of 1783–84. "This palace, for it is honored with that much too splendid name, is at this time almost in ruins; the inhabitants of the town took away everything they could make use of, carpets, pannels of glass, locks, iron utensils, and the like, until watchmen were finally installed to prevent the carrying-off of the house itself. The state would be glad to sell it, but there is nobody who thinks himself rich enough to live in a brick house." Problems of the palace concerned neither the Confederation nor the young nation very long, for it burned in 1798 and was not put back to right till well into this century.

New Bern's clock tower—by night a landmark, a bright and well-lit local moon across the water—read 2:15. A male and female mallard sat upon a worn timber as I passed through the open railway trestle and moved on into one of the greatest of our eastern rivers, the Neuse, the ailing Neuse.

With a certain historical trepidation, the Ted Williams motor and I pushed the jonboat upriver, toward the New Bern Fertilizer Company. A crane was lifting and then lowering pilings into place from a barge held fast by a blue tugboat. On the New Bern riverbank was an enormous magnolia in bloom, its ivory blossoms calling to mind an egret rookery, like Monkey Island up in Currituck or Phillips Island in the Haystack Marshes of Newport River closer by.

It was a flat calm, with water and sky equally blue and silver. I might have gone miles upstream, but something turned me round. Back on the Trent, as I was looking at some little palmettos on the bank and watching a kingfisher in a yaupon tree, I fouled the prop again in those grass mats. Two men, both of them bare chested and showing some gold, went roaring by in a low-to-the-water speedboat, kicking up side spray but no rooster tail.

Out of summertime nowhere came a thunderstorm, a great single cracking clap sounding out terribly as I rounded the airport, and I pulled back up to the Brice Creek landing in a warm driving rain. Now I was not alone. There was a man in a green ball cap and blue jeans and a blue shirt, along with his straw-hatted old mama. A Methodist preacher named Graham Royall from Vanceboro up north of New Bern was there, too. His calling had also carried him to Harlowe, on the back way over to Beaufort, and to Fair Bluff, a blackwater hamlet on the Lumber River far to our south. Reverend Royall's particular interest was down-east architecture, so we stood in the rain-dripping wilderness and talked about shed roofs and porches for a spell. He was a canoeist, and kept his wallet in a plastic bag.

The blue-shirt man spoke up: "Well, I reckon it's about high tide, long about now."

"Here?" I said. Tides hadn't occurred to me this afternoon, nor should they have. Where we were standing was forty miles up the Neuse, which empties into Pamlico Sound, not the sea, and a few more miles counting the Trent and the creek itself. Wind, not moon, piles the water up thisaway, and unpredictably so. Nonetheless I said: "How much tide *is* there here?"

"Eight to ten inches," he said. "A foot if it's a *good suck*." He and the others were just waiting for the rain to pass before going back out on the creek, but I wanted to prowl other reaches of the forest and so went on and slid the jonboat atop the car. There were ditches full of Croatan's *cafe au lait* storm waters yet to see, a stretch of ferns and wild blue iris along Little Road, a red-tailed hawk there, too. When I said something about coming back to Brice and going upstream next time instead of down, the blue-shirt man just shook his head and said,

"In June for-*get* it! Place'll be full of powerboats. These folks that live in these big houses down the creek, they'll come up on you, pass you at forty miles an hour within four feet, and just *wave* at you."

John Lawson was why I had turned around out on the Neuse. Or, rather, John Lawson's fate, which bore out the truth of a brooding remark in Joseph Conrad's *Heart of Darkness*. Marlow, the narrator, was speaking of pre-Christian England in comparison to the serpentine Congo of colonial times a century ago, but I would hasten to bring the Sound Country before Marlow's court there on the deck of the cruising yawl *Nellie* the night he said of the Thames,

"And this also has been one of the dark places on the earth."

On December 28, 1700, the day after his twenty-sixth birthday, John Lawson left Charleston, his home of only four months, and set out for the Carolina backcountry. He was explorer-with-portfolio, representing the Lords Proprietors—the eight Englishmen who owned the realm, this Carolina colony that was only a decade older than Lawson himself.

He and his party canoed up the Atlantic coast, turning up and in at the Santee River, his guides a succession of Indian men he called Scipio (of the Seewee tribe), Santee Jack, and Enoe Will. He had precious little guidance beyond these men—there were no maps.

The elongated, swooping *C* trail of Lawson's party led them into northern, now North, Carolina just west of Waxhaw, arced east then north, hung a right at High Point, and headed in beeline to the Sound Country. He was astounded by the plant, animal, and birdlife, and was generally a fascinated observer of the many Indians he met along the way, like the Tuscarora hunters of the coastal plain. By the time he reached English habitation, around present-day Washington and Bath, he had covered most of six hundred miles in fifty-seven days. At Pampticough River he rested as a guest of planter Richard Smith, whose daughter became by Lawson's last testament "my dearly beloved Hannah Smith," his intended but never his wife. Lawson in taking her as his near-wilderness lover was going native, though not nearly as native as what the wilderness had in store for him. Perhaps John and Hannah were just living out the pastoral fancy of the Byronic quatrain:

> They together on an island lived.
> A natural love they had.
> And a natural love, though it's not good,
> Lord, neither is it bad.

It was the end of February, 1701, and how long Lawson lingered at Smith's we do not know. Lawson did apply for land hereabouts on the Ides of March, as revealed by the town records of Bath, just downriver from Washington. Or by the records of what would *become* Bath after this same applicant Lawson surveyed, laid out, and cofounded Bath, our state's oldest town, incorporated on March 8, 1705.

But before this, Lawson dropped down to the confluence of the Trent and the Neuse, where the Indians had a town called Chattoka. Apparently no one there minded having the peripatetic Englishman around—Lawson went up the Trent a little ways, a half mile or so, and built a house on some high ground overlooking a creek even now called Lawson's Creek. Ere long he wandered north to Roanoke Island and looked over the Ralegh colony's fort, at what little remained of his forebears' handiwork a century and then some after Ralegh's colonists had vanished traceless but for the single word they had carved upon a tree without elaboration: CROATOAN.

Lawson and presumably Hannah drifted back to Bath, where he built a new house on lots 5 and 6, fenced himself and his woman in, got to be Pamticough clerk of court, and partnered up with a jurist and a physician in the construction of a "horse-mill." John Lawson was becoming a leading light in the colony.

He was also writing a more or less true account of his life on the river and deer trail and Indian path. Lawson's book, *A New Voyage to Carolina*, was brought out in London in 1709.

While he was in London on the business of his book, he met a Swiss businessman, Baron Christoph von Graffenried, who had heard wonderful reports about Carolina from one of Lawson's bosses and tacit benefactors, Lord Proprietor the Duke of Albemarle. Von Graffenried also had absorbed the 1706 Joshua Kocherthal report on relations between the English and the Indians in Carolina: "complete friendship and good understanding."

The Swiss—Von Graffenried was accompanied on this mission by one Michel—struck a deal with the English. Queen Mary would pay the transport of 650 German Palatine refugees who were currently crowding London, and two of Carolina's best—Lawson and his co-horse miller, Christopher Gale—would get them to America. The baron had bought 17,500 acres of Trent and Neuse waterfront from the Lords Proprietors, another 1,250 acres from Lawson. Once in Carolina, the Palatine labor force would, under John Lawson's supervision, get the town of New Bern going. Von Graffenried would follow with more settlers, a smaller group from Switzerland.

It was January 1710 when Lawson and the Palatines sailed from Gravesend. Half of them died on the stormy thirteen-week crossing. Once they reached the relative maritime safety of the lower Chesapeake, they were set upon and plundered by a French privateer. Depleted in every way, they now staggered overland. Down on Chowan River Thomas Pollock—another Lawson friend and ally—looked kindly and took pity upon them, refurnished them, and shipped them on to the site Lawson had picked, old Chattoka, now New Bern.

Von Graffenried showed up in early September 1710 with a hundred Swiss and saw no shine or newness at all about this version of Bern. He found it a place of "sickness, want and desperation."

Some of what Von Graffenried must *not* have heard about the "goodliest land" was the high level of political strife in the colony during the early 1700s—a virtual civil war with Quakers mad at Governor Thomas Cary, then allied with him. This was on top of some bad crop years, and all was aswirl at the time of the baron's arrival. Council leader Cary was essentially deposed once Edward

Hyde was appointed as the first governor of—officially—*North* Carolina in December 1710, but the enmity did not end there—a force under Cary attacked a Hyde army at Thomas Pollock's Chowan plantation the following June.

John Lawson stayed out, or at least aside, of Cary's Rebellion. Pollock removed himself to Virginia, then after a spell so did Cary, and the colony proceeded under Hyde. What Lawson could not sidestep, though, were the Indians, of whom he had easily observed: "They are really better to us than we have been to them," adding presciently: "The Indians are very revengeful, and never forget an injury done, till they have received Satisfaction."

Indeed, in 1701, the first year he was in Carolina, Lawson heard from Pamlico natives about the "wicked" Englishmen who "threatened the Indians for hunting near their plantations." There were armed conflicts with the Coree in 1703 and with the Meherrins in 1706 and 1707; and by 1710 the Tuscarora were petitioning Pennsylvania over abject land theft, kidnapping, and human bondage. Why Pennsylvania? A rich and active Indian slave trade had already provoked the Pennsylvania assembly, in 1705, to legislate against "further importation of Indian slaves from Carolina."

Perhaps Lawson and Von Graffenried set out up the Neuse in September 1711 to find its headwaters, its source. Or perhaps it was to study where to shoot a new road up to Virginia. Lawson originally proposed the trip, according to the baron, "hinting there were plenty of wild grapes which we could gather for refreshing ourselves. This statement, however, was not strong enough to prevail on me." Even so, with Lawson assuaging Von Graffenried's legitimate fears about Indians, telling the Swiss land baron "surely there were no savages living in that branch of the river," they left New Bern for the interior, taking two weeks' provisions, two friendly Indians as aid and insurance, and two black oarsmen.

One of these friendlies was on horseback, paralleling on land the progress of Lawson and Von Graffenried and their watercraft. When this Indian went to cross the river, he rode right into the Tuscarora village of Catechna, now Contentnea.

"What are you doing with that horse?" the Tuscaroras asked him.

"Bringing it to the Surveyor-General and the Baron, who are going upstream," he answered.

This admission created a general alarm in Catechna. The Tuscaroras seized the horse and bade the New Bern Indian to warn his intruding employers to go no farther into Tuscarora country. When the Indian bore them this message, Baron Von Graffenried said,

"I do not like the looks of things—we ought to turn back at once."

John Lawson just laughed in his face.

And then Tuscaroras swarmed out of the jungle and out of the Neuse River and came roaring upon them. Having warned the New Bern Indian, then followed him back to Lawson and Von Graffenried, they now force-marched the men through the brush, briers, brambles, and mires of those lowlands, and brought them, in the middle of the night, before King Hancock back at Catechna on Contentnea Creek.

Lawson and Von Graffenried were tried, with forty elders their jury.

Amazing as it seems, they were acquitted.

They might have walked out of that fateful council chamber, but there were other forces at work, and it was not to be.

The Lawson–Von Graffenried exploration of the Neuse, a modest and innocuous fortnight outing by design, had blundered into a serious native muster for war. No sooner were they acquitted by the Tuscarora—of trespass? of general, intrusive annoyance? of serious crimes committed by other Europeans, crimes too long unpunished and unavenged?—than Cor Tom, king of the Corees, came at Lawson with a host of complaints.

John Lawson, exhausted and probably emboldened by the judgment of the elders, met Cor Tom's ire with ire of his own, and this undiplomatic action was the last protocol in which Lawson had a voluntary say. The incensed Tuscaroras went into council of war, now, sentencing Lawson and Von Graffenried to death but granting Von Graffenried a stay after he threatened them with retribution from his guardian, the queen of England.

Lawson made no such claims for himself, and had no such luck. His spleen already vented at Cor Tom, he now assumed a stoic posture and let come what may.

What came has never been known for certain. Von Graffenried heard about but did not witness the torturing of Lawson—Indians found a razor on Lawson and threatened to cut his throat, so Von Graffenried was told, adding that "the small negro," one of the oarsmen, corroborated this. But Von Graffenried also heard Lawson was hanged, or was burned. William Byrd II (who as a boundary commissioner for Virginia in 1728 showed a respect for earlier work done by Lawson, uncommon to the point of uniqueness for that inveterate Virginian) brought the slit-throat story forward in time, but Lawson's friend Christopher Gale, writing only eight weeks after Lawson's death and also trusting "Indian information," said:

"They stuck him full of fine small splinters of torch wood like hog's bristles and set them gradually afire."

The day after they had killed Lawson, the Tuscaroras told Von Graffenried that the Sound Country Indians were massing for war, hundreds of Tuscarora, Mattamuskeet, Pamlico, Neuse, Coree, and Bay River warriors. And they were speaking with decidedly unforked tongues.

Eleven days later, at dawn on September 22, 1711, this Indian army conducted a broad, murderous assault on the region between the Neuse and Pamlico. The attackers were pitiless in their mayhem: eighty infants were slaughtered; women were laid on the floors of their houses and staked to death; houses were burned, stock killed or driven off.

The Tuscarora War had begun.

Colonel John Barnwell in January 1712 marched a force of South Carolinians three hundred miles, beat the Indians in two battles near New Bern, and besieged Catechna for ten days before agreeing to a truce on account of the presence of white women and children in the Indian fort. For this truce Barnwell was roundly criticized and coincidentally not paid for his efforts—whereupon he kidnapped and enslaved some Indians for his pains and, having gained the appellation "Tuscarora Jack," stole away back to South Carolina.

The Tuscaroras resumed their attacks in the summer and fall of 1712, and now yellow fever, too, was carrying off hordes of Carolinians, including Governor Hyde. A second South Carolina force won a "glorious victory" at Fort Neoheroka at Contentnea Creek in late March, 1713, and the earth here has held both colonists' musket balls and the remains of the Indians' provender, charred peaches and acorns, for most of three centuries since.

Those Tuscaroras who weren't put to death by scalping, burning, or what the Virginia governor called "exquisite tortures," and those who weren't enslaved drifted out of this landscape, some probably to Indian Woods, the Tuscarora settlement that exists nowadays as a Bertie County township far to the north of New Bern and Catechna. This was the reward to Tom Blunt, leader of a wing of friendly Tuscaroras, apparently the effective price of protection for the Albemarle region, which did not suffer in this war as badly as did the Neuse and Pamlico. The Tuscarora were the sixth nation of the Iroquois, and they were gone from Carolina altogether by sometime in the early nineteenth century, gone off faraway to upstate New York.

Their name is yet upon us: in the little crossroads a few miles west of New Bern; on a building-side sign just east of Kinston that reads TUSCARORA YARNS; at the scouts' Camp Tuscarora near Newton Grove; on Tuscarora Avenue, the road in the Cabbage Patch section of Elizabeth City where I first heard them spoken of; and abbreviated as "Tusk," the name of the tiny Core Sound fish camp where Ann went often as a girl.

One of the places settlers fled to during the war was Captain Brice's home, on the south shore of the Trent River, hard by the creek to which *his* name is tied. Marlow was right: there are freshets from a fountain filled with blood, and these eastern streams are among them, or have been. On this one bright May afternoon, I looked up John Lawson's river and for an instant saw the bend in the

Neuse that lured him on for good, ill, and eternity, and as I made my own way—pounding the jonboat over the mysterious and haunted waves this brief history still sets in motion—back up to Captain Brice's and Brice Creek, I could say, out of homage to both Lawson and King Hancock, in the tongue of the Tuscarora because John Lawson went among the Indians, like Thomas Hariot had gone on Roanoke Island before him, and learned their language and wrote it down:

Oonutsauka.

I remember it.

Next day driving along N.C. 101 on the way up to Havelock, I looked out over the potato fields all aflower, the very emblem of eastern Carolina's springtime promise. I met Carolyn Kindell, Ann's sister, at the New Bern airport, and took this young biologist on yet another field trip into the Croatan, this time aiming for Great Lake.

A pileated woodpecker let out its *kuk-kuk* cry as we roamed down Catfish Road. We stopped to admire a nice stand of pond pine along a branch between Little Road and Sheep Ridge Lane, none of them all that tall and their old tops windswept flat. She cautioned me against figuring how old they were by their height, the way we gauge loblollies. "You can't tell their age—could be *real* old. The forest has such a wide variety of nutrients, water regimes—some of them live a long time, and just don't get beyond a certain height."

White bells were in bloom, and, intermingled with *Gordonia*, or loblolly bay, with its occasional red leaf, so were the swamp magnolia (*Magnolia virginiana*), the sweet-bay magnolia with its fragrant flower. In a tractor tread beneath a power line, small sticky dew droplets of sundew (*Drosera*) were growing. "They love it here," said Carolyn, adding: "Mowing mimics fire." Also thriving thereabouts were yellow trumpet pitcher plants (*Sarracenia flava*), a couple dozen in one group standing tall, and purple pitcher plants (*Sarracenia purpurea*) as well, with their tall magenta in-folding flowers.

Such a wilderness as the Croatan is a feast at almost any time of year; certainly it is so in the spring. This is no less a jungle than the Great Dismal, its riches no less apparent: a male indigo bunting; the short pond pines and taller loblollies through which the sand road to Catfish Lake went winding; pink *muhlenbergia*, or muly grass, in bloom along both sides of Sheep Ridge Lane at Black Swamp Road; golden ragwort; fleabane with small daisylike flowers; woolly mullein, looking a mite like lamb's ears—"Let's pick em," said Carolyn. "Pick em like cabbage and *eat em*!" She said this with a laughing relish, reminding me for a moment of those cannibals in *Heart of Darkness* who spoke with similar enthusiasm about Charlie Marlow's dead helmsman as the small steamship pushed up the Congo. We took two lefts, first on Holston Hunter Road, then on

Pitcher plants

Seaborn Road, passing *Gordonia* thirty to sixty feet tall that was towering among pines no taller. A black racer went shooting across the road, and swallowtails were coursing about as we passed a pocket of longleaf pines, some mature, twenty or thirty young.

Coming upon Great Lake by car was a lot like plying one's way along by canoe in a canal filled with sand, like driving in the loose sand on a sea beach. There was a good deal of side-to-side sway, sinkage, and a just-plain general uncertainty about the forward progress of the car. Occasionally along the six- or eight-mile Great Lake Road, there were dips and swales that seemed of sufficient size to swallow a modest vehicle like our VW station wagon with the turtled jonboat atop.

The little put-in was at a thirty- or forty-yard cut, a small channel that led through willows and reeds, following red vertical channel markers to the lake itself, a bullfrog watching us on our way out. We tied up and went walking in a boggy sweet-gum woods straight across the lake from the landing, then cruised north along the eastern shore and had lunch in the cypress shade of a little beach on the north shore. There was a fortune of ospreys on this side of Great Lake, one mother chasing around *scree*ing at us when we drew near nest #188, her fierce and piercing cry almost belittling the sharp call of the hawk, and reminiscent of the mother sitting her nest on Brice Creek the afternoon before.

Just through those woods was Ellis Lake, sometimes called Lake Ellis Simon, after the man who ran the hunt club Camp Bryan back in here for so long, one more of the formerly great number of Sound Country waterfowling hideaways that attracted and interested many a man, including the fellow who most often took aim at the clear and Elysian space beyond outfield fences: Babe Ruth. Duck hunting interested the Babe, at least from dawn to dusk, when he would pile his big self into his touring car and repair to New Bern and hand out nickels to children and carouse with the night life of Old Chattoka.

Carousing closer to where we were was a large population of alligators over there through the woods, gators cruising that other lake, I reckoned, for the unlucky duck or the young osprey flopping down into the lake waters, not having learned to fly fast enough to survive one of these patient and rapacious saurians.

I wondered: maybe it was the fish hawks, the ospreys, that had lured the brilliant homegrown photographer Bayard Wootten of New Bern out here to Great Lake to shoot. Mrs. Wootten—designer of the original Pepsi-Cola logo, rambling chronicler of Southern folklife and domestic architecture both low and grand—was once caught here by the lens of another, standing by her tripod and wearing her full turn-of-the-century rig—broad-brimmed hat and white blouse, long black dress and all—in two and a half feet of water.

Fierce and noble as an eagle, *Pandion haliaetus* fishes all the waters of the

Bayard Wootten, Great Lake, Craven County, about 1910

world, save those of Antarctica. "I have seen the great nests of this one-species family in pine trees on Japanese islets, on sea cliffs near Gibraltar, on spruce islands in the Baltic, on Mexican headlands, and on eroded pinnacles in Yellowstone National Park," Roger Tory Peterson once wrote. They fish with the keenness and dedication of men and women casting the Carolina surf for blues in the spring and fall, or lying out in camouflaged blinds and boats for ducks and geese, and when they stoop and drop with talons open and thrown forward and hit the water at up to forty miles an hour, their handlike raptor's claws closing, it is a better-than-even bet their prey is in hand. One close lakeside observer of this single-species family saw an osprey "fly off with a three-foot eel and carry it to a feeding perch a quarter of a mile away." There is a danger, though, in this powerful grip, for the occasion is not infrequent when an osprey locks talons on a fish too heavy and is dragged underwater and drowned, both carcasses then married for eternity like Ahab and Moby Dick.

(opposite) Osprey

Their nests are enormous stick-built affairs, running to hundreds of pounds, and they pile them on chimneys, on platforms on channel markers and radio towers, on the broad-spread branches of pine and cypress. Gone are the days, at least in our realm, when men dynamited them out of these avian leaseholds, and gone, too, are the days when DDT residual in fish got into our ospreys and threw off their reproductive systems and thinned their eggshells well into the 1960s. Ospreys mate and seem to pair off for as long as they both shall last—up to twenty-five years—filling their pith-thatch nests with three eggs a season, eggs that vary from white to a pattern that looks like an ovoid, sepia moon, as if the craters were cinnamoned. And David Lee, the man who once saw that eel air-freighted, thought that because ospreys return to the same nest but not together and not on the same time or day during the spring mating season, "they may bond to the actual nest site as much as they do to each other."

On the water again, we stopped not too far out from the beach, warping alongside a fifteen-foot cypress with spreading branches and a top feathered like a ming tree. Osprey nest #179 was built not atop the tree like so many of them were, but halfway up—it was nothing for us to make the boat fast and climb up and peer into the nest: there, lungs and hearts pumping against the heat of the day were three osprey goslings, golden brown with white stripes in their feathers' coloring. In a few weeks they would favor their folks, white heads with black masks, and be ready for flight, but for now this diminutive raptor triune was all in a heap, tired from the hard and steady work of *growing*. Above—and not too far above, either—the mother circled and *scree*d, so we left her chicks panting and gasping, right where they belonged this May day when balmy was becoming beastly hot.

I *had* been lost here: not on some remote Indian midden led there and marooned by a congenial if crusty fellow-sailor on shore leave from a ship called *Mystery*, but somewhere else altogether, somewhere between the big green burgeoning Croatan jungle of the May-time present and the hideous bloodlettings of that Tuscarora War begun one long-ago September and recently recollected *in situ*, a history far beyond my own and far beyond that of anyone or anything now living except for a few Sound Country cypress monarchs. Now over Great Lake, above and beyond the flight of the osprey, there came the beating of other wings, the air-slapping sound of an enormous helicopter, a pulsing and percussive reminder of the modern moment and a war just ended near other waters in the Persian Gulf far away.

We find ourselves on the entrance of a vast plain
which extends west sixty or seventy miles. . . . This
plain is mostly a forest of the great long-leaved pine,
the earth covered with grass, interspersed with an infinite
variety of herbaceous plants, and embellished with
extensive savannas, always green, sparkling with
ponds of water. . . .

—William Bartram, *Travels through North
and South Carolina*, 1791

Tar

· ·

What sort of place? This sort:

Looking for the old Onslow County–New River homeplace where my grandfather Page had been a farmboy, I pulled the oyster-white station wagon into the clearing out in front of Joe Powell's TAR LANDING GROC. late one autumn evening in 1973, our tires clicking over the flattened bottlecaps that paved the ground. John Foley and I left my brindled dog Jake in the station wagon and walked on inside.

It was a long narrow building with creaky wood floors, bare lightbulbs and glass counters, and a space heater, redolent of cheese and of salt- and pepper-cured hams and sausage meats hanging from exposed rafters, the whole drill of a country store; and of the two men there—one in his sixties, the other older— I asked:

"Got any idea where the old Page place was?"

They frowned at each other. "Page place?" one of the men said.

"That's right."

"What was you lookin for it for?"

"My grandfather grew up here, around here—this's the first time I've ever been by."

"Grandfather, no kidding."

"No," I said.

"Well, now, let's see. There was a Page," the older man said. He was sitting on a bottled-drink crate, and had brightened considerably as we entered the store. "And I think he was a Robert, or a R. W., something like that, sound like your people?"

"No, that wasn't my granddaddy—he's J. A."

"J. A.," said the older man. "Don't b'lieve I ever knew him. This one here was Robert or something."

"He anywhere around where I could talk to him?" I said. "Might be a cousin."

Both of the men shook their heads, and the younger of the two said, "Naw, that family moved out I spect it's been thirty years ago, and that's the last Page I ever knew of in this country."

I was stunned, stopped cold, mystified. I could not accept that these men had never heard of my grandfather, the man whose hand guided the building of the Bell Tower and Wilson Library and Kenan Stadium in Chapel Hill; who had learned carpentry and masonry and, as he later said without a trace of hubris, learned to be a master builder, after he had grown up on a one- and sometimes two-mule farm that I just knew was within throwing distance of this little country store; whose mother and father were big country people with the same size feet, and what served their marriage well was that she wore his new brogans around the house to break them in while he was getting the last of the good out of the pair he was wearing in the field; who worked for the army during World War I in the cold of coastal Fort Caswell, at the end of the spit of land called Oak Island down across the bay from Southport; who remembered two seasons of pig harvesting on Smith (later Bald Head) Island that netted more than thirty thousand pounds a season ("What did they do with it?" my aunt Sister asked me. "I believe they ate it," I said), wild pork from that salt-marsh and maritime isle; who remembered the Redshirts riding into Tar Landing and Richlands and Jacksonville during their successful black intimidation campaign of 1898; and who broke his arm once, falling off a mule and cracking it so badly that the forearm bone was jabbed through the flesh and skin of his lower arm like a spike, and he rode to the doctor and medicine that were six hours away on the same mule that threw him in the first place. . . .

There in the old store, to where maybe he had run for plow points or a sack of flour or a little handbag of hard candy, I stood motionless and still could not believe these men of Tar Landing had not known my granddaddy or at the very least known *of* him. Sensing my disappointment, which was keen, the older man stood up from his bottle crate and shook my hand and said,

"Well, it's good to know you. I'm Joe Powell, I'm seventy-three years old, and I can stand on my head on a basketball."

"You can *what*?" I said, and I glanced at Foley and could tell nobody'd ever said such a thing to him, either.

"Said I can stand on my head on a basketball."

"He *can*, too," said the other man.

"Come out here, I'm gon show you," Joe Powell said.

Then he reached around behind the cash-register counter and came up with a two-thirds-inflated basketball, held it forth gripping the indention and waving it in our faces, and headed for the front door. "Let's go!"

"That's all right," Foley said.

"You don't have to do that," I said. "We believe you."

"Naw, you don't. I'm gon show you."

It was bell-clear that he *was* going to show us, so, while Joe was picking out just the right place for his impromptu gymnastics, I walked to the car and got a camera, rousing the slumbering dog as I did. I got back to Joe Powell just as he found his spot, a small six- or eight-inch-wide gulley at the side of the parking lot, where he could get the ball down and lodged so it wouldn't roll and kick out from under him quite so easily while he was going upright, upside-down.

"Okay!" he shouted. "Here I go!"

He leaned over, put his bald head into the ball's shallow concavity, and went up—but only about halfway—and then he caught himself with his feet and one knee. "Nope, nope! That ain't it! Watch me now!" He did the same thing again. Then again and again—in all about eight or nine times, waving Foley and me down whenever we tried to talk him out of what we were sure was going to be a broken limb, a self-smitten hip or thigh. He stood up, stepped back from the point of action, nodded at us as if he had figured out the problem at last.

"Boys," Joe Powell said, "it must be that medicine I been takin. Got me to where I can't balance good."

"Well, then," I said, "maybe next time."

"Oh, no," he said, "I'm still gon do it—that's just why it's takin me so long."

At last he went up, held for a moment, and flipped on over, sent himself sprawling out on his own mercantile ground there, like his head somehow fired, in the outrageous goofiness of his display, and projected him off that old crimped roundball a height and distance commensurate with the value of the idea. "The wonder 'tis not that 'twere done well, but that 'twere done at all," I recalled Doctor Samuel Johnson's remarking on another occasion. Foley and I helped him get up and brush himself off, and by then even Joe Powell was allowing that maybe it *would* be next time.

Then Jake the dog started sounding off.

"Whose dog's that over yonder in that car?" said Joe, heartened by the canine distraction.

"He's mine," I said. "Just a mutt."

"Well," said Joe, "let's have a look at him."

Leading him by his rope trace, we got Jake on out of the wagon and let him stretch and prance around over the bottlecaps. "That's quite a dog," Joe said. "Yeah, I like a good dog like that."

"Thanks, Mister Powell."

"Yessir, that's my kind of dog. Sure is. I'd make a squirrel dog out of him, 'f he was mine."

"I reckon he'd do all right on squirrels," I said, but I had my doubts.

"Oh yeah, oh yeah," said Joe. "You wanna trade?"

"Trade?"

"Dogs."

"Trade dogs with you?" I said. I harked Jake back into the car.

"That's right," Joe Powell said. "Come on, I got a good dog, best dog there is, I'm gon show you." And he started tugging at my elbow, pulling me back toward the store.

"But I don't want to trade dogs," I said.

"Come *on*!"

He led us not into the store but around its side, and there waiting patiently, tethered to a doghouse, was a brown and black shepherd. "That 'ere dog," Joe Powell said, setting it free.

"Good boy, good boy," I said, rubbing the dog's head. "What about him?"

"That 'ere dog hates fire, *hates* it! Pulled a baby from a burning house one time, that's right, sure did, saved that baby's life—on account of that's how much he hates fire."

"No kidding."

"Sure's I'm born."

"Well, that's something else," I said.

"And you ain't got to take my word for it, neither," he said. "I'm gon show you."

Joe Powell produced a brown-paper grocery bag, folded and flat, and the shepherd immediately tensed. "Y'all stand back now," he said, and all three of us backed away from the dog, and then Joe fetched a Zippo lighter with an embossed pheasant on its side from up out of his pocket, lit it, and, once it was good and aflame, sailed it from about ten feet away right at the dog's head.

The shepherd leapt into the air, teeth bared and growling, clapped its big jaw onto the bag, and came to earth slapping at the flaming bag with both his forepaws.

"See there! See there!" Joe Powell stamped and cried.

In less than ten seconds the shepherd had put out the fiery bag and now stood over his smoking victim, still batting at it. The air was thick with paper smoke and with the ugly pungency of the dog's singed whiskers and burned hair.

"Didn't I tell you?" Joe said. "Didn't I?"

"We got to get going," Foley said, eyeing the dog and man hard with a New England look that could peel paint. They didn't have this in New Hampshire.

"Well, now you seen him," Joe Powell said. "How bout a trade?"

"No, thanks," I said. "But if I did want to trade, tell me—what would you get out of it? My dog can't do anything like that."

"Oh," said Joe, "that's just it. That shepherd, he can already *do* all that stuff. Don't matter about yours, not a bit. Cause, you see, I'd get all *my* fun outa *train-in* him!"

Back in Chapel Hill a week or two later, I told Granddaddy Page about my short sojourn in Tar Landing and about Joe Powell's antics. I thought my grandfather would be glad, if not proud, that I had wandered by his old home, but as I described the oddball scene to him, he grew increasingly detached and somber and in the end was not amused. Much later, I realized that he understood full well my appreciation of the basketball headstand and the fire-eating dog, but that he wasn't at all sure I understood something larger that loomed behind those entertainments, something that he had lived with in surfeit there and elsewhere in the coastal lowlands eighty years earlier, an isolation and loneliness that inexorably if not inevitably led to a certain amount of loafers' glories and idiots' delights. All he said at the time of my Tar Landing report, though, was one even-handed, sympathetic, sad remark:

"Son, people way out in the country sometimes," he shook his head, "sometimes they just don't have a whole lot to do."

'Twas not always so.

Nor was this a commonplace, the air of the coastal plain pungent with the smoke and smell of a dog's burning hair and snout whiskers. Our piney woods had fire, sure enough, but they were far more redolent not of the burned hair of an oddly disposed dog but of the smoke of the big and broad-burning natural and rejuvenative wiregrass fires that lightning sent—bestowed upon, even—the longleaf pine savannas, whose wiregrass gave quail good cover and whose seed fattened wild turkey and whose strands as fuel burnt off the scrub oak and sweet gum and whatever else, hardwood or vine, that would shade out and destroy the young longleaf pine; and, once we knew how to blaze angled, arched cuts (called boxes) and thereinto bleed and collect resin off the great longleaf, and how to cook and distill its pitch and its sap, then our woods were redolent, too, of the smoke of tar kilns and turpentine distilleries; and well before we were ever called Tar Heels, because our boys stood their ground in the Civil War as if they were tarred to it, we were widely known as tar people—*Tar Boilers*, Walt Whitman called us. Pine tar was who we were. Like Tuscarora, it was, and is, all over our geography: Granddaddy's Tar Landing, the same name again down on Stump Sound, yet again on the eastern end of Bogue Banks—Tar Landing and Tar Landing Bay—where Ann's mother once ran a fleet of condominiums named Tar Landing, Ann swabbing their decks—small wonder that more river and sound landings so called in their day did not adhere.

But there is still a Tar Corner up in Pasquotank, named after a barn a farmer once slathered with the stuff, painting his plunder house with preservative; a Tarkiln Creek in Pamlico County; a Tarkittle Ridge on Cedar Island in Carteret; a little Cape Fear River town of Tar Heel; and Tar River itself running easterly from the foothills upstate down to Pamlico River and Sound. It is thick in our ever-expressive language, as both substance and activity therewith: "They *tarred* and feathered so-and-so and rode him outa town on a rail." "They're gonna *tar* the road sometime soon, I hear." "Oh, Lord, now you're *tarred* by the same brush that he is." And so what if it was a Georgian rather than a Carolinian who devised the great, inanimate Southern stoic, the Tar Baby? "Ol' Tar Baby," wrote Joel Chandler Harris, "he don't say *nothin'*!"

It was the longleaf pine that made such tar people of us, that made our Southern veins run and pulse slowly with this sludgy blood. For, though money may never have grown upon trees, it certainly grew *within* these, and we had them aplenty. The longleaf, *Pinus palustris*, is to its lesser cousins the slash and loblolly pines as Hyperion is to a satyr, as sequoyah to a cedar. The big splayed-open cones with their thick scales grow to nearly a foot in length, and the needles to almost a foot and a half, forming up spherically in boughs so that a single longleaf tree has the look of a topiary displaying a close-clustered world of green planets. A stand of longleaf seems a careful and divine sculpture indeed, with an even more awesome molding than the rounded canopy of a maritime live-oak forest. Our coastal-plain woods two and three hundred years ago were vast and nearly unbroken reaches of longleaf pine, their lands veined by streams, dimpled with shining ponds, and threaded through here and there with a few narrow traces, cartways, carriage paths. Pine Barrens as a formal name may have stuck only in south Jersey, but we Carolinians were the barons of barrens. Not for nothing was a great stand of Onslow County longleaf turpentined in the nineteenth century under the name of the Rich Lands. Before the forests were bled out for resin and charcoaled out for tar, the volume of Carolina pineywoods produce was somewhere on the far side of incredible, and the multiforms of its resin flowed through our ports, paying the way for the many, lining the pockets of a few.

In 1610, only three years after Jamestown's founding and Pocahontas's celebrated saving of Captain John Smith's neck, the official "Instructions for suche things as are to be sente from Virginia" made clear to the colonists what their major quarry was: "Pyne trees, or firre trees are to be wounded within a yarde of the grounde, or boare a hoal wth an agar the thirde pte into the tree, and lett yt runne into any thinge that maye recyue the same, and that wch yssues owte wilbe Turpentyne worthe 18L Tonne. When the tree beginneth to runne softelye yt is to be stopped vp agayne for preserveing the tree." And there was more: "Pitche and tarre hath bene made there and we doubte not but wilbe agayne . . ." Another text of the time, the "Booke of the Commodities of Virginia," brought up "Hard pitche, Tarre, Turpentine, Rozen" all in the same breath, and, as the Sound Country quit Virginia and became Carolina in the 1660s, these naval stores became staple Carolina produce and remained so till the second quarter of this century.

Naturalist John Bartram saw black men building tar kilns east of Lake Waccamaw in 1765, and they could hardly have been the first to be getting into the business, or even close to it, for in that same decade 50,000 barrels of Carolina tar and pitch were annually shipping out through the Cape Fear River port of Brunswick, below Wilmington, both towns being major tar-taps to the world—sealing ships and tarring rope around the globe.

Touring the Confederation in 1783 and 1784, the German doctor Johann Schoepf saw at the head of Pamlico River our Little Washington, a port of thirty houses to which New Englanders as the "middlemen and freight carriers" of America were routinely bringing in "cyder, cheese, apples, gingerbread, rum, sugar, iron-ware, and trinkets which they exchange in small trade for pelts, pitch, tar, and the like"—through Occacock Inlet (Ocracoke) and across Pemticoe Sound (Pamlico). "Such a lonesome country," said Doctor Schoepf, "all sand-flats and pine forest . . . an ocean of trees." Carolinians, he observed, were enjoying considerable gain from turpentine, tar, pitch, resin, and turpentine oil. He saw that one man running 3,000 turpentine boxes in a forest of 12 to 15 acres could roll up 100 to 120 barrels by summer's end, charging sixteen shillings or two Spanish dollars a barrel, and, discussing the relative merits of pitch and tar, said pitch kept well and brought more money for fewer casks. Then Doctor Schoepf, casting his eye on the piney-woods practices of that day, gazed with an accurate clarity and foreboding into the future as well:

"It is certainly no hard matter to grow rich in a short time, if it is regarded as indifferent in what state one leaves the land to his heirs."

Novelist George Higby Throop, who enjoyed both hospitality and employment as a tutor at Scotch Hall, the Capehart family's upper Albemarle Soundside plantation, had his narrator in *Bertie*—Captain Gregory Seaworthy—observe of the piney woods in 1851:

... and my horse gave some signs of weariness as he 'padded the way' in the silent shades and utter loneliness of the giant pines.

O! those Carolina roads! extending leagues on leagues, with never a crook descernible by the eye, flanked by thick-set pines that have been blazed and scarred by surveyors and tar-makers; level as a house floor, and sometimes as hard; musical at times with the hunter's horn, the hounds in full cry, or the notes of a thousand birds, thrown into fine harmonic relief by the low bass of the wind as it sweeps through the lofty pines. O! those Carolina roads!

Several years later, journalist–landscape architect Frederick Law Olmsted, traveling in our coastal plain, wrote:

I was now fairly in the Turpentine region of North Carolina. The road was a mere opening through a forest of the long-leafed pine; the trees from eight to eighteen inches in diameter, with straight trunks bare for nearly thirty feet, and their evergreen foliage forming a dense dark canopy at that hight [*sic*], the surface of the ground undulating with long swells, occasionally low and wet. In the latter case, there was generally a mingling of deciduous trees and a water-course crossing the road, with a thicket of shrubs. The soil sandy, with occasionally veins of clay; the latter more commonly in the low ground, or in the descent to it. Very little grass, herbage, or under-wood; and the ground covered, except in the road, with the fallen pine-leaves. Every tree, on one, two, or three sides, was scarified for turpentine. In ten miles, I passed half a dozen cabins, one or two small clearings, in which corn had been plant-ed, and one turpentine distillery, with a dozen sheds and cabins clustered about it.

Olmsted (who would plan Manhattan's Central Park, Brooklyn's Prospect Park, Vanderbilt's Biltmore Estate near Asheville, and Pinehurst in the Carolina sandhills as well) was visiting and viewing our piney woods—"turpentine or-chards," he called them—in the 1850s, at the height of all this resin and tar pur-suit. In its three centuries of Southern primacy, the turpentine business clearly came to have as complex and colorful a human culture as tobacco one day would, and here was the Yankee eye upon it and all its division of labor, assay of forestland, assault on timber. He saw hands cut "boxes"—angled slashes in tree sides for resin to collect in—in ten minutes' time, a day-rate of seventy-five to a hundred. They were cutting well into the cambium layer of the tree, stimulating tissue growth near the wound and, with it, the increased flow of resin; they cut the boxes in winter, then cornered or streak-cut trees steadily from March till November, going up the tree to heights after a few seasons sometimes in excess of twelve feet; the men "dipped" or emptied the so-called boxes a half dozen or so

Porte Crayon's *Scraping Turpentine,* **1857**

times a season, a dipper being a flat blade in the shape of a trowel. A "crop" of turpentine was 10,500 boxes, and a "drift" was one-fifth of a crop; with each tree getting boxed from one to four times, it took 4,000 to 5,000 trees, 200 to 250 acres of piney woods, to make a crop. Once it was cropped—boxed, chipped, and dipped—it was barreled. Olmsted saw black coopers making pine-turpentine barrels "hooped with split oak-saplings," $1.50 to $2 for six or seven of them a day. And, since he was on Southern tour twenty years after the introduction of the copper turpentine still—before which most crude turpentine got shipped out through the Cape Fear, the sounds, or Norfolk for distilling faraway—he saw something Doctor Schoepf hadn't, a piney-woods refinery in action:

"At a fifteen barrel still, I found one white man and one negro employed under the oversight of the owner. It kept employed twenty-five men hacking and dipping; running twice, that is, using thirty barrels crude turpentine, a day. Besides these hands, were two coopers, and several wagoners. The wages of ordinary practiced turpentine hands (slaves) are about $120 a year, with board, clothing, etc., as usual." At one distillery Olmsted saw a "congealed pool of rosin" of more than three thousand barrels "glistening like polished porphyry." Elsewhere, he watched the kiln-charring of pinewood till the coaled wood expressed its tar, which ran out of the kiln in little trenches for collection and ladeling into barrels.

"This," judged Olmsted, "is an exceedingly slovenly process. . . ."

The abject mess of tar boiling notwithstanding, this visiting Yankee in King Longleaf's Court wasn't treated badly. Once, he left the stagecoach and made his own way—and better time—by shank's mare, fetching up at eventide at a long one-story cabin, Mrs. Barclay's, and judging it "right cheerful and comforting to open the door, from the dark, damp, chilly night, into a large room, filled with blazing light from a great fire of turpentine pine. . . . As soon as I was warm, I was taken out to supper: seven preparations of swine's flesh, two of maize, wheat cakes, broiled quails, cold roast turkey, coffee, and tea." After dinner, Olmsted was put into "a house by itself" where there was also "a great fire" and "a stuffed easy chair" and "a tub of hot water, which I had not thought to ask for, to bathe my weary feet. And this was a piny-woods stage-house!"

Porte Crayon, that picaresque knight-errant and belle-lettrist of the antebellum Southern road, fell among the tree-tappers as well, and here the quick-sketch artist found a feast for the eye. He observed turpentine barrels standing here and there about the great woods in pairs, waiting to be carted to market on two-barrel drays, and he also saw signs and symbols of the great forest's future in the present before him:

"When the trees have been recently blazed, the square-cut markings, white on the black trunks, strikingly resemble marble grave-stones, and the traveler may imagine himself in a vast cemetery."

Our visitors from William Byrd II forward have often noted how slack many of our people are, or can be, when left to our own devices out in the eastern wildernesses, living in a state so close to nature that it seems only natural for a man to lie about half the day and only to rise when the strength is sufficient to beard the daylight at the crack of noon, hang one's head dolefully on the top slat of a dilapidated fence and, as Byrd put it, "gravely consider whether or not to take a heat at the hoe." Well, Olmsted—who put the shiftless "vagabonds" at a social station well below the "turpentine farmers"—did better at Mrs. Barclay's than Crayon did a few years later at the home and hearth of Mr. and Mrs. Squibs.

Squibs was a turpentine gatherer who, when Crayon happened along, was in the process of getting drubbed by his infuriated wife, the source of her fury being that Squibs, having run through his latest turpentine money, then made off with some of her hens' eggs and sold them for whiskey, a pint bottle of which he had secreted in an old boot in his cobbling workshop. When he offered Crayon a pull (after Crayon booked himself into the Squibs's cabin for the night),

Crayon made only a pretense of drinking, whereupon Squibs said, "Here's luck!" and jammed the bottle neck into his mouth. Mrs. Squibs caught him— "The hand of the Amazon reached in and took the bottle. Crayon expected to hear it crash against the house, but he only heard a string of some ten or fifteen disrespectful adjectives, followed by the noun 'HOG.'"

At dinner—corn bread, sweet potatoes, yaupon tea, which also carried the nickname of Japan tea—Mrs. Squibs ran her husband down steadily. "He would neither mend shoes for the neighbors nor for his own family. He would scrape a couple of barrels of turpentine now and then, carry them to town, waste half the proceeds before he got back home with his scanty supply of meat and groceries. As long as these lasted he would never lift a hand to any thing.

"The only defense made by Squibs was confined to a few miserable winks at his guest. He at length ventured to remark that turpentine was very low now— scarcely worth scraping.

"'Low!' said she, with flashing eyes. 'Low! What's the price of *eggs?*'"

Crayon was away early next day to Little Washington, which he found "a flourishing place of four thousand inhabitants" doing "a smart trade in the staples of the State—turpentine, cotton, and lumber. It has several extensive establishments for sawing and planing lumber, and for converting the brute turpentine into its various derivatives."

He rode up to Greenville on Captain Quinn's *Governor Morehead*, a small steamer "of rather queer build," a boat that would be burned by federal troops a few years later in the same Potter's Raid that torched the Rocky Mount Mills and ended Tar River commerce for the rest of the Civil War. Crayon then walked overland to the Wilmington and Weldon rail line, through "the same interminable pine forests, boxed and scarified by the turpentine gatherers, with the barrels standing about in couples among the trees, and frequent tar-kilns in process of erection, or smoking and smouldering toward completion."

So it went. *De Bow's Review*, in the summer issue of 1862, adjudged the state of our Sound Country woodlands relative to resin-tapping while engaging in a remarkably generous explanation and exculpation: "Scarcely a good tree in North Carolina has escaped this operation. . . . But so poor were the lands and so great the profits of labor, and even of the land, in the turpentine business, compared to other available products, that capital thus invested has generally yielded more profit than agriculture on the richest lands. Therefore, it is neither strange nor censurable; but altogether judicious, while these great profits were to be obtained, that nearly all the labor of this region was devoted to making turpentine, instead of enriching and cultivating the soil. . . . However, the juncture is now reached when this formerly most profitable turpentine business must be gradually lost."

In Paul Green's Pulitzer Prize–winning play *In Abraham's Bosom*, set in a late-nineteenth-century turpentine stand, a black laborer named Bud proclaims early on with he-man bravado, during midday dinner in the piney woods: "Picking cotton! Dat 'oman and chillun's job, no reg'lar man mess id dat. [Waving his hand at the woods behind him.] Turpentining's de stuff."

So cut, cut, cut went the boxers, cornerers, and chippers, and, lo, at what a rapid clip *gradual loss* came to coastal-plain Carolina! Arguing for improved methods in collecting longleaf resin and gum for turpentine in July of 1915, a chemist and an engineer in the USDA's Forest Service declared that the supply of longleaf in the South "suitable for turpentining is very nearly exhausted." A price spike in the naval-stores business during 1911 sent turpentiners scrambling and cutting into as much as three-quarters of their "round" or previously un-notched, untapped timber. There wasn't much raw material left to waste, and the USDA foresters were seeing the end of the box method of gum collection, its replacement by the use of metal cups. "The first systematic attempt to improve the method of collecting gum," they wrote, "was made at Bladenboro, N.C., by W. W. Ashe in 1894. A comparison on a limited scale was made between the French cup and gutter system and the box system, and the results showed a gain for the former of over 20 per cent in the value of the products collected."

But all that was happening was keeping a little more of the goods from going down the drain. The geese were busily eating the seed corn and the great garden kept shrinking.

Speaking in City Park, Southern Pines, North Carolina, in the spring of 1923, a forest engineer felicitously named Thomas P. Ivy saw the demise of the great longleaf forests. The conifers, or gymnosperms, were the most ancient of trees, with only four hundred species remaining in the world (one thought of this recently when several hundred pines of a species thought extinct since the age of dinosaurs turned up hale and hearty in a remote Australian cove). Here, during the Warren Harding era, was Ivy's report on the great Southern pine: of four hundred billion board feet in the original pan-South forest (Ivy was an engineer, after all), only one-fifth was left.

Still, Ivy was hopeful. "Even now in its depleted condition," he said, "it yields annually 25,000,000 gallons of turpentine and 800,000,000 pounds of rosin." At that late date, he somehow believed *Pinus palustris* could return in quantity to the South, and that its remedial effect would extend beyond forestry and into the land of lint. "The reforestation of the Costal [*sic*] Plain will restore the disturbed balance in the insect world and thus check and put an end to the pest activities of the cotton boll weevil."

The good hope was not to be realized in any broad fashion, though Engineer Ivy was that spring standing in one of the few places—the Sandhills—in North

Carolina where one might still be convinced that it could or would be. At Weymouth, the estate of writer and fox-hunter James Boyd, now an artists' retreat and Nature Conservancy piney-woods preserve, Ivy saw at least one longleaf pine of 110-foot height and a diameter at breast height of two feet, four inches, near the size limits of the species. Nowadays one is grateful for glimpses of these great trees, such as are still in Weymouth Woods, still in the Croatan, still in Onslow County at Camp Lejeune, still in Bladen Lakes State Forest in Bladen County, still in the Green Swamp, in small colonies and isolated individuals.

One may even be modestly grateful for an iconic elixir of the pine-stuff, standing at the domestic ready among more modern tinctures and dopes. In our medicine chest, Ann and I keep a cake of Grandpa's Pine Tar Soap and a small, two-ounce bottle with a pine-green label and a white cap, looking for all the Carolina world like a miniature bottle of white vinegar. "Pinee," says its label, "An Unmixed Oil of the Long Leaf Pine." A firm named Ag-Mark down in Teachey—the Duplin County home of legendary Tar Heel pine-high skyer Michael Jordan—produces Pinee, which is 100 percent pine oil ("Containing 91% Terpene Alcohol"). It is for dressing all kinds of scrapes and abrasions, burns and insect bites of the nonpoisonous variety. It is *not* to be taken internally, but if it were and if it tastes like it smells, then Pinee is a nearly direct transfer of essence from strong, astringent pine needles into the bottle itself. One Carolina woman of recent vintage said it would make you "heal up and hair over."

There has always been a medicinal air about the pine, well before the heartsick patient for whom the gypsy Madam Rue prescribed Love Potion Number 9 sang, "It smelled like turpentine, it looked like India ink." Hunters used turpentine and axle grease to dress their bear dogs' wounds; flatwoods mothers slapped fat meat and a drop of turpentine onto their children's hands to draw splinters out. Olmsted in the 1850s said: "The turpentine business is considered to be extremely favorable to health and long life. It is sometimes engaged in by persons afflicted with pulmonary complaints, with the belief that it has a remedial affect." And in *Bertie*, novelist Throop reported: "Did the colonel growl with the rheumatism, she was loud in the praise of spirits of turpentine, hot vinegar, iodine, and British oil."

So indigenous and endemic was tar in our country's culture that when the blockade-running steamer *Kate* inadvertently imported yellow fever to Wilmington from Nassau during the Civil War, in August 1862, the collective wisdom of the town was that they should burn tar in barrels placed on street corners about the city, that tar smoke and vapors might medicate the very air and drive the pestilence back to its own clime and latitude. Nearly 450 deaths later, autumnal cool and first frost ended what the billowing tar barrels could not, and we knew then that pine tar, though a powerful commodity, was no medicinal match for a plague.

Strange that this beautiful tree is so nearly gone: *Pinus palustris*, whose seepage caulked ships and cured ropes and fought yellow jack and bee sting and rheumatism, too, and whose pith as poles and planking built the South and that grew or had grown in such an astonishing and capacious carpet across the whole of the coastal plain that where we now must look for relict individuals and colonies were once whole forests that few travelers saw without falling into melancholy and short-sighted boredom and assaying as "endless" and "unbroken" and "monotonous" this biggest of North American big woods.

The great Carolina naturalist B. W. Wells, ten years after forester Ivy called so hopefully for the reforestation of the South with the longleaf, wrote the epitaph of the land of the longleaf pine. Coming from a man both intimately aware of and acquainted with what he called "the natural gardens of North Carolina" and a man not given to invective, a bitter one it was, too:

"And now this noble original forest, one of nature's most unique products of the ages in North America, is gone—rooted out by hogs, mutilated to death by turpentining, cut down in lumbering, burned up through negligence. No 'Save the Pines League' was ever formed to rescue any of it. Not a part of this great natural wonder, worthy of the name forest, remains intact within the state's borders."

We are not alone in our worship of the big resinous pine.

There is a bird abroad in these forests famous for its love of the longleaf's resin, its natural and uncooked tar. This is the rare red-cockaded woodpecker, *Picoides borealis*, that nests in longleaf cavities of its own construction, marked by the resin flow below the hole, the resin made milky by exposure to the wind and rain, pollen and dust.

In the small stand of longleaf on Millis Road in Carteret County's Croatan Forest, no less lovely for its diminutive size, I have seen the viscous milky flow on the trunks of longleafs that are home to this bird, the sap flow extending a foot or more down the purple-brown pine bark below the woodpecker's home hole in the trunk twenty or thirty feet above the wiregrass forest floor. As much as any other creature here in God's own pitch-pine garden, more than most, this woodpecker is flying, feeding, nesting, breeding, and in every instance *depending* upon this savanna companionship not merely for some particular diet or avian livelihood but for its very existence. Since *prima facie* only a bird can have a bird's-eye view, an even better look at things in this woods than a turpentiner or even a peripatetic Yankee landscape architect like Olmsted, what, then, does the red-cockaded woodpecker see from his resinous dugout on high?

Young longleaf-pine and wiregrass savanna, Cedar Island National Wildlife Refuge, November 1996

It is a long watch he, or she, must keep, for the big ornamental cone takes its time—two years—getting up to size, then sends its maple-like seed spinning down with cotyledons enfolded and flattened into a wing and with its small ball of meat and strength then growing flat on the earth, for several years looking like a big head of fescue with pine needles for grass blades—the grass stage, time of the tap root and the near-surface webbing spread of its ancillaries. This time of growth is evidence that the plant puts its faith in patience and endurance, like Faulkner's mule that would work for you patiently and faithfully for ten years for the chance to kick you once—so the longleaf, having risked little thus far, could finally in one kick of growth, one surging burst, leap upward by dint of genetic design to overcome the danger of fire, shoot upward without branching and having risked its slender trunk to ground fire for as little time as possible.

Wilmington welcomes President William Howard Taft, November 1909

At the Millis Road savanna, I noticed how the longleaf at grass stage hardly looked any different from the wiregrass sprouts around it. Also sprouting out and putting forth there were white-tufted *Zigadenus*, and the forest floor was so open and clear you could walk easily through these woods all day, though its border was a serpentine curve of impassable pocosin. A good breeze was soughing through the longleaf pinetops, and the day felt cool in here even at eighty degrees.

Decorative blue rings, foresters' paint, marked the longleafs where red-cockaded woodpeckers had staked their claims. This "small and most particular king," as naturalist Janet Lembke calls the bird, wants virtually no other home but a fully matured longleaf ailing from red-heart fungus and needs a range a mile and a half in diameter for a colony of only a dozen. But the circle around the little black and white bird with the diminutive red cockade is not closing in upon him alone.

Outside Millis Road savanna, on nearby N.C. 24, rolled a force of sand-camouflaged Desert Storm humvees and trucks bearing some of our national military force back home, servants as they, and we too, were of another crude commodity and of a very different distillation, now that the world has long since turned from tarred lines and ropes and hawsers and the constant maritime need for caulk. For the war just past had been fought not over the Southern pinelands our military moves through ceaselessly and trains in constantly, but over buried carbon fields far away, and in the bright and treeless deserts no bird, not mourning dove or woodpecker, there flew.

The Big Empty

· ·

Lower Carolina

In the big, empty section of the southeastern coastal plain that comprises such places as Warsaw, Burgaw, Calypso, Tomahawk, Beautancus, and Beulaville, Granddaddy Page once found work for a spell, just after the turn of the century, supervising the renovation of one crossroads community's jail. He stayed at the small hotel, took his meals in the little dining room there, and, as he was both new to town and dealing with the improvement of an important and valued local edifice, he met the hamlet's agrarian and mercantile leadership rather quickly.

The second or third Sunday he was in town, Granddaddy had dinner after church with one of these prominent citizens and his comely wife. As they parted, Granddaddy—in his linen suit not only the best-dressed man ever to fireproof a courthouse but also one of the most genuine and genuinely courteous—shook hands with the gentleman and responded to the lady's "We certainly did enjoy dining with you, Mister Page" with the innocent remark:

"Well, I certainly hope I'll be seeing more of you."

To which she said, "I'm sure you will," and that was that.

Not long afterward, there came to Granddaddy at the hotel an invitation from this woman and her husband asking him to join them and a couple of dozen other kindred friendly spirits for a big Sunday afternoon dinner on the ground some miles out of town at a popular swimming and picnicking spot, a Shall-we-gather-at-the-river? that pleased my grandfather, getting the little envelope when he called for his key at the desk after a long day of bricks and mortar.

When the day came and Granddaddy arrived at the convocation, he in his Sunday finest riding up on a rented horse a little after the appointed hour, he was not surprised that he had in the course of his first month in town already met most of these folks.

He was stunned, though, to find them all stark naked.

As the new arrival and attendant, his presence had been quickly noted, and the option of backtracking was not to be his. He dismounted, and the lovely woman who had issued the invitation came confidently approaching him and said,

"Mister Page, we're so glad you could come out and join us for dinner and a swim."

Quickly re-cementing his composure, the man who was well on his way to being a master erector bowed modestly and dealt with the moment directly and unapologetically, observing to her with a wry smile:

"You know, when I told you, back in town the other week, that I hoped I'd be seeing more of you, I had no idea that I'd be seeing *so much* more of you . . ."

His talespinning went no further . . . but I don't believe my grandfather took them up on their big municipal nudism, this immersion with the leading lights. It wasn't like him, and it certainly wasn't a condition of his brief employment re-engineering their hoosegow.

Along these relaxed lines, though, I remember there being in the 1970s a purported nudist colony at Grissettown down in Brunswick County, just far back enough into the myrtle and pine thickets to be a substantially mosquitoey place for the exposure of human hide; and in February 1996 at nearby Longwood, there was a reported first-ever Christian Nudist Conference, religion *au naturel* featuring "Amazing Grace" in the pines as well as naked Christian karaoke, according to a piece that ran in the faraway *St. Louis Post-Dispatch*. There was even a celebrated attempt in the 1980s at establishing a nude-bathing beach—some Fire Island come south, or South Beach Miami come north—on Bird Island just below Sunset Beach, but what my grandfather witnessed if not partook of preceded this buff-life private and public by seventy years.

The coastal plain was not new, even in my grandfather's time, to a certain amount of carnal pleasure in public bathing, and this not only at sea beaches and river shores. None should forget those baths and springs—like Shocco and

Panacea and Chalybeate—that flourished during the nineteenth century, and some, like the mineral Seven Springs resort on the Neuse, well into the twentieth. And if there were some proclivity and tradition, among a portion anyhow of those who went to these mineral wells, for nude bathing and bare-assed marination, and if they engaged themselves in it, inviting newcomers to join in and swell the flock of New Edenites, so what? Who else, after all, was out there rattling around in this big, empty country to come upon them, to witness, to object?

This lonely stretch of eastern Carolina is the valley of the Northeast Cape Fear River, and the Cape Fear itself. Three large roads run down through it, north to south, but there is not a single city here, and few towns of any size. This is cucumber and pickle country, home to both the Mount Olive and Cates brands, and though it is topographically almost tableland flat, some of it nomenclaturally has a vertical slant: here are Maple Hill, Pink Hill, Snow Hill, Potters Hill, Pleasant Hill, and Rose Hill—where writer Reed Wolcott found so many forthcoming speakers for an early 1970s oral history. The region is also home to Duplin Wine Cellars, the biggest and most successful of the latter-day scuppernong squeezers. Faison is the childhood home of scholar and coastal-plain social critic Linda Flowers, and two of North Carolina's best contemporary black writers also grew up hereabouts: Pulitzer Prize–winning dramatist Samm-Art Williams in Burgaw, which he immortalized as Crossroads in *Home*, and Prix de Rome–winning novelist Randall Kenan, whose hometown Chinquapin became Tim's Creek. In Kenansville itself, Liberty Hall is seat of the Kenan family, which has for generations sponsored and underwritten the nation's first public university, upstate at Chapel Hill, where novelist Kenan honed his craft.

Back in Faison, Verna Taylor, who as keeper of Magnolia Hall and also as magistrate has kept an eye on the inside information of everything from Beautancus to Calypso, claims the strawberries here are the best in the world because they grow "after the clay ends and before the sand begins." Blueberry orchards along South River thrive in the lowland loam, and a Burgaw outfit packs both blueberries and scuppernongs by the thousandquart.

Just as George Washington once sought to fill the Great Dismal Swamp with German, Dutch, and Palatine farmers, so, too, have land and labor factors tried populating this place. Presaging Washington's efforts by two generations, a crowd of Pennsylvania Welsh in the 1730s moved into the low divide between the Northeast Cape Fear and the Cape Fear Rivers, enough of them that their area came to be called "the Welsh Tract." One Malatiah Hamilton laid out an unnamed market capital for the Welsh Tract in 1740, a settlement incorporated in 1791 as South Washington. Then in 1840 it moved a mile to seat itself on the

Strawberry festival, Wallace, Duplin County, 1936

newly completed and momentarily longest rail line in the world, the Wilmington and Weldon, and renamed itself Hiawatha—it is now merely Watha. So much for honoring a great president and a fictive Native American. A few miles away is Penderlea, a New Deal project whereby the federal government divided 10,500 acres into thirty-acre tracts and put nearly 150 farmers on the land here, even built them a lake—thereby making some sort of Rooseveltian good out of the failed post–Civil War efforts of carpetbagger E. R. Brink, who sold fifty farms off this same Penderlea property to New York City dwellers before a Wilmington bank foreclosed and reconstructed Brink out of the mail-order real-estate business.

Better luck at the same game was experienced some miles south by Hugh MacRae, the energetic Wilmington entrepreneur who—having built legendary Lumina pavilion at Wrightsville Beach *and* the electric trolley out to it—created the outlying truck-farm communities that would inspire Penderlea: a 6,000-

acre Dutch agrarian colony he got going early in the twentieth century at Castle Hayne, another at Van Eden; an Italian and Polish town at St. Helena; a Germans' and Hungarians' New Berlin, now Delco; a Greeks' Marathon; and a Poles' Artesia.

If fecundity were all it took to people a land, though, this little region would be overrun. The section is so empty because it is so *wet*. Angola and Holly Shelter Swamps between them are together nearly the size of the Great Dismal Swamp, and the broad Black River swamps just to the west are as legendary for their two millennia–old cypress monarchs as they are for dividing parties of canoeists—legions of whom put in yearly at Ivanhoe, as we have, and other landings—and sending them mystified into disparate apparent channels that all turn out false and then losing them for discomfiting spells of time.

Coming southeast along N.C. 50, smallest of the roads—counting 421, 117, and 40 as well—that run down through here and out into lowland waters, I first saw this big, empty province one April night thirty years ago. It was the spring of my junior year in high school, and Tom West and I had set out to spend Easter on the coast, staying with Tom's father in a small cottage on Topsail Island and pier-fishing. In Tom's noisy, dull-green late '50s Volkswagen beetle, we left the red-clay country of Chapel Hill in late afternoon and came down out of the piedmont by N.C. 55 to Newton Grove, the wagon-wheel roundabout where we loaded up on 20-cent gas, picked up N.C. 50, and rolled on the rest of the way toward Topsail Sound and the sea.

Somewhere in the flatlands near Chinquapin, silver phantoms came streaking one after another across N.C. 50, just really screaming across the highway ahead. We slowed and saw that our ghosts were fast-moving boxcars in a northbound train, their long paneled sides catching our headlights aslant so that they were just bursts of silver speeding over the two-lane blacktop at a dark crossing. It took several seconds for us to realize what was what, and to neophyte pilgrims the moment was arresting and intense.

"Damn!"

"The hell?!"

"You see that damn thing?"

"I couldn't tell what the hell it was."

Out of earshot and range of all authority except gravity, we were busy working on our cussing. The world was wide open and very large, and even larger was the great mass of things we didn't know: as we bounded through Holly Ridge on the way to the sound, we didn't know that George Washington had spent the night at Sage's Ordinary a mile south, just a century and three quarters ago to the month! Nor did we know that less than two dozen years ago a city of sixty

Breaking new ground, Dutch settlement of Van Eden, Pender County, about 1913

thousand soldiers trained for anti-aircraft warfare at Camp Davis here, though it was the freedom they'd won us that propelled us down the road.

We finally rolled into Topsail about 9:30, and Tom's father, who had already been down at the beach for awhile, seemed happy to leave us to ourselves.

"Dad," Tom said, not five minutes after we got there, "we're gonna go out and see what's going on."

Ten minutes later we found the dance.

There were twenty or thirty cars—some late '50s two-door coupes, a few Chevy Impalas and Ford Fairlanes, a woodie or two—halfway off the paved road, or up in the driveway of what I recall as a large cottage with a concrete carport and patio. There was either a jukebox or a very big and loud record player, and you could get cold drinks for a quarter. It was just a house party, but it seemed like an open-air club. The forty revelers were high schoolers, or not far from it.

Tom and I made our way to the drink box and stood around like most everyone else, watching the half-dozen dancing couples. What light there was was dim and blue, but you could see a certain amount of crowd-teasing going on: randy-dance bottom-to-bottom twisting, performance making-out during the slow-shuffling soul songs.

"Say, who y'all know here?" Some fellow in the dark, checking us out.

"Nobody. We just stopped by, is all," I said.

"Where you from?"

"Chapel Hill."

"Oh yeah?" He liked the sound of it, was impressed in a tossed-off way, and asked: "Y'all go to Carolina?"

Now see how the road to confrontation and intimidation and violence starts with a single simple misrepresentation. Alone, I wouldn't have risked it, but it was so easy—and so much better in a world where self-confidence and cool were equivalents—to answer as Tom West did:

"Yeah, we're freshmen."

"Well, hey, that's cool!"

"Yeah!"

"Y'all raise a lot of hell up there, don't you?"

"Hell, yeah, we have some times," Tom said, "lemme tell you!"

Our stature enhanced, our part in some great wild legend of Carolina affirmed, we shut up and watched the dancers. I don't think we were there more than half an hour, but it was long enough. Toward the end of that time, couples fell away from the dance floor, some wandering off into the dark dunes, till at last there was only the light scrape of two pairs of weejuns over the concrete pad.

The woman of this last dancing pair was a sultry redhead about seventeen. She was as confident and at ease with her eye-catching self as the ocean, and with the least effort was clearly the most provocative presence there. Her dancing was relaxed, languorous really, little more than a lithe, sensual sway. Her slight smile gave nothing away, and Tom asked our new friend her name.

"Jeanette," the other said. "And that guy she been dancing with, she don't go with him."

"Well, who *does* she go with?" Tom said.

"She don't think she goes with anybody, but this guy Gene's coming over—he thinks she's *his* girl."

This should have given us pause at the outset. We should have known better.

Soon a dull red '57 Chevy BelAir with a charcoal gray top rumbled by and turned around down the street and pulled up and stood idling before the cottage a few moments. The driver left the car running, got out, and stalked out onto the small dance space.

This was Gene, no doubt about that. He stood there for a few more moments, incredulous that Jeanette kept on dancing with the other fellow. He looked like he was considering whether or not to cut in, and Jeanette just smiled at him in a noncommittal way, almost as if she'd never seen him before.

People reappeared and they crowded in, shrinking the dance floor's diameter by five or six feet. Gene started talking, with real energy but not very loud—the music was still up, so you couldn't hear what he was saying, just that he was threatening and abusive.

Suddenly the little joint was as hostile as it had once been inviting. Jeanette stopped dancing and stepped back, and the two boys moved in on each other. Gene was sturdy and worked up, and he was busy berating the other fellow. When someone killed the music, it looked like a fight for sure. Then Jeanette without comment took Gene's arm, and the two of them walked back to his car and drove off into the night, leaving all of us in stunned silence.

The music came back up, but there was in it neither cheer nor anticipation. The hostility lingered, the main event had just driven away, and the party was over.

Saturday morning was beautiful, bright and cloudless and just a little brisk, in the high 50s. We ate a big breakfast and drove the Volkswagen down to the south end of the island, where we rolled up our pants legs and seined for minnows.

The waters inside Topsail Inlet were frigid, or we might have lingered and really loaded up. But once we had a scant bucketful, we stopped back by the cottage and picked up fishing rigs and went on up to spend the day on the Surf City pier. If we caught anything but skates, I don't recall, but I remember that getting our lines tangled back under the pier with fishermen's lines on the other rail was all the excitement for some hours.

The day heated up, though, and the chill went out of the breeze, and the salt-sea air got as balmy as it ever does in April. The languorous Carolina spring we all of us ache for from Christmas on had begun, and so had the savoring of it. Low-country men and boys were out in force. Old women, their faces lined and leathery beneath duck-billed caps like my grandmother Simpson always wore up at Nag's Head, sat here and there on rude benches and worked one or two or three lines.

There was a surfer in a black wet suit that gleamed silver in the sun, and a few boys our age watching from shore, all of them wearing sweatshirts and jams, painfully bright as if each fellow had taken a short spin on a primary-color wheel before hitting the beach. Their heads would turn whenever some taut-thighed girl ambled by, apparently oblivious to them and to the effect of her two-piece suit, huge and now almost comical in concealing all the acres of womanflesh that today's few strings and strands reveal.

And Tom and I watched it all, these tiny moments of Pender County passion, of courtship as endless as the waves boiling by below us. We watched and joked as if our being way out at the end of a patch of planks on matchsticks in the surf gave us not just a God's-eye view of it all, but God's own detachment, too. And it did, up until Tom jabbed me in the ribs and hissed excitedly:

"Look! There she is! It's *her*!"

"Who?"

"Jeanette! The girl from the dance."

Yes, it was, and she was walking out our way, toward the end of the pier, in a promenade no more hurried than the light mid-afternoon breeze. Was she pretty? Was Elizabeth the First? Of course she was—the loveliest thing in Surf City, which was the entire known world just then. She was a redhead, born to rule, a portrait of self-possession and unstudied grace, and now, as she had effortlessly converted the pier into her court, we were her fops, her fishing fools, and she was ruling us.

Jeanette had world enough and time.

Had she been alone as she walked our way, Tom and I might well have been delivered by another of her courtiers into the depths of Holly Shelter Swamp some miles inland before the night was out. Or merely sunk in the Intracoastal Waterway.

But she was being escorted by a boy cousin, also about our age, and thank heaven for favors in any size or denomination.

We spent hours together, the four of us, walking up and down the fishing pier, on the beach, eating hot dogs and chili in the little six-booth canteen on the pier's land's end, Tom being boisterous and witty and charming in a raffish way, Jeanette amused and fed and inordinately fussed over without her making the first request. The only words I can recall her saying were, "Yes," and "Sure."

Did she want to get another hot dog? Yes. Did she want to walk up to where they had that dory skiff beached? Yes. Did she want me to run back and get her another drink? Yes. And before long it was about nine o'clock, and did she want to go ride around for awhile?

Sure.

The two-lane tarmac at Topsail went from northeast to southwest, and so did we. Down, then back up, and then down again. In and out of the parking lot at the pier, one of us stepping out and fetching for the rest. Back by the patio-dance scene from the night before, where it was all quiet on the shagging front.

Who cared whether the party was open or closed? Want to ride around some more? Sure. Go back to the pier, see what's going on? Sure. It was great fun, an enormous good time, and in all those hours with our sweet, mischievous, truck-load-of-dynamite Pender princess Tom and I made only two mistakes.

First, we confessed that we were only high school juniors.

And, second, we let Gene spot us—with *her*.

The Chevrolet's bright lights flared out of the darkness behind us, putting odd light into the Volkswagen through the oval rear window and light at odd angles from the rear-view and side mirrors. Gene had roared up behind us with his lights out, and we hadn't heard his engine over the high grind of our own. We were doing forty when he caught up with us, not four feet off our rear bumper, and flipped his lights on.

Jeanette took notice, but she floated during this event in an amnion of immunity and calm and betrayed neither annoyance nor appreciation at Gene's assault on us land-pirates of romance.

We sped up, to maybe fifty or fifty-five now, and Gene was right there, riding our bumper. He would thrust and brake so that the '57 Chevy seemed to lunge and feint, its headlights jumping menacingly and its chrome-thatched grill voracious like a cannibal's mouth.

The three of us boys laughed—adrenalin will out—and Tom floored it and got us up to sixty or so. We were topping out now, and Gene behind us tired of rear play and went fore, all windows of the Chevy down and Gene's four henchmen leaning out yelling and giving us with magnificent hormonal verve eight hands worth of the All-American unidigital salute. Ten generations of life in Holly Ridge and Sneads Ferry had bred and built a war machine for which we were no match.

We had certain advantages, though, and Tom found them quickly. His wheelwork was terrific. Once Gene was in front of us, he slowed down, and Tom braked hard, whipped us around. We could turn faster, and we could run off into the sand shoulder and not get stuck. The Volkswagen was another mile and a half north after this maneuver before the hungry heart in the Chevy bore down on us again.

Into a trailer park north of Surf City Tom slipped, and Gene followed gamely. But Tom led the Chevrolet into a maze of clotheslines and swing sets before sliding alongside and between two tight trailers and zipping back out onto N.C. 210.

That play won us two miles.

Had we been swifter in matters of car-chase sweepstakes, we would have bugged out to the beach itself, and the night would have been ours. Instead we pulled into Ross's Texaco, where the man who wore the star wanted no part of our car or Gene's, either. Both vehicles emptied. Jeanette sauntered over to speak with Gene, and her cousin followed along and stood with the rest of the homeboys. No one approached us.

About five disorganized minutes of yammering passed over by the Chevrolet, after which Jeanette climbed into the front seat of the Chevy next to Gene. All the others glared at us, and then they, too, got into Gene's car. Jeanette's cousin came back to us.

"Gene thought she was going riding with him tonight, but I don't think they want any trouble. Come on," he said.

"You know all of them?" Tom said.

"Yeah, all but one. They're all right. They're just messin with us."

Jeanette had played us for fools, I thought, but there was an unconcerned look on her face, neither relief nor delight, as she moved from our camp to theirs. She was in motion and in command of no less than eight young minions.

Gene peeled out with a vengeance, laying rubber two hundred feet. The boys in the backseat gave us hard, abusive looks, and Tom called out after them, though we all knew none of them could hear his words over the squealing wheels:

"So your daddy buys your tires! So *what*?!"

The three of us sat staring at the cups of coffee on our booth table back in the fishing-pier restaurant. Tom wanted to know all about Gene and his gang. I listened, but my main interest was in being off the hook and done with that crowd.

My sense of relief lasted less than fifteen minutes.

In they trooped, in fact needing more satisfaction than they'd gotten back at the Texaco station. Jeanette trailed in, sat on a stool over by the short counter, and idly joked with the soda jerk. They let her cousin out of our booth—"This ain't got nothin to do with you," one of them said—and loomed over us, fiery-eyed and possessed of all the home-court advantages. We were in a tight spot, and I daresay we knew it.

"Who the hell are you guys?" Gene laid into us. "What do you mean, coming down here, trying to snake somebody's girl? Ought to beat your ass, you sonofa-bitches! Hell, I will! Come on, speak up, Big Time!"

Mortified, Tom never lifted his eyes from his coffee cup. Mine alternated between my feet beneath the table and whoever was speaking. I tried to be as expressionless as possible. The people's tribunal was in masterful session, and just beyond the canteen door was a long and handy plank for us to walk.

"Tell us you was college boys! You ain't no more college boys than I am," Gene said, and there was a hateful superiority about the way he delivered this egalitarian declaration. In the short time since we parted company, Jeanette had clearly been debriefed—and we ourselves unmasked.

"Bunch of high school Harrys."

"*I'm* the only one around here goes to college," said a slim gawky blond fellow off at the end of the group. The rest of them nodded, smartly acknowledging him, and I took heart. My old daddy told me when I was still in grade school that you might not be able to stop a fight, but you can sure postpone it as long as you keep talking.

"Oh, yeah," I said, "where do you go?"

"Richmond Polytechnic Institute," he said, looking down his nose and adding slowly, "R-P-I."

It so happened that behind me in Mrs. Sommerfeld's matrix algebra class back in safe and sound Chapel Hill sat a big funny man in his twenties, a fellow who had been in the marines and had returned to get his high school diploma. Once he had mentioned that he'd taken a semester or two at RPI between service and coming to high school. I played the only available card.

"I know a fellow went to RPI, last year I think."

"Oh, sure," Gene's thin lieutenant replied belligerently. "Who?"

"Ex-marine name of Bill Marx."

"Bill Marx?"

"That's right. Sits right behind me in math."

"Well, goddamn—you know Bill Marx?" To the others he said: "He knows Bill Marx! I can't believe—hey, wait a minute, what's he look like, your Bill Marx?"

I hoped to hell there weren't two of them.

"Tall, curly blond hair, always crackin jokes."

"Damn if that ain't him. That's him all right. Bill Marx, yeah, he's a good old boy. Hey, that's cool!"

Then he reached over and shook my hand.

"Hey, you guys're all right. Hey, we didn't mean nothing, just trying to find out what's going on, you know how it is."

I did now. I think he exceeded his authority. Gene should have been the one to exonerate us. But the other three were clearly relieved not to have to start a rumble, and the tension vanished.

"Aw, hell," Gene said, disgusted with us and his gang, and, if he had any sense, with his vixen Jeanette. Counting the dinner we had bought, the car chase, the antics of the jealous lover, the dramatic confrontation and the farcical denouement, she had gotten what must have been fifty dollars' worth of entertainment without spending the first nickel.

"Aw, hell with em," Gene said. "Let's go."

After they left, our spirits recovered quickly, and Tom regained his swagger. We drove back over the bridge across the Intracoastal Waterway, where the marshes narrow between Stump Sound to the north and Topsail Sound to the south and where the ferry-flat used to be, back to the mainland, then spent a while riding around an old deserted concrete airstrip now all grown up in little maples and pines, and finally took Jeanette's boy cousin home.

In the thirty years since that night I have been all over the Sound Country—high and low—of eastern North Carolina, but I never have gone back to Topsail

Island, for Gene did warn us forcefully as he went out the fishing-pier-canteen's door:

"Don't you come back down here and pull this kind of shit again. Next time you're gon get your ass kicked."

"Oh, leave em alone, Gene," said the thin blond fellow. "They know Bill Marx."

On a Saturday late in March, 1996, Ann and Hunter and Cary and I put our white canoe into the dark Black River at Ivanhoe, many miles away from Topsail, across the early '90s burn of Angola and Holly Shelter and three decades away from the mad Topsail dash for Jeanette. It was a blue-sky day in the low sixties, a cool sunny day after an inordinately long winter, and if it were a quieter, steadier time than the long-lost day when we had squired the redhead around, it was no less exhilarating.

On the way down we had passed the neon signs for Madame Valerie the Plain View Psychic, and we passed fields of last year's cotton, brown sedge in it all bowed over in the same direction. Odd manufactories loomed at the far sides of big fields, in little notches cut from woodlands for which the main roads seem but minor and insignificant interruptions: Lockamy's Pottery Works, a concrete casting affair, with a life-size Jesus as the leader of a big pack of gray-cement yard art, and a pallette yard by a pond near Spivey's Corner.

Spivey's Corner was home to an agreeably ramshackle eatery called the Green Top Restaurant, with little hips at the end of its lime-green tin roof. The Corner has made itself famous as the "Hollerin Capital of the World" by staging a National Hollerin Contest on the third Saturday of June each year. Across the highway from the Green Top, though, a marble, grave-like marker proclaimed that this was the "Hollerin Capital of the Universe," and I thought for a moment that was a mighty and perchance hubristic grab at the title in a universe where an explosive nova like the Crab Nebula might be giving off the occasional high-volume intergalactic yell. Some powerful competitors *do* wind up here, though. My old friend Jake Mills once heard a fellow upstate in Chapel Hill telling it in Merritt's Store that he'd *tried* to enter his wife in the hollerin contest, but the officials wanted to assign her a *handicap*, saying she'd have to holler through a sheet of asbestos to make it fair for all the other contestants. To date, anyhow, no one has upended or undone Spivey's Corner's claim of universal primacy in the bellowing realm. Here if nowhere else one came to hear "Amazing Grace" shout-yodeled by bib-overalled choristers for nonproximate audiences, to hear long-haul dinner invitations offered to far-off recipients by people used to (or whose immediate predecessors were used to) speaking familiarly with field hands at distances of a mile, or two.

Black River, March 1996

There was smoke in the air, coming off the charred ground where farmers were burning the brush out of their ditches, and there were great dust clouds out over the big fields, reminding us it'd been blowing a gale over the sounds earlier this week. Holly glistened in the woods, and the maple was just pinking out in this most reluctant of springtimes. I saw an old cedar as fat and spread out as a lowland live oak, saw, too, how the soil color alternated dramatically: now black, now nearly sand-white.

At tiny Ivanhoe, testament to the nineteenth-century fascination with the works of Sir Walter Scott, we took county road 1007, a two-lane blacktop that had been *adopted* by the Black River Organic Farm, and were ready for the river itself. A light dirt road a half mile below Ivanhoe led down to the dark-water landing, past one of the biggest pines in all Carolina, a loblolly, three and a half feet in diameter at breast height, its enormous girth continuing much farther up, and a wide, spreading crown.

Then we were on the river, a jolly foursome paddling upstream against the rapid Black River flow. There was always something to see in a woods, even more so in a river forest. In and among the winter-gray gum and river birch, the understory was beginning to green up. Switch cane moved in the light breeze, and we heard the *kuk-kuk* cry of a pileated woodpecker. Ann spotted some cypress knees well gnawed by beaver.

After a couple miles Ann and I pulled and poled the canoe to rest in a wet woods off to the river's side, Hunter objecting that we'd never find our way back out. We were in only one foot of water, and in that shallow spot the clear moving water of the Black in sunlight was like a liquid amber, at its darkest like strong, steeped tea, with some subaquatic heart-shaped leaves growing on the bottom.

Now it was early afternoon, and the Carolina sky could not have been bluer. Another half-mile upstream we stopped and marveled at a single maple, gloriously pinked out against the blue and framed by hundred-foot pines. The eye-popping purity of those colors was more than worth the Black River's price of admission. In the gum swamp above and beyond the bridge we snaked about, watching a white-throated sparrow and a wood thrush and a towhee move ahead of us, Ann pointing out all the sculpted patterns, the ripples, buttresses, and wings on the bottoms of the cypress. Up the river bluff here was a huge sawdust pile, the tailings of an old sawmill now derelict. Running up on the shore, on a small mud-tongue of land, our quartet ate cheese sandwiches and pecan sandies here in the drowned swamp woods and just plain loafed about in what was also a grove of a couple hundred cabbage palmettos all in the fan stage, a young plantation in this shallow backwater.

Going back down with a six- or eight-mile-an-hour flow was a lark, more steering than paddling—though we took a twenty-minute sidetrip into a cypress and gum slough well leveed off from the main stream of Black River, and into a twenty-acre lake of the river's own making off to its southwest side. Once more ten-year-old Hunter proclaimed our impending doom—"We'll never find our way out, *never!*" he said over and over again. So it might well seem, in the leafed-out late spring and summer, but the sight lines of a swamp woods in winter are usually fine enough to keep one's bearings—and wits—in good order.

It was a bald cypress monarch that drew us into the slough, one of the storied, many-centuried veterans for which Black River is legendary—its *Taxodium distichum* the oldest stand of trees east of the Rockies—one of those famous big lunkers that got away from the broadax and the crosscut and the chainsaw because of its difficult berth in the river swamp, or maybe due to its abject hol-

(opposite) Out of the channel, Black River, March 1996

Bald cypress, Black River, March 1996

Ivanhoe Landing, Black River, March 1996

lowness. This was a four-foot cypress, maybe eighty feet tall, with numerous holes in it not from pileated peckings and carvings but left by limbs that long ago fell away from the tree's trunk. As we paddled around it, thirty feet out from its base, I could see into one limb hole and out another that briefly lined up with the first, blue sky beyond and me looking through a thousand-year-old tree, the walls of time opening wide upon thin air and space.

Downriver a ways were a pair of cedar-sided fish camps with screen porches, one of them sporting a green county-road sign, of the new style, identifying the lane as

RAGGED ASS ROAD

Below that we stopped for a few minutes to look about a beaver lodge, and then, still heading down, the swift current slammed us broadside into the bushes as we turned to make a cut through flooded woods a quarter mile or so above the landing. After putting the womenfolk ashore, Hunter and I went paddling downstream another eighth of a mile or so before turning for the sprint up, and Hunter's calling back to Cary alerted and set in motion a nine-year-old country boy as yet unseen and unknown by us—he was just roaring down the lane to the landing on his All-Terrain Vehicle as Hunter and I nudged the canoe ashore.

The boy was cheerfully uncommunicative, though before he roared off again I shoehorned out of him that his father was the owner of a blueberry farm there.

Would that they were most all of them berry farms down that way, for something this big section is not empty of is porcine population. Below Clinton, pig houses lay low across the fields, and about the countryside were neat hanging signs at the entrance to many a farm with silhouetted blue-green pigs and the corporate name Prestage over the top. There was a superficial neatness, cleanness even, to the look of this pork-feed-lot modernity, but as the great outrageous spills from swine-waste lagoons into the New and Neuse Rivers during 1995 and 1996 well showed, no eastern waters are really safe from oversaturated dikes and farm-sludge floods.

Pack the canoe and pray for rain, but not too much of it, lest one more dike give way and one more overtaxing of land and water do in for all time some of the oldest trees in America. At sunset we left Ivanhoe, driving past a big stand of pine and wiregrass, and, where the Tomahawk Road hits N.C. 41, we slowed for a moment at the silver-gray marker that bespoke a Revolutionary War gun factory near here, run (till the Tories destroyed it) by John DeVane and Richard Herring. I remembered Bill Herring, who grew up on the Black, telling me that one of the last if not *the* last steamboat that came up Black River calling on its landings sank upstream of his family's place about 1920, at a point called Clear Run, and how at low water you could still see the ribs of the old boat. Still on the way from Kerr to Tomahawk, we passed the Tom-Kerr Buck Club, a hunting lodge with kennels surrounding it, passing, too, a stand of young longleaf pine as we drove away from the beautiful Black River and its cypress older than America, more ancient even than all the nations of Europe, and went north through the big empty spaces toward Garland in the gloaming of late March.

They found Joe's body,

They found Joe's head!

They buried 'em both,

But he's not dead!

On a dismal night in a dismal swamp,

You can see his lantern shine!

—Simpson & Wann, "The Maco Light," 1976

Maco

· ·

Southeasternmost

One tarpitch September night my friend John Foley and I fell victim to the lure of old lore and went looking for the Maco Light, a phantom luminary of long standing, west of Wilmington on the north shore of the Green Swamp. There were no signs, no concessionaires, no historical markers, nothing to guide us to the exact right place, so we stopped at a small store and asked, just one more pair of searchers in the unmapped spirit-ether of southeastern Carolina.

"You done passed it, bout a mile or so back," the counterman said. "Take your first left, go a little ways, pull over by the tracks. It'll be some others there, just like you."

"You ever seen it?" I said.

"Oh, yeah, everbody round here's seen it. I quit countin how many times."

"Do you think it's a ghost?" Foley asked.

"Now, I didn't say that," the other said. "I'm just tellin you I *seen* it. As to where it's some kinda *ghost* or just a buncha *kids* or somethin, they ain't never figured that one out."

"Well," I said from the door, "we'll see what we see."

"Oh, you'll see him, I reckon," the counterman said, looking up toward the ceiling. "They say he likes a black dark night."

We wandered over to the railroad tracks that were only to be there a few years more, parked the oyster-white station wagon, got out and sat on the hood, and awaited the Ghost at Maco Station, for more than a century one of North Carolina's most popular and enduring supernatural phenomena, dating to a fatal train wreck in 1867 at the small rural station then called Farmer's Turnout, fourteen miles west of Wilmington on the line serving Wilmington; Florence, South Carolina; and Augusta, Georgia.

We were alone at Maco Station, reviewing the evidence in the dark.

Conductor Joe Baldwin, riding in the last car of a wood-burning train and discovering that his car had come uncoupled, died while waving a lantern from the rear of that car in a failed attempt to signal and stop a second train coming up from behind. One witness saw Baldwin's lantern fly clear of the train wreck, land and right itself in the adjacent swamp, and burn on. Shortly afterward and continuing over the generations since, a flickering light has appeared regularly along the railroad tracks in the vicinity of the 1867 collision. This light has always been believed to be the ghost of Joe Baldwin—who was decapitated in the wreck—looking for its head.

"Sometimes the light is so bright," a Miss Frankie Murphy once said, "that you can almost read by it."

Though we weren't trying to read anything, we were looking hard and longingly down the steel rails, looking east as the counterman advised, wondering how far away, or how near, the ghost would be when it made its undead perambulation. I recall seeing a carbon-vapor light some ways away, a light that waxed and waned beyond a big willow swaying in the evening breeze, and I remember how the crickets and tree frogs were roaring, as they do, holding sonic sway over the surrounding countryside.

Ghost is bound to be used to this, I thought. Might be somebody from one of those trailers down there north of the tracks, I thought, somebody who comes out four, five nights a week and swings a lantern, playing ghost just to keep the ghost hunters pouring in. Foley was thinking along the same lines, but then who would keep doing that kind of prankstering, year in and out, for nothing other than a specter of artistic satisfaction? And there wasn't anybody living in trailers down there in 1867, when this thing got going.

Cover of darkness is the magician's cloak. We sat upon a white car we couldn't see and knit ourselves into the lining of that cloak, talking low as we waited on about spectral lights up and down the coast: the ghost maiden's fire-fly lamp in the Great Dismal Swamp, the Okisko Light on the Swamp's southern edge, the lanterns hung upon the necks of Outer Banks ponies and nags—the ghosts of ships-that-never-were luring real vessels into wreckage and phantasmic piracy . . . there was no shortage of side files of these subjects, certainly none that two men peering into the ink had any trouble calling up.

Presently an automobile turned off U.S. 74/76, the east-west federal highway that parallels the train line, and moved slowly down N.C. 87 toward us, pulling in alongside about fifteen feet away. Whoever its occupants were, they remained within the vehicle. Whether or not they could see us now, certainly they had made note of our presence when their headlights washed over us as they parked.

We were still and undisturbed for a short spell.

Then someone cracked open a rear door and that threw the dome light upon them, two older couples, as a man got out of the backseat saying:

"Yeah, this is it. This is the place all right."

"You sure, Horace? There's a lot of places like this, you know—railroad crossings in the middle of nowhere," said a second man, the driver.

Now they all got out, all of them talking, the women too. "This doesn't look like anything." "Better be good, Horace." "What does he look like?" "You remember what time of night you saw him?" "Was it scary?" "Was it worth it?"

"Oh, you all give that ghost a chance," Horace said. "We'll see him." Then he called out to us: "Y'all over there?"

"Right here," I said back.

"How long you been waiting?" he asked.

"Forty-five minutes or so," I said.

"Seen anything yet?"

"Not yet." When I said this, the women groaned, and the driver allowed:

"Damn, Horace. Peg and I could be having a drink back at the hotel right now."

"How long you boys gon give it?" Horace asked us.

"We got all night," Foley said boldly.

"Well, *we* don't," said one of the women.

"Oh you hush," said Horace, and then it was quiet for a few minutes.

"When did you say you saw this damn thing?" said the driver.

"Well," Horace said, puzzling aloud, "it was right before the War, must of been about '38, '39." All his party let out a disheartened arc of disapproval.

"You said a while back," one of the women recalled. "You never said it was *that* far back!"

Another car made the turn off 74/76 and drove our way, pulling in cater-cornered to us and Horace's crowd. A black family clambered out noisily, one of the children shrieking into the night: "C'mon, Mister Head-Cheese! I'm ready for *you*! Lemme see that big ol' head-cheese of yours!"

"Be quiet or he won't come," warned the little boy's mother, and the family moved a bit down the tracks.

"Head-cheese?" Foley asked me, laughing a little.

"Could be, by now," I said.

It was nearly ten o'clock now, and every several minutes or so another car would pull into the Maco Station parking lot: a young couple who'd clearly had more than ghost hunting in mind and who were astonished by the gathering crowd; another family or two; a car of double-daters out on a tear. Before long there were nearly fifty people convened at Maco, drawn into the spectral net by the lure of ghostlore and the promise of an appearance, a sighting! The small boy was still crying out into the night about head-cheese, only now he was running ever-increasing distances down the tracks, scaring himself, then sprinting back to his parents. Foley and I had left the station wagon and moved up beside the black family, and it was something of a natural wonder how convivial it all was, everyone from seven to seventy reporting on previous visits—"No, didn't see him that time, that was the third time I was here, but I did see him the next time I came"—and speculating on if or when Old Joe Baldwin might show tonight.

"That's it, Horace," came a woman's voice. "He's not coming, we're tired, let's go!" There went the evening's first and only defectors, and it was easy to understand: Horace, who had worked for a shipping company thirty-five years earlier, had lured his wife and their cocktails-and-dinner companions out from Wilmington on a lark with the good tale of Old Joe, but when the lark had not risen and sung they all got querulous and needed more balm. Foley and I were impressed, really, that they had lasted nearly an hour, and even more amazed that when they finally jumped the gun and left, they missed the main event by less than five minutes.

"Whoahhhhhhhhh, oww, Mama!!" cried the little head-cheese boy, running back our way. "Mama, he's *after me*!"

The apparition flame appeared perhaps fifty yards down the tracks from the chorus of us, and the boy was halfway between when it did. We were all agitated: Look at it! Can you see! There it is! Oh, man!

Joe Baldwin's Ghost was the flame and glow of a kerosene lantern, a light that was simply *there*, as if someone holding such a lantern with his back to us simply turned around. We saw nothing move into place, no match-light flare. For a half a minute the light bobbed from side to side just slightly, made a small upward curve several times, bobbed some more, then inscribed an arc, flew to the tracks' side, and vanished.

Did you *see* it? That was real, I saw it! Better'n last time! What'd I tell you? Think he'll come again?

"I ain't afraid of you, Mister Head-Cheese!"

"You hush up with that, now—you want to get yourself *haunted!*"

We all pulled together, the cloak of night and mystery and wonder settling upon us and uniting us. We were witnesses, we had all seen! Now we were hoping for another visit, another glimpse into beyond the beyond! All hearts beating as one: come on, Joe, come on out again . . .

But come again he didn't, and the crowd of attendants rapidly shrank, till it was once more Foley and me. Then it was midnight, and even our stalwart selves had had enough, and we gave Maco back over to the tree frogs and the owls and the spectral surrogate of Old Joe Baldwin.

Railroadmen back in the 1870s and 1880s reported a pair of Maco lights at work, lights that would come together, but that ended after the earthquake of 1886. Over the years, the Maco Light has been bright enough to fool many railroadmen into stopping their trains thereabouts, and, to remedy this schedule-thwarting effect of the ghost, signalmen at Maco used two lights, one red, one green. While President Grover Cleveland's train was wooding and watering up at Maco in 1889, the president saw the two signal lights, asked about them, and got the full story of Old Joe Baldwin. In the spring of 1964, the South Eastern North Carolina Beach Association contacted para-psychologist Hans Holzer to come to Maco and investigate Joe Baldwin and his light, and after his visit Holzer gave an apparent certification of the phantom conductor, citing the consistency of his nocturnal returns.

I made quite a few myself, like Horace, getting friends and family to wander out from Wilmington or up from the Brunswick beaches to seek the light. I also got increasingly emboldened, to the point of striding one night in near march-time down the tracks far beyond where the head-cheese boy had ever gotten to, seeking a trestle in the swamp that someone had told me of.

"Whoahhhhhhhhh!" came the cry again.

A pair of fellows westbound at a clip equal to mine slammed right into me, and we fell helter-skelter down onto the roadbed and crossties. When we got back to our feet and allowed ourselves relieved, nervous laughter, they warned me of yet another party that I might run into directly, adding:

"But you ain't got to worry none about em—they're from Morehead, they're *cool!*"

I went another quarter-mile east. I didn't see the crowd from Carteret County, but I did have the thought that the ghost might appear between me and my car back up at the road crossing. This was a disquieting notion, and suddenly my '55 Chevrolet BelAir drew me back to it like an electromagnet.

Since the railroad tracks were torn up in the late 1970s, the light has "greatly diminished, if not completely disappeared," Cape Fear Museum historian Harry

Warren told me. Someone approached me backstage in Washington not long ago and declared that she and her husband *owned* the Maco Light, or at least the land where it had long appeared, and that they were now putting an industrial park there.

Can a ghost doomed to an eternity of headlessness and endless nocturnal search have run its course in less than a century and a third?

Can Old Joe Baldwin get a witness?

Maybe a quarter million or so, and I am proud to be amongst that number, so I can honestly say:

I saw the light.

To light in the vast wet plain of Green Swamp beside and below Maco one must find an island, one of those high-ground hummocks large enough to carry a name like Kentuck Island or Honey Island or Bearpen Island; and, of all the Green Swamp islands, the one that people hear of and remember the most is called Crusoe.

Its name clearly has all the conjure power of the castaway, the half-dead and washed-up-ashore, and when I used to make the run regularly down from Whiteville to Sunset Beach, I would always turn off at the Last Chance, the little nabs-and-beverage bin at the north end of N.C. 130 where a pair of tall blonde women stood behind a broad trough of crushed ice and flipped splayed-out six-packs up out of the ice and into paper sacks in a most precise and flamboyant performance, and I would always tune in the local AM station there to absorb some of the isolated voodoo atmosphere and glide right through the western Green down N.C. 130, down through the Crusoe jurisdiction, just to hear talk like this:

"Sister Brown," said the announcer, when he quit preaching long enough to pitch pork chops and palmists, "Sister Brown is not your ordinary reader—she is a religious holy woman and she can help you with whatever your trouble in life might be. Are you disappointed in love? See Sister Brown! Men, are you afflicted with lost nature? Sister Brown can help you! Disputin with your relatives? Problems with money? Or both? Sister Brown is the one can help you out! Listen, people—you do not tell Sister Brown who your enemies are—she . . . will . . . tell . . . *you*!! Don't delay, friends, see Sister Brown to-*day*! And she has plenty of free, private parking around back, so all visits are con-fi-dential!"

Crusoe Island was on down the road, past the sign of the black bear announcing its sanctuary, and half a dozen miles or so off 130 from Old Dock, a sand-ridge tongue between the black Waccamaw River, the blackwater outflow from the Carolina bay Lake Waccamaw, and the Green Swamp—just the sort of place a handful of French might hide out and seek solace upon their expulsion

from moiling, tumultuous, revolutionary Haiti in the early 1800s, the same decade that saw the prison death of the ex-slave rebel Toussaint L'Ouverture and
the assassination of his collaborator and successor Dessalines.

There had been no Sister Brown to tell Toussaint who his enemies were, at
least not all of them. Only trickery and betrayal occasioned his capture by the
French, and Dessalines, emulating the enemy Napoleon and crowning himself
emperor and, also unwarned by Sister Brown, fell to bushwhackers. But what
made the landed white foes of these black rebels fly to North Carolina, to swamp
Carolina, even as the revolution was falling apart? If Sister Brown knows that
in these latter days, she hasn't said yet—and it can be hard to find her from a
distance, since in the Whiteville yellow pages the only such businesswoman
now listed is "Mrs. Dixon, Palmist, Famous Psychic, South College Road, Wilmington."

Even so, back on Crusoe Island in Green Swamp, the Carolina French, the
closest social claim to Cajuns we have, are here now—or at least their heirs and
assigns are. A. M. Waddell, a lawyer, thespian, and journalist, saw some of these
French Carolinians when he wandered Waccamaw just after the Civil War. He
met Old Willis and his daughter, saw the Anne family and "their men, Armand,
Pascal." (While he was back in the Green rummaging around, Waddell also observed a shingle operation near Lake Waccamaw, black men bringing shingles
out of the swamp woods by mule tram and moving their produce across the
Lake on shingle flats; and he learned from the shingle rig's white owner of a recent vote that had gone 200 Republican, 1 Democrat. This Waddell, future congressman and rabble-rousing white-supremacist Democrat, who would lead the
campaign that resulted in the disenfranchisement of black Carolinians as well as
in the installation of himself as martial mayor of Wilmington after the infamous
armed Cape Fear uprising and slaughter of blacks in 1898, would certainly have
marked well such a lopsided political accounting, and its meaning.)

Perhaps the Armands and Pascals that Waddell saw *weren't* French. Twentieth-
century wonderers about Crusoe and the Green have asked: Were they the last
progenitors of a band of pirates who fled here to hide out? Or the remnants of a
coastal Indian tribe penned in by European settlement? (A community of Waccamaw Sioux, which lived near but not *in* the Green at Buckhead near Buckhead
Swamp and Slap Swamp of Columbus County, produced the renowned quilter
Miss Lee Jacobs, who won a state folk heritage award in 1996 for the grace, color,
and originality of her work—"Try not to put the stitching where a toe'll get
caught in it," Miss Lee advised.) Or the latter-day families of Civil War draft-
dodgers who, being poor and scarcely out of indentured servitude themselves,
refused to fight a war for slavocracy? Who were they who lived lost to the world
way back in there?

"Mrs. Marley is convinced that they are descendants of French ancestors," wrote University of North Carolina professor and producer Frederick Koch of folk-playwright Clare Johnson Marley of Cary, who had written *Crusoe Islanders: A Drama of the Carolina Low Country* for Koch's course. "Many of the old islanders claim lineage from one of the French-Haitian refugees and are familiar with the story of the escape from Haiti." That may be, or may have been, but a half century has passed since *Crusoe Islanders* bowed on the boards of Playmakers Theatre in Chapel Hill in July 1943, and those old islanders Koch mentioned are at least two generations gone now. A few words from Robert Ruark's 1961 memoir *The Old Man's Boy Grows Older*, though, may corroborate the French connection: "On some islands in the vast sea of tangled growth were clumps and clusters of humanity who had escaped first from the French Revolution to Haiti, thence from Haiti to Wilmington, thence from Wilmington to sanctuary in the swamps. Some were inbred and idiotic from isolation. Nearly all had French names and spoke a French patois not unlike the Haitian creole. In the swamp, the Green Swamp, there were panthers and bears and alligators, wild hogs and wild cats."

What of Mrs. Marley's "Low Country" drama itself? Her play sheds little light on the cultural background and history of the Crusoe islanders, portraying instead a 1918 foreground in which a mother and daughter wrap bread loaves in cabbage to bake and are essentially trapped and saddled with way too much sense of place and in which the menfolk are depraved xenophobes. Ma Bella tells a timber cruiser, an outsider who has gotten lost in the swamp while "scaling trees for the government," about her mate who "ain't got nary bit o' use for nothin', 'ceptin' a jug o' corn likka and a passel o' houn' dogs." Jed Tolliver, identified in the *dramatis personae* as "a degenerate," is the man to whom Bella's husband trades bear hides for whiskey; Tolliver (whose name as a corruption of Taliaferro, or "sword bearer," recalls the similar transmogrification of Faulkner's Scotch Urquharts who in rough Mississippi became Workitts) offers to lead the timber cruiser back to civilization, but merely takes him to a spot of cattle-drag quicksand and merges him with the environment. Bella, confronting Tolliver over the murder, quickly follows the cruiser into the sucking mud, and swamp daughter Kathy—she with the blue dayflowers in her hair—is at closing curtain left alone between Tolliver and her harsh, ruined father Obediah. It is a bad scene.

Most Crusoe visitors that I know of have fared considerably better than that bogged-down timberman. My sister Susie, down in Whiteville in the 1970s clerking for Judge Pou Bailey, went touring in the remote portions of Crusoe once, and was well received everywhere—she was, however, in a squad car, a sheriff's deputy her escort. My friends the Smith Boys, Big Jim and Neal, canoed up on the Spivey clan, who were only too happy to sell the Smiths a cypress paddle for their continued safe passage down the Waccamaw. Other old friends, Laurel and Charlie Sneed, used to sit in on music sessions at a store out in Crusoe Island, and they swore to me by candlelight at their cottage in Shallotte one night long ago that it was a Cajun-style chanky-chank they could hear well within the string-band music of the islanders.

Boatman and writer Franklin Burroughs, coming down the Waccamaw River from the lake a few years ago, also floated in on the Thomas Spiveys, younger and elder, and got a practical lesson on foot- and hand-adzing a cypress-log dugout from the younger (who, when not digging a boat, might be operating a dragline or building a bridge or, more likely, trapping snakes somewhere from here to Virginia or Georgia for the university zoological trade, and who propelled his own dugout with a paddle "no longer than a pizza spatula and with a considerably narrower blade, managed with one hand," according to Burroughs). Presently Burroughs drifted on down out of the Green Swamp, down a Waccamaw lower in water level since the Waccamaw Lumber Company and the St. Regis and the Georgia Pacific were in the swamp cutting and draining, enough lower so that steamboats, which once made their way as far up the old "Wocoma" to Freeland on high water, could do that no longer. Down the dark Waccamaw, where men once poled log rafts (at a dozen logs to the clamp and a dozen clamps to the raft) for a week to make it down as far as Conway, South Carolina, then walking back to their Carolina families with their reward of boughten goods—tobacco and marbles and candies and maybe a little something in the way of cash.

Just west of Lake Waccamaw is a tiny community called Red Bug, which reminds me that, though Tick Bite is a crossroads near Kinston, there is no shortage of ticks in the Green Swamp—my wife Ann once came out from an afternoon turned around in the Soups section of the Green with forester Tom Perry, both of them absolutely covered with ticks. Whatever other bugs thrive herein beyond chigger and tick, there have over time been enough of them to engender and board one of the insectivorous gems of all botany:

Venus's-flytrap.

To the Londoner who in 1768 had given some flytraps to him, the great Linnaeus wrote: "I never met with so wonderful a phenomenon," a remark the equally great Darwin later echoed, calling it "the most wonderful plant in the world."

This particular swamp, pine, and wiregrass corner of the world—all within a 75-mile radius of Wilmington—is the entire known habitat of the Venus's-flytrap, and both the plant and a good bit of the land that supports it have been protected thanks to the efforts of the North Carolina Nature Conservancy, owner of the 16,000-acre Green Swamp Nature Preserve. And, though policing many thousands of wild acres against poachers involved in filching the small insectivore may be even more difficult than hunting up the swamp distillers of yore, the state of North Carolina has in recent years taken a tougher and more active role in saving the flytrap from extinction, both on the books and on the ground. In April 1991, Sergeant Milton McLean and other wildlife officers collared three men who had made their way into the depths of the Green on mountain bikes and who at the time of their arrest had more than a thousand Venus's-flytraps illegally in their possession. The numbers of the day in this free-boot economy were: $1.50 a plant to the collector, $3 retail in town stores selling them as houseplants. Long gone are the days of my youth when I was easily able to mail-order a Venus's-flytrap for home use and then set it out in my mother's neo-Victorian living room in front of polite company, and let it eat.

The little semibog bug-biter looks like a green velvet bear trap with eyelashes, lashes that are in reality triggers. Osmotic pressure keeps the trap open against its own tense pith but gives way when these triggers get a double touch, causing the two open halves—with their bright red, voracious interior—to feign a wilt and let the flytrap's woody springs snap shut on prey that can be as large as a grasshopper.

With its range cut in half, the flytrap is now called by the state a "species of special concern," and the law as of June 1991 set fines for illegal, unpermitted collection at $100 to start, escalating to $1,000 a plant for recidivists. Botanist B. W. Wells, who only sixty years ago saw no endangerment for the species, flagged Venus's-flytrap as "the most unusual of unusual green things."

In the exotic land of Maco, Crusoe, and Last Chance, of Sister Brown and Jed Tolliver, nothing is stranger than this—not French swampers, not Whiteville conjurers. No voodoo or mojo, whether Haitian or homegrown, is more mysterious than the little green low-growing flytrap of Venus. "We were here before you were born," says a sign behind the bar at McSorley's Old Alehouse on New York's East Side; true and impressive enough, but the flytrap was here before the human *race* was born, licking its chops over primeval deerfly wings and Mesozoic mosquito legs and nibbling away at clouds of Jurassic gnats. For a mouthy thing, though, the plant vocalizes nothing, or perhaps does so by word and deed too subtle for the latter-day breed that sends ham-fisted flytrap trappers afield against it.

You do not tell her who your enemies are—she will tell you.

I didn't listen to the plant I set upon my mother's mahogany drop-leaf table thirty years ago, but to its kin, its cousin still out in the wilds of woolly Brunswick County these days, I am all ears. She could be blind and still be a swamp seer without peer, and if there is a message coming from the mute *Dionea muscipula*, I do not wish to miss it this time.

Wandering around lower Brunswick County one cold January weekend in 1985 on a *King Mackerel* study tour, Jim Wann and I were staying at Hughes Marina and Motel, an unassuming fisherman's flophouse down by the waterway at Shallotte Point, enjoying the nearby presence of the big-prowed shrimpers and butterfly nets though hating to hear how many commercial fishermen were turning to offshore contraband pickups as a better way than fishing to make a go of things. We came back to fetch a second car, which we'd left at the motel while we roamed the county with our friends from the now-defunct *Free Press*—on our windshield was a scrawled note, called in to the Hughes desk by the *Free Press* editor:

"Barge hit Sunset bridge—come quick!"

The bridge in question, if not *in extremis*, was the old pontoon bridge Mannon Gore had slapped across the waterway thirty or forty years ago, connecting the mainland to a long causeway out to Sunset Beach, our penultimate barrier island before Little River and South Carolina. One lane wide and with a small white tender's shack, it rose and fell with the tides, so, depending on where you are in the endless cycling, you either drive up over a peak or sink down into a trough or just roar across flat. A cable and winchworks floated it open for snowbirds, pleasure craft, fishing boats, and barge trains, and though the forces of speed and greed have fought for years to scrap the homely old clunker and replace it as most all others have been replaced with a high-span flyover, other forces have stood beside the rude bridge and fought this major change to a standstill—a draw over the bridge.

I have sat out in Homer Foil's nearby yard, an oak-covered rise on the mainland side of the waterway looking out across the mile-wide emerald marshes, the only interruption in the great plains of green being the tidal creeks with their dark, oyster-encrusted pluffmud banks and the chalk-white egrets rising up and wheeling about as they follow the shrimp and minnows. In the western marsh was the lone hermit's shack, to which I jonboated a load of amped-up, curious boys many years ago. Homer heard from a neighbor, who used to go out by boat and play in it when he and his friends were little, that federal agents once came and fired on the cabin to chase the hermit away. Nothing breeds reflection and speculation so much as staring at an empty house, and nothing cracks such a mood, especially there under the land-side live oaks at Homer's board-and-batten cottage, so quickly as an air-horn operator trying from his boat to awaken the bridge tender in the tender hours of night, the boater so frustrated once his air horn died he then screamed himself hoarse till like his failed alarum he too ran down:

"Hey! Hey, you! YOU IN THERE!! Can't you hear me, you lazy sonofabitch! Wake up and OPEN THIS GODDAMNED BRIDGE!!!"

Nothing worked for that pilgrim. Sunset, as the flyover-bridge opponents would say, is not that kind of place: If you are in a hurry, what are you doing here? In an earlier time, native opponents of a new, private bridge that was built to run from the western end of Sunset over the marshes and flows of Mad Inlet to the lower-coast end of North Carolina—Bird Island, owned by Greensboro money but inhabited then as now by only shorebirds, myrtle scrub, shell-scarfers (you could generally walk across the inlet at low tide) and the occasional clutch of those exhibitionistic stripped-naked swimmers—came to the structure under cover of darkness, kerosened it and torched it and burned it away, the fire leaving only the charred creosote pilings standing for years into the future as monuments to local intransigence and an ancient and militantly proprietary interpretation of riparian and other property rights.

"Sounds serious," I said about the barge and bridge to reporters Mark Smith and Deborah Crane, who studied the note unhurriedly and somewhat bemused.

"Maybe," said Mark laconically. "Guess we'll have to run by there." The Sunset bridge was only a few miles away from Hughes Motel, and they lived just down the waterway from it, not even a mile farther, at Bonaparte's Landing.

"We don't get too upset anymore by notes like this," Deborah said. "See, our editor once left us a note about a double murder and naturally we got all fired up, but turned out it was only two dogs had gotten run over out on Highway 17."

This call, though, was real. When we reached the little crossing, there were already several dozen vehicles stalled on either side of the breech. The pontoon bridge was stuck askew, and a pushboat and barge were laid up in the marsh. When Smith and Crane's story and photographs ran in the *Free Press*, the heading with full merit was:

THE BARGED-OUT BRIDGE

The Sunset bridge stayed barged out for six weeks, but, even so, automobile traffic still managed to float across the waterway. Brunswick County dragooned a ferryboat from the state, graveled a slip aslant of the causeway, and appropriated Bonaparte's Landing as the mainland terminus. No one would have wished for a bridge-slamming boat wreck, but, since it happened whether it had to or not, it was something of a sight to see, and from Homer Foil's proximate yard you could even feel the lower part of the Sound Country relax back into the sleepier side of itself that recalled the not so long ago years just after Hurricane Hazel had swept the southeastern beaches clean in October of '54. There was little left out on the ocean side of Sunset except an old wooden fishing pier named after the then-still-visible-at-low-tide wreck of the *Vesta*, a Civil War blockade runner and contraband hustler that had run afoul of wind and tide and come to permanent berth aground in south Brunswick.

One August evening in 1976, Homer and I were out stargazing on the new Sunset Beach Fishing Pier, the trestle to glory that replaced the Vesta, and Homer said of the old wreck resting somewhere below us: "I recall being able to see an old boiler sticking out from the sand, but now the beach has built up and out so you can't see a trace of it anymore." So we looked up instead, into the dark universe above us, bright with stars, and charted the Big and Little Dippers, Draco, Hercules, Lyra, Cygnus, Aquila, Delphinus, Cassiopeia, Andromeda, Triangulum, Aries, Pegasus, Perseus, Capricornus. Shark fishermen came out in the midnight hour, threw buckets of guts over the side, set their lines, and all fell promptly asleep in sleeping bags at the end of the pier.

If there seemed to be a slackwater spirit, a Sound Country ease to it all—the barged-out bridge, the blockade-runner wreck, the snoring shark fishermen—perhaps there really was such a thing. Builder and old-time Carolina salt Bill Hunt loved to stand out on the beach-cottage porch a half mile from the pier and hold forth with tales like the one about why his Laurinburg friend Judge Dickson Phillips was known widely among their crowd as "Thinslice." "He'll have us all over to his place," Bill once said, "for ham and all, and he'll slice that ham so thin you can read a newspaper through it." An odder ease and sociability was evidenced by the speakeasy nature of one of the state whiskey peddlers in that district, who in trying to lower the stocks of his slowest-moving wares used to offer the perceived likely customer a sample china coffeecup full of Coco-Ribe, a vile looking coconut-and-grain agglomeration, saying:

"Yeah, Saturday mornings, tell you what I *do*—pour me about three fingers of this ol *Coco-Ribe*, mix it all up with a bunch of pineapple juice, turn on the cartoons, look out yonder over the marsh, and just let the world go on and float *a-way*!"

One of the most genial of the Brunswick marsh hawks was a curly-haired fellow about sixty named Frank Nesmith. We met him at his dock on Bonaparte's Creek near the pontoon bridge, Ann and Cary and I, on an August afternoon a year ago, and spent the rest of that hot day roaming the broad marshes in his fourteen-foot skiff. When we passed an old trawler lying halfway over on its side at the edge of the waterway, Frank said: "It does me good to see sights like that, still around here—let's me know that not *everything* looks like millionaires have got ahold of it yet."

This was the week the laughing gulls changed their head color, from charcoal to an oyster white, and there were crabs in the pots with new blue shells. Down the back side of Bird Island we boated, toward Little River and the last of North Carolina. Just as Mad Inlet at Bird Island's upper end has moved southerly by nearly a mile, a descending dune field easily showing in aerial photographs Mad's steady move, so too have Little River and *its* inlet migrated well to the south over the forty years since Hurricane Hazel. Just before we beached Frank's boat on Bird Island near the inlet, we slowed to watch the birds coursing one Little River sandbar: royal terns and gulls, a dowitcher, some skimmers.

Not far from the Little River jetty stood a curved-top, rural mailbox on a post in the dunes, a sandy park bench nearby, aimed out to sea. Frank Nesmith said this was the "kindred spirit" mailbox, and bade me, "Go on, check the mail." Inside lay a spiral notebook holding *ex tempore* scrawled thoughts and reflections, not of Frank's but from the walkers out on this strand. Many entries were signed, many were anonymous, many alluded to a *sense of timelessness* the writers had felt here, and all were dated. Their variety was wild:

Dear Kindred Spirit,

I found my second home on a beach in North Carolina—for 22 years I've been a rural mail carrier, mostly in Minnesota . . .

Dear Kindred Spirit,

Please let Bird I. remain the same. Please don't ever turn it into a regular beach because it's such a special place . . .

Dear Kindred Spirit,

The only cool thing about this island was the naked lady.

Dear Kindred Spirit,

I have been told the Kindred Spirit can pretty much solve any problems. . . . I am in a very controlling relationship, where if I could get out I would . . . it would be very much appreciated if the Kindred Spirit could help me . . .

Dear Kindred Spirit,

Help me win the lottery.

and

Dear Kindred Spirit,

Why are you so far away?

Good fortune led me some years ago to a rocking chair on the front porch of Jim Smith's little inn on Fourth Street in Wilmington, just two blocks west of the Sixth Street house with the two-storied bay window where my mother was born one Ides of March, at a time when there still were a few old veterans—men and women—around who had lived through the Civil War, when Wilmington had been the last Southern port open and open only because of the powerhouse pounders, the Confederate cannon downriver at Fort Fisher, which kept the Union navy enough at bay for a raffish bunch of daredeviling sailors, blockade runners, to move in and out of the Cape Fear. Sit on Jim Smith's porch and stare past the old church graveyard where the long dead sleep beneath the big live oaks, and look down the hill to the wharves where Market hits the Cape Fear, both branches of its draining and flowing now married and with conjugal force roaring toward the sea, and know that when the greatest artillery pyrotechnics and ballistics display this continent has ever known fell upon Fort Fisher in January of '65 and collapsed it, the South was finally closed to the world and the end of the war was at hand.

I had just played piano around the corner at Thalian Hall, behind whose chalk-white columned portico was a velveted and balconied jewel box of a theater, and the gracious reward beyond the honor of the thing and the paycheck of it too was these few moments of looking off through space and time from a side street of what for two centuries anyway was our state's greatest port and city. A couple years earlier, after another night on the Thalian boards, our crowd had gone out for awhile into the bright, cheerful, agreeable din of the Cafe Phoenix down on First Street, with its faux marble and narrow balcony and Italian-sausage-and-capers sandwiches, a hot Bohemian draw specializing in a meld of theater and film and rhythm-and-blues society. Lawyer Richard Wright from the outlying sweet-potato town of Tabor City (or *Razor City*, as Ron Hyatt said they used to call it when he was playing in the Border Belt minor leagues, where "Some were on the way up, some on the way down, and some like me just on the way *out*," adding, "They'd *slice* you down there at Razor City, slice you right down to *frying* size!") was, through all the considerable cross-talk, convincing our *King Mackerel* collaborator Jake Mills that the two of them were cousins, a conversation that continued the next morning and ended in accord amongst the mimosas at a nearby bungalow on the Front Street bluff overlooking the Cape Fear River. But that was another night.

So was the evening director Jim Colman and I, after filming all day along the waterfront, enjoyed an outdoor balcony dinner of grilled grouper at Roy's Riverboat and sat talking about the little river tour boat *J. N. Maffitt*, named in honor of a particularly bold blockade runner, and about the wharfside street preacher who'd kept intruding upon the tour group led by a straw-hat and cane fellow who looked for all the world like a large version of Truman Capote and haranguing them:

"I want to tell you bout *Jesus*, cause you let *him* be your guide now and he's gon take you where you *need* to *go!*"

And we had talked about the Fort Fisher Hermit, dead now, who appeared to fort tourists in years past and made his living off coins that folks tossed into an old frying pan he kept sitting out near his warren in the old seaside fort's sand-and-earthworks. "Yeah, he was a failure at everything," historian Harry Warren had said to us earlier that day, "till he became a hermit, then he was a runaway success at that. Had himself an old frying pan, always kept a few coins in it for people to add to, and they *did*! No telling how much loot that old man made with that frying pan."

That was a quiet night, though Jim had noised it up for himself by going around the corner and shooting pool till 2:00 A.M., losing eighteen dollars in the deal. I had left him to it, walking back up the hill to Jim Smith's porch, reflecting how odd it all was, my mother's family had been so long tied to this old town—Granddaddy learning his builder's trade here after the Pages left the Tar Landing farm in Onslow County and moved to the city; Mama having been born here; her Edwards cousins Eugene and Furney Durwood (who was named for a relative of his parents but was always called F. D.) clerking and then owning and running the Miss Lucy B. Moore Florist Shop and converting flowers and ferns into good fortune; her less-fortunate cousin Graham, who used to let the air most of the way out of the tires and take Mama riding on the beach out at Wrightsville, cutting figure eights in the sand, till World War II called him, and his aircraft, with the entire crew looking groundward for survivors of a crash in Central America, then itself flew slam into a mountain and the sole survivor of *this* crash recalled only that Graham had looked up and seen the face of that mountain and exclaimed "Oh, my God!" and that was the last of it; and years later, in the First Baptist Church at Fifth and Market, my grandfather's bringing my mother and uncle and me to witness his baptism (or rebaptism—for someone had lost his *bona fide*, or letter of membership in the church) one blasted hot Sunday in the summer of 1967; and now in the 1990s my mother and the same uncle and their older sister having a running discussion (not to say argument, though the talk possessed as much energy as if the issue were both contemporary and burning), the issue being whether or not Mama could legitimately remember (as opposed to having heard so much she really only *thought* she could remember) the Monkey Man, the organ grinder, who used to move up and down Market Street when my mother was scarcely more than an infant in the early 1920s.

One evening, sitting out there on the porch so engaged, I heard a blood-curdling yowl from a child, urgent shriekings from others too, coming from the far side of the graveyard, and I bolted across the street without thinking what I would do to whomever I might meet in the halfmoon dark, and tore through the old grave slabs, getting hit in the head by hanks of Spanish moss hanging low off the big live oaks, shouting "Hey!" as loud as I could while running over the dead.

"You shut up you, who you?!" came a voice from beyond the graveyard fence. It was a black woman.

"What's going on over there?" I shouted back.

"It's nothing!"

"Who's that hurt?" I said.

"Nobody's hurt," she answered.

"Well, it sure sounds like it," I said. "That's why I ran over here."

"No, it's just a little boy, his mama's gone off somewhere and he don't know where she is—he's got scared and started cryin, that's all."

"You sure it's all right?"

"It's all right, Mister," she said. "Thank you."

"Good night, then," I said.

"Good night."

I went back and sat on the porch, a bit winded and still wondering what sort of domestic scene I had just entered, however briefly. Jim Smith came out to see what was afoot, and he sat down and joined me. Jim was a big curly-haired man, a Westerner, who had worked for Ford Motors many a year before circumstances that he seemed more in control of than not sent him abroad along the southeastern coast studying port towns for their climatic likelihood as whereabouts for a high-grade hostelry. Wilmington won out, and it agreed with him mightily.

"I ever tell you about old Jack down the street, what happened to him?"

"I don't believe so, Jim," I said.

"Well, it's the damnedest thing," he said. "Old Jack, back when he was about seventeen, was out in his boat in the ocean here by himself, setting nets, and the boat hit something, he never knew what, and the collision pitched him out of the craft and into the winter water. His boat drifted swiftly away from him in the sea, and he was on his own a mile or two out in the Atlantic, but he swam for it and hours later, incredibly, he made it to shore. Jack had no idea where he was—it was dark, and he had washed up on an uninhabited stretch of shoreline. He took off walking and he walked right into a swamp.

"Meanwhile, his empty boat had come ashore, been found and reported, and when his family heard about it, well, they knew how far out he'd've been working and so naturally they assumed the worst and figured he'd drowned.

"Well, Jack was walking all night through that swamp and after a bit he heard someone, or some *thing*, following him, keeping pace with him, taking steps to match his own. So he sped up, as best he could slogging through knee-deep mud, you know, but when he did, whatever was following him sped up too,

177
Maco
. . . .

same as Jack. He was mortally exhausted, thought he'd survived drowning only to wind up getting done in back in the swamps by a bear or some crazy person or something. When it got to be daylight again, he stopped—and his pursuer stopped—and then he figured out what it was. It was his own steps, the muck closing up noisily with a sucking sound that he had been mistaking for the footfalls of another.

"Got out of that swamp and found a road, and while he was walking up that road, drenched, frozen, all covered with mud and about to drop, here comes a deputy sheriff, pulls up alongside of Jack and calls him over, saying:

"'Hey, buddy—you heard of anybody drowned down this way?'

"Jack thinks a minute, then shakes his head and says, 'No, sure hadn't,' and keeps on walking. The deputy drives on down the road away from him, turns around where it dead-ends at the swamp, and, when he passes Jack going back up the road, same direction, the deputy slows down and says 'You look like you might could use a ride, fellow.' And Jack says, 'I'd 'preciate that,' and climbs in the squad car.

"So now he's getting warmed up and kind of coming around after all that exposure—the sheriff's man still not knowing this was the victim he was out searching for—and they're riding back towards town when here comes Jack's family all piled in a couple of cars heading down to the shore to throw a wreath in the sea there where Jack's boat had turned up. And Jack sees them and yells to the deputy, 'Hey, could you turn around and follow those cars!?' which he did, of course, and threw his siren and lights on and they had a big tearful reunion right there on the roadside."

Jim stopped and shook his head. The Wilmington night all around us was quiet, balmy.

"I asked him once," Jim said. "Asked him, 'Jack, when you were out there, you ever think of just . . . giving up?'

"'No,' Jack said. 'I knew I was a real good swimmer. It never even crossed my mind.'

"That man's a house painter in Wilmington today," Jim Smith said, rocking on his port-town porch, "and they say he does a real nice job."

Knowing that the harbor lights were lit and aflame across the bay at Southport was enough to pull my cohort Jim Wann and me ofttimes down out of the red-clay country and back into the coastal plain. Throughout the '70s we were drawn there by the flashing night beacons, red and green, by the wheeling spokes of the Oak Island Light, by Bald Head Light's low steady lantern, and by the moving specks out on the water that were the running lights of whatever craft was abroad when we got there to the place where the roads ran out and there were no more roads till Africa except the most ancient of all, the roads on the trackless sea.

"What's *in* Southport?" people would ask us. "I mean—there's no *beach* there."

Well, to start with, it was a nice ride down, slinking around out east of Fayetteville on the Wade-Stedman Road (where there was still a property-line sign saying NO TRESPASSING, BY ORDER OF ATLANTIC COAST LINE though there hadn't been an ACL for a generation because the Seaboard Air Line merged it into itself and made the Seaboard Coast Line, and now even that is gone, into the Chesapeake and Ohio, the Chessie, the C&O, which even in abbreviation reminded one of the predecessor canal emanating from Georgetown, but all of which is rolled into CSX, an acronym fit for nothing but the Wall Street stockticker, with its unsingable rhythm devoid of any and all mystery) and then running along the north side of the Cape Fear through Cedar Creek and down through the Spanish-moss clump of a village that is Whiteoak, and crossing the great erector-set steel-trestle bridge over the Cape Fear at Elizabethtown (the same bridge caught on film not too long ago being dynamited and sunk into the Cape Fear) and there picking up N.C. 87 to Maco and skirting the Green Swamp and going on into Southport itself, which was then still Brunswick's county seat.

Little old Southport, with its enormous and overarching live oaks and its Old Whittlers' (a.k.a. Old Liar's) Bench down by the wharf near where the *Frying Pan* lightship docked. One right turn and there on the water was an eight-room, faded-green cinder-block motel, the Riverside—not the Cape Fear Inn, where upon the lawn is a small grave and headstone for My Love Pierre, the motel owner's late, lamented pet spider monkey that not only had the run of the place but also had its own room—the just plain Riverside, and that is where and what it offered and was.

No, there was no beach there, that was across the way, out beyond the wide waters that Southport's verandaed and widow's-walked homes gazed over and turned their morning faces to. What there was on the main street was an A M U Z U theater, now closed, and next to it an Old Curiosity Shop, run by an old fellow who was something of a curiosity himself, a biggish white-haired and mustached man named Bomps Pancoast, who wore a porkpie hat flattened on his head.

"Come on in here," he said to me one morning when I was out walking. "Whatever you were looking for, I got it."

"I wasn't looking for anything," I said.

"Don't matter. I still got it."

Old Curiosity Shop, windows still taped after Hurricane Bertha, Southport, August 1996

And so he did. After a slow tour through his musty, dusty store, I bought from Mister Pancoast two mock-crystal sherry glasses, a willow cane that seemed far more related to some soft-shoe routine than actual support of its bearer, and — for my old friend Jake who has been showing up here in Southport since he was a boy — a small face-of-a-man paperweight that looked like what I imagine Caliban to be and was the size and color of a piece of charcoal.

On another trip we called upon James Harper, who with his wife Margaret ran a much-celebrated newspaper named the *State Port Pilot.* We were on something of an assignment ourselves, for the *Carolina Financial Times,* our question being: Was a University of North Carolina geology professor's prediction of an imminent 7-point-Richter-scale earthquake with Southport as epicenter having any particular effect, economic perhaps, on the town? I had already asked a waitress at the edge-of-town waffle shop what she thought, and in a voice of panic she said:

"If I didn't have to have this job, I'd go pick up my little boy and hightail it outa here!" She had looked around to see if anyone overheard her, then sighed, "But I got to work. Take your order?"

When a little while later at the newspaper office we sat with Mister Harper, a small, jovial, incisive man, he laughed at our inquiry and said, "No, no, nobody around here's upset about that!" Then we told him about the waitress, and he allowed as that was too bad, people getting affected by what some pointy-headed

Treasures, Old Curiosity Shop, Southport, August 1996

prof up in Chapel Hill had to say. He thought that was kind of a half-cocked thing to do, predict earthquakes—this was early 1976—as that was not a business with much reliability attached to it.

"I'll tell you an earthquake story, though, if you really want one."

"Sure," I said.

"Well," said Mister Harper, leaning back in his swivel wooden captain's chair, "this was when the earthquake of '98 hit Southport. People came streaming out of their houses, into the streets. And they all ran, I mean *ran*, down to the old cemetery—just down the street here, you ought to walk on by it, you'll see the same thing those old-timers did that night—anyway, they all formed up in a big mob, ground shaking every now and again, people crying, praying, all of them there at the cemetery because they thought—I mean, the whole town thought—that it was the Judgment Day and there was going to be the great Revelation and all the graves were going to open up and all their dead relatives and friends were going to fly up and, you know, be made whole!"

He paused a moment, and in fact he had told the tale with such exclamatory enthusiasm, since he was speaking of rather excited people, that it sounded like something big must have really occurred, like maybe not *all* the graves but possibly one or two or so came open and raised at least a few dead. Then he went on:

"Course nothing happened. The earthquake passed and after they'd stood

Steamer *Wilmington*, Southport, early 1900s

around and waited for half the night, they all gave up on Judgment Day and went on home. But this new earthquake this fellow's calling for? Nobody's given it much mind, around here. You want to know what folks around here're upset about, I mean *really* upset? *Corncake Inlet!*"

"Where's that?" I said, but I was thinking, What's that? As coastwise as I had been raised, I had never even heard of it.

"Oh, it's up above Bald Head." He waved his arms in an easterly direction. "All the fishermen used to go out through Corncake, but you see now it's all shoaled up and you can't get through there and they have to go out down the Cape Fear. And to hear 'em talk, anything that's wrong with anything around here, somehow it has to do with Corncake Inlet closing up! Fishing's off, the catch is down—Corncake Inlet! Nothing's been right since the Corncake closed up. They want the Corps of Engineers to dynamite it, or dredge it, or something, anything to open it up. Then there won't be any more problems in Brunswick County, once they reopen Corncake Inlet. I'm not kidding—that's the big thing around here. I hear a lot more talk about Corncake than earthquake."

I remember one of the hands on the Fort Fisher ferry saying he wished it wasn't his shift right during the time the earthquake was supposed to hit, but I also remember he rolled his eyes after he said that and lit a pipe. I remember giving a short ride to an elderly, hitchhiking inebriate who only talked about how much hard work he'd done in the fish houses, cleaning and boiling fish over the years. If there were bad catches these days, he didn't seem to know about it. Rather, he recalled working for a week, that's right, he said, a whole week without sleep, till he finally on the verge of collapse went over to where all the fish were dumped, found him a giant flounder the size of a bed, flopped out on that flounder, and slept for three whole days!

And I remember going over to Bald Head back in the '70s, right after the State of North Carolina lost its last best chance to get and hold that big piece of island and sea beach for the people, right when a self-proclaimed low-density, hidden-by-the-trees beach development was starting. Someone from the Carolina Cape Fear outfit carried us over the water in a runabout and showed us a nascent golf course and tapped his impatient foot while we climbed the rickety, winding wooden stairway inside Old Baldy, the short tawny lighthouse—with its keystone-arch doorway and tall windows spiraling up around the shaft to follow the stairs and its irregular dark patches of exterior discoloration that looked not unattractively like wormy wood—set on the island's northwestern point a good mile or more from Bald Head, the broad and open sand flat to seaward.

The salt air, breeze, and spray that are free in this part of the world always make such small-craft transits a real joy. But it was clear—more from the pinched and hurried demeanor of our corporate host than from the golfing-village design he showed off—that the people who would purportedly move here would not be the sort of Carolinians, if they were Carolinians at all, who slept on grand flounders or walked about with willow canes or buried the family monkey in the yard.

Still, as Thoreau said, there is more to day than dawn. I knew I would come back to this corner of the Sound Country, whether there was an earthquake supposed to go on or not. The road that goes through Maco Station leads here, and I have ghosts of my own to hunt up, like the old birdmen Pearson and Brimley watching curlews on the Oak Island beach nearly a century ago, and Grand-daddy Page working over there at Fort Caswell and freezing through the First World War and relishing that feast of wild pork the soldiers hunted off of Bald Head. It was a big island out beyond all those harbor lights that had drawn me here, and there was much more of it to see. I knew if I got tired I could always stretch out on a king mackerel, and call it a cot.

One gorgeously gloomy November Friday twenty years later, we wended our family way toward Bald Head, catching up with the backside of a stormfront along about the Northeast Cape Fear, where the mistletoe grew clumped and clustered in the short oaks and cypress. The geese were in their southbound *Vs* over Brunswick River, and in the swamps and pinestands, in the Town Creek sa-vanna too, the storm's thick late-autumn mist clung to everything, and the sand stretching beneath the oak and pine and myrtle scrub around Boiling Springs Lakes had the look of wet cement.

Through this cold mist and spray we all rode over the big river-mouth bay on a sixty-foot passenger ferry—Bald Head now being a private village unto itself—that left Southport from a special slip a mile or two outside of the real town. The ferryboat's name was *Sans Souci*, but the boat and the slips at either end of the transit belied the name—that considerable care had been taken and not inconsiderable money spent on Bald Head Incorporated was evident at every turn. The little harbor and marina looked like a movie set, its newness and superimposition making it seem not quite real and full of pretense of being something and somewhere else, like the convenience store's name: Island Chandler.

But there is nearly always a beyond and a back of beyond, and past all this sleek modernity was Old Baldy and a paved path lying over the turn-of-the-century tramway, the Federal Road laid long ago to carry materiel two and a half miles to the other end of the island to build its other lighthouse, the Cape Fear Light that Oak Island Light eventually replaced. That afternoon after everyone was all ensconced in our Cape Fear Riverfront cottage, outdoorsman Manley Fuller, my son and little girl and I lit out walking east down the Federal Road, into some of the best of the Bald Head jungle.

Here where the wild pigs once roamed were now wild cucumber, Carolina laurel cherry, witch's broom on a red cedar—a big green upward spray coming off a gall that occurs on only one in ten thousand trees. We saw paper mulberry and sabal palm in the woods and, running alongside the road itself, the bright decoration of all the silverling (*Baccharis halimifolia*, also called sea-myrtle) seedpods busted, a thick platinum-white spray. Dogwoods, cut off the island in the 1950s for textile shuttles, are thicker now than then. The children were en-

Palmettos, Bald Head Island, about 1905

thralled by the pearpad cactus and ate its jammy fruit. They might have chewed the bark of the toothache tree—John Lawson's *pellitory* or pilentary, whose spiky-cork bark cools like ice—but we kept walking and they only ate but so much of the landscape.

Turning back at the rise maybe halfway across the island, we then drifted down a lane to Bald Head Creek, the tidal flow that separated Bald Head from much smaller Middle Island. In the marsh across the creek from the floating dock we stood upon was a seventy-year-old clapboard fish camp on stilts, somebody's humble tumbledown lodge, undetailed except for a door on the south side and a small square window on the east and all of it looking like it had last been painted a generation ago. Posted next to it was a state marine CLOSED TO SHELLFISHING sign. Later I learned that this was an old government boathouse, made free use of by the few island residents in days gone by, now even more abandoned than it might seem—the channel of Bald Head Creek, which had once been to the north of the boathouse, was now shifted completely to its south. But at the moment I first saw the unglorified shed, I thought: now *here* was vernacular architecture, like the hermit's shack in the Sunset marshes and the hunt camps in the Great Dismal Swamp and in the great Alligator River wastes, nothing like the fanciful and pristine immediate antique of the structures that greet pilgrims to this place, just an old cottage to leeward now open to all comers and all weathers.

An egret went wheeling across the dull gold marsh like a fleck of ivory turning in the wind, pure white against the tall loblollies behind, and I felt the old lift of heart one feels when the honest-to-God real stuff is near.

Next morning the sun brushed a wash of gold over the water-side homes and the dockpilings of Southport, and a little later, after the wedding (Cousin Sue and Keith's) whose party we swelled, Hunter and I lingered on the beach of the sandy Bald Head itself, the plain of the island's southwestern point, skipping oyster shells in the surf when the water was slack. Later still, I turned the older children loose with bicycles and maps and took off with Ann and our little Cary for the far end of the Federal Road.

A small brick powerhouse there at the road's east end was all that remained from the operation of the Cape Fear Light, a thin shaft held in place for more than half a century by a skeletal steel frame so strong that it took repeated dynamitings to be dropped and decommissioned. Out on the beach beyond, the pink and blue sunset sky was mirrored in the wet sand, and in the sheen of this sandy mirror, too, a quarter moon was rising. My daughter pointed us to Cape Fear, the small, slightly hooked lazy-*J* point of land disappearing into the rip of Frying Pan Shoals, and I went walking with her out into an inch of water at the very tip of the Cape till with quick and counterbalancing common sense she urged us,

"Back, Daddy, go back!"

So back we went, retreating from the vast triangulation of breakers rolling over the shoals to the horizon and beyond, the riptide waves spraying in the November wind everywhere. That night after everyone was safe in bed back in the riverside cottage, I sat up looking out across the Cape Fear River and watching, hypnotized for no small time, the steady four flashes of Oak Island Light. When the same Captain Charlie Swan who had long manned Cape Fear Light came out of retirement to throw the first power on at Oak Island in 1958, what he lit

Cape Fear River pilots' tower, Southport, August 1996

was for its time the brightest light in America. Not just coastal North Carolina, or even the eastern United States—in all America!

Who all has roistered here? I wondered. All those free-range cattle that the owner-planter Smith set out here before George Washington was sworn in as president; all the hogs and sheep that came later; all the river pilots, some of whom guided blockade runners both above and below the Smith Island range of marsh and ground that includes Bald Head, and their sons and nephews, pilots too, in a nearly closed union they called the Combination; all the bathers and beachcombers around the Pavilion during World War I when that generation's land developer called Bald Head "Palmetto Island"; bootleggers and more hogs and goats and a one-armed hermit named Archie Mac and his mule Molly, who lived over on Bald Head Creek near the Coast Guard boathouse; truck-farmers and market gardeners, dogwood cutters, dredgers, fillers (the leader of the development whose runabout had ferried us from Southport to Bald Head in the 1970s had also actually sent a barge loaded with heavy equipment, dozers and so forth, to work on Bald Head *before* the State of North Carolina cleared his permits), golf-course builders, board-and-batteners, golfers, cyclers, and just-plain amblers and other light-seekers like myself.

Come now the four flashes in one quadrant rolling level with the world, now come on a clear night to the ghost at Maco still after a century or more seeking reunion with himself, now come to the barred owl coursing the depths of Green Swamp, now come to the small craft in the inlets of Shallotte and Lockwood's Folly and Shallotte Sound too, now come shining on a plane even with the sea through the window panes of pilot houses plain and grand, outbound and homeward, and now come to me as to all who range widely abroad the earth and her seas and pray God have mercy on the mariner.

I'm climbing up

On the rough side of the mountain

I hold to God, his powerful hand

I'm climbing up

On the rough side of the mountain

And I'm doing my best to make it in.

—Rev. F. C. Barnes and Rev. Janice Brown

of Rocky Mount, North Carolina,

"Rough Side of the Mountain," 1985

Rough Side

· ·

Out beyond Belcross and the potatolands, on u.s. 158 east of Elizabeth City as Camden County is becoming Currituck, there was in my boyhood a small country gas station with a live attraction: Cuff the bear. He was a big black bear who stood in his shelter, a small hut open in the front from waist height up, looking as if he were going to serve you up a barbeque sandwich or a snow cone. In fact he was addicted to Coca-Colas, and no telling how many six-ounce dopes my family passed his way, Cuff taking the green bottle from you as you quickly retreated. For there was over his window on the world this warning: "Hello. My name is Cuff and I like fingers!" Sometimes Cuff was staked out closer to the highway, chained to a metal rod in the ground. He chugged down a Coke in just a matter of seconds, threw the bottle down, then reached out for more.

I remember my father coming home from court one evening and telling me that Cuff had escaped, gotten away into the swamps. What would happen to him? I asked. My father shook his head—he didn't know. But when he told me that men and dogs were hunting Cuff, I knew without admitting it that that was the end of the civilized bear. A few days later, Daddy said they'd caught Cuff raiding a hoglot and shot him dead. I cried about all this, for I felt like I knew him, and he'd never so much as taken a nip or swipe at me. By the next time we rode east toward our little shingled shanty at Kitty Hawk, I was merely wistful when I looked at Cuff's old enclosure, empty now but with the I LIKE FINGERS sign still up and in place. Soon that pen was torn down, and for a long time now the station itself has been gone.

Not so some other animal pens that always haunted me, haunt me still: these were the long pony-shed barracks of the migrant laborers who worked the steady and successively maturing crops, coming up from Florida on U.S. 17, the Ocean Highway, in old and overcrowded schoolbuses, encamping all across the coastal plain, passing through Pasquotank and then disappearing after potatoes were in, reappearing I reckon up on Virginia's eastern shore, coming back our way to chop cabbage. I remember them hanging on the stall doors of those pitiful apartments—languorous, exhausted, children half-naked, most of them black but probably in those days some Indians among them too, where nowadays they'd be Mexicans, or Haitians, and somewhere back then something strange and rough and ill-fitting lodged in me without intention as I compared the living quarters of these creatures:

Cuff the Bear lived better than the migrants.

Jake Mills and his son Mark and I were down near Woodard, heading for the Sans Souci ferry on a fishing trip. It was very early one morning in May, and in the clarity and muted brightness of the longslant morning light the old farmsteads, the white clapboard bungalow homes with the broad porches and kerosene and propane heat tanks outside, the unpainted barns, all looked entrenched, good and rooted in place, and I thought nothing of the familiar Carolina country sights till Mark exclaimed noisily:

"Man, it looks like the De-*pression* around here!"

And then in an instant I saw eastern Carolina as Walker Evans had seen and shot the South, neglected, ill-maintained, full of ruins great and small, evidence everywhere of the shortage of care or cash or both. For every Somerset Place or Hope Plantation, well-restored grandee lodges and halls, there were a thousand, or *ten* thousand, dilapidated sheds, shacks, shanties, tobacco barns, falling in. I thought about all the times I have gazed across a quarter-mile of corn- or beanfield stubble in the fall and seen some one-room country little shack faintly lit by the scant yellow light of candles, or kerosene or oil lanterns, and thought, Yes, lovely old sight of a Southern night, that, but all in the eyes of the beholder. Nearer to that flame was someone, probably but not definitely black or Indian or mestizo, who couldn't pay a light bill and maybe never had or never would, or never would again. And I thought, too, of other, larger ruins, all the old I-houses, the old plantation houses empty, that one could see clear through, and the sets of twin chimneys standing after a fire or a house had fallen in, then one or both of them leaning a little more through each set of seasons till there remained nothing but a pile of bricks and mortar, or the even more doleful single chimney alone in some field.

"There's nothin but haves and have-nots down there," a New Bernian remarked to me about the Carolina east one day, and not long afterward another son of the lowlands, fishmonger Tom Robinson of Atlantic, said to me with no shortage of conviction, "What the east needs is a big dose of land reform." The disparities are wild, and certainly always have been. On maps that portray the presence of poverty in the American South, the counties of the Carolina east achieve a hegemony like that of the Mississippi Delta, with far more dwelling as have-nots than haves.

Land reform? The main, evident version of it involves consolidation, mostly by timber interests that have colonized eastern Carolina and set out enormous monocultural loblolly pine plantations. Despite a number of small but significant experiments in turning tenants into freeholders, like the planned agricultural communities at Penderlea, Tillery (where poet Jim Seay once conducted a poetry workshop on the shipping dock of the Tillery Casket Company), and Scuppernong Farms, a strong, landed Jeffersonian citizenry across the seaboard of the coastal plain is still *videri quam esse*, to seem rather than to be.

I saw the hope for it at the Edenton Feeder Pig Coop in the early 1970s, where black men and white worked together and established a state grading shed and market to help small pig farmers keep from being victimized by "pinhookers," buyers who cruised the country lanes and took advantage of the farmers by buying their pigs on the dusty spot at sorry, undermarket prices. But the swine-herd reality two decades later is high-volume, industrial hoglots that make the sixty- and eighty-pig pens of Pasquotank and Currituck of my youth look like matchboxes—these fantastic feedlots of the 1990s are there to serve new and massive lowland abatoirs.

Watching Edward R. Murrow and his camera tracking up the Ocean Highway of U.S. 17 that ran right by my daddy's door, I felt enormous discomfiture, watching Murrow as he interviewed a friendly-as-could-be eastern Carolina potato farmer who said Oh, these migrants, they wouldn't live any other way even if they could, they don't want any responsibilities, they're like children, they're the happiest people in the world! I remember the church group in Chapel Hill after Morrow's film *Harvest of Shame*, flaying that farmer and running him into the ground and even though I suddenly wanted to defend him, not what he was saying but just *him*, because he could have been my cousin and he was all right, decent enough to his own kind anyhow, I knew he was as dead-solid wrong as could be about those sub-tenant, sub-share migrant workers (just as all the other fourteen-year-olds watching the legendary Murrow work the easy mark

knew that farmer was wrong): Nobody wanted to live in a pony shed with lousy water and no commode let alone shower and all in all worse off than a Coca-Cola-swilling show bear just down the road. Nobody with a choice chose *that*.

Any more than all those black Africans had chosen two hundred years ago to show up in Tyrrell or Washington County working for Josiah Collins who had the swell wrap-around porches to sit out upon and regard Lake Phelps, or Scuppernong, and who needed them to dig his system of canals to run his four-story low-head water-powered grain mill and carry the flow off his fields so he could impress Edmund Ruffin and everybody else who stopped by and be the most flamboyant planter in eastern Carolina and have his family for spells of time speak nothing but French around the house and put on so many airs as to infuriate his close neighbors the Pettigrews, who as planters were themselves no slouches, just couldn't keep up with the Collinses, though they did produce the brilliant, ascetic Johnston Pettigrew who went off to Chapel Hill and Berlin, Madrid, and Cuba, off to Charleston and from that city of Southern firebrands to the South Carolina legislature where he led the minority in opposing a re-opening of the foreign slave trade, and Lord knows might have someday gone off to the White House had his region not become a nation unto itself and sent him forward at last as a leader in Pickett's charge at Gettysburg, where he was wounded and then, gut-shot in the retreat that followed, was dead at dawn less than two weeks after the great loss.

But before all or most of all that there was among those Africans, whose labors underpinned the whole affair, a homesickness so pure and deep for another jungle on another continent that it drove some of them to sing the songs of their homelands at night till, overcome and overwrought by their own fervid keening, they set out from Somerset and strode into Lake Phelps as if with a conjurer's blessing and charm, as if believing they could now walk on water or swim all the way home or to something and somewhere at least better by far than the brute life they had been living under force, though if they ever saw a country in Africa again it was not Ghana but the undiscovered country of death, for they drowned, exchanging one wretchedness for another, as people will do.

Somerset fell to abandonment, ruin, and other owners after the close of the Civil War, the Collinses themselves no more capable of controverting time and history's course than Faulkner's Sutpens, and then at last to the 4,000-acre plantation that had operated most of the nineteenth century under one family's name came Scuppernong Farms, a small-farm settlement in the 1930s that has left less mark on the lowlands than the empire upon whose ruin it was built.

And if this rough side of God's country here and in other eastern precincts

(opposite) Lone chimney, Halifax County, September 1996

has stayed rough and still resists shine or polish over 130 years since Appomattox and a half-century since FDR, to where enough of it in enough spots could cause someone at a casual glance on a beautiful May morning to say: "Looks like the De-*pression* around here!" (like that off-plumb trailer down on N.C. 904 near Old Dock where a gape-mouthed woman always seemed to be standing in the door as if employed to do so, giving a long-suffering Tobacco Road look toward the flood of upstate tourists streaming through her tobacco and yam country on the way to Brunswick beaches, and whether hers was a look of despair, disdain, or just plain old uncomprehending disbelief, who ever knew?) then how in the name of the Almighty whose tenants we all of us are could a black woman named Redford lure hundreds of descendants of Somerset slaves back to this rough side of creation, back to the shores of Lake Phelps for a reunion that turned out not angry, vengeful, or down but both joyous and proud, and so moving to all that she has done it yet again? And how—against all the back-breaking sharecropping of sound and sea, as laborers purse-seined the pogy—how could a pair of folklorists named Luster lure a dozen black net-men, chanteymen, to the stage dozens of times to sing again the old songs, the *Bye-bye, Sweet Rosie Anna*s, and pull in mime the old nets, this also a reunion, a dignified rejuvenation that carried this chorus from Front Street and the Maritime Museum in Beaufort to 57th Street and Carnegie Hall in New York City? And how could a playwright from Burgaw (who said his first friends in New York City amazed him with all their talk about teenaged love-making in the backseats of cars because all *he'd* known at that same age was grappling between the corn rows, glad to be so engaged) sing so lovingly of that scratch, small-farm life? What was it that brought any of them *back* to the rough side of the Sound Country in fact, memory, and art?

The answer is as simple as those fields the poet found his manhood in: rough as a cob, this was home. And Samm-Art Williams said he knew when he got on the bus at Port Authority in New York City one night along about the third week of December and the bus was packed and everyone on there was carrying shoe boxes of chicken and tins of baked goods—cornbread and cookies—and bottles of wine or whiskey just enough to last the night because come morning they'd be home, he knew that was his story, too, and that when he wrote it, it would come out simply as *Home*, and through his farmer Cephus Miles of Crossroads, North Carolina, Williams would sing:

"I love the land, the soft beautiful black sod crushing beneath my feet. A fertile pungent soil. A soil to raise strong children on. . . . I love the land. I love touching the crops. And gently holding each plant in my hand. And feeling the love and care that Grand-Daddy, Uncle and me put into its cultivation. When you hold a plant, you can feel the heartbeat of God. I love the land."

Though he would then sing a little more, and a little rougher:

"Ever skin a catfish? It takes talent. You use wire pliers. Catfish don't have scales. A tough skin. And watch out for his mouth. He's sharp around the mouth. You can get a gash cut in your arm that will rival the best laid razor scar you ever saw."

Even with all the inequities the Sound Country knows and has known, violence has not been a habit of coastal life, or a strong trait in the character of coastal people. Still, when coursing the long ledger, one sees a gracious plenty of astonishing moments of mayhem, murder, and the movement of contraband, to wit:

Because an Indian apparently filched an Englishman's silver cup when Ralegh's explorers under Grenville and Lane were first sailing in the Carolina shallows in July 1585, the English then torched the Indians' town of Aquascogoc southwest of Mattamuskeet and fired their crops. This single, primal episode—both incident and response—prefigured John Smith's difficulties with Powhatan twenty years later as well as John Lawson's death-by-torture and the vicious Tuscarora War that ensued here in the Sound Country 126 years later; and it set a pattern in immigrant and Indian dealings of approach, communication, a flaring trouble, attack, counterattack, and reprisal *ad infinitum*. And though no one will ever solve its mystery, the very disappearance of Ralegh's Roanoke Island outpost—the legendary Lost Colony—is in main theory laid to slaughter, enslavement, and absorption by the Indians somewhere in the coastal plain of Carolina or the tidewater of Virginia. One cup of silver, and how many of blood?

To prove out the Sound Country as an exemplary rogues' harbor, it took the dark heart of a man from elsewhere altogether, Edward Teach of Bristol, England. Captain Teach, or Thatch, in 1718 briefly ruled eastern Carolina and the shipping lanes lying just over the barrier banks and shoals. Teach, better known as Blackbeard, the literally fuming pirate with his battle-face beard full of incendiaries and smoking punts, for a spell used with impunity the small Sound Country ports of Bath—where Governor Eden was made to entertain if not endorse his forceful and well-armed guest—and Ocracoke—where the brigand met his fate.

By the time Blackbeard was engaged in the Battle of Ocracoke, in November of 1718, he had corralled and captured his minor rival, Stede Bonnet, the "Gentleman Pirate" of Barbados, and made Major Bonnet a collaborator by trading ships with him, Blackbeard taking Bonnet's better-armed boat, and forcing the naval militias of both South Carolina and Virginia to invade the Sound Country with the clear intention of exterminating the brutes. Charleston's William Rhett took Bonnet at the mouth of the Cape Fear; and Lieutenant Robert Maynard of Virginia caught Blackbeard inside Ocracoke Inlet, where the pirate, after cutting

Maynard's force up with cannonading shrapnel-fire, then ran aground and afoul of Maynard's still-superior numbers once Maynard's sloop bore down on Blackbeard. At the end of the battle and the day, Blackbeard's head decorated the sloop's bowsprit.

These piratical operations also set something of a pattern. Blockade runners evading the federal navy at Frying Pan Shoals and Cape Fear supplied the South through Wilmington and kept the Confederacy alive till three months shy of Appomattox. During Prohibition, a rum runner's misfortune in foundering on the Outer Banks and spilling its goods spawned a waltz-ballad, "The Night the Boozeyacht Ran Ashore," sung to the melody of "Sidewalks of New York." White liquor made in the then-great swamps between Pamlico and Albemarle Sounds — East Lake rye, Skinnersville corn — moved easily by small craft to pick-up points where by automobile and truck the swamp sauce roared off to such markets as Norfolk, the navy-town queen of Hampton Roads.

The Old Dominion paid us back. In 1953, down-east revenuer Garland Bunting went after a latter-day speakeasy right on the serpentine Pasquotank River, set up, he said, by "a bunch of wild people who had moved from Virginia into Camden County." Bunting feigned two rounds of drunkenness, then let the barkeeps haul him out back to a waterside cabin, where they robbed him and left him. Years after he had walked away from that less-than-savory round of evidence-gathering, he speculated that if his swampy hosts had known his true purpose, he would have been "catfish bait."

In more recent times, legion are the tales of shrimpers regularly and not un-intentionally netting bales of offshore marijuana bound for Sound Country safekeeping and distribution. "Between 1979 and 1983," Richard and Barbara Kelly reported in their book *Carolina Watermen &c.*, "customs agents seized forty-one vessels, five aircraft, and fifty-five vehicles involved in smuggling drugs into Brunswick County." And, mind you, not only marijuana — a down-east woman I know fairly stumbled upon a jettisoned four-pound, zipper-lock plastic bag of cocaine out on the long empty strand of north Core Banks. The cargo has occasionally fared better than its bearers. Near a small wharf and fishing operation up a creek in the isolated Pamlico Sound–side village of Mesic, half a dozen shallow graves turned up occupied in 1973, and lack of honor among drug smugglers was the cause of death.

Human contraband in long supply moved into, and through, the Sound Country swamps in the generations before emancipation, runaways skirting patrols and dogs as they sought ports with outbound vessels to freedom at their wharves, colonies of marooners setting up and staying on in the fastness of wet wilds from one end of the coastal plain to the other. Samuel Huntington Perkins, the Yale-trained tutor at Lake Landing plantation on Mattamuskeet in

U.S. revenue officers attack smugglers, Masonborough, New Hanover County, 1867

the late 1810s, knew of "Frequent instances . . . of them fleeing to the woods & swamps and subsisting for years on food there found or conveyed to them by their former fellow sufferers. Not long since a woman was discovered in the centre of the Great Dismal Swamp. There she & her six children had lived for years preferring the horrors of such a place and the enjoyment of freedom, to the comforts [of] civilized life when attended with the loss of liberty."

On occasions when fight prevailed over flight, the offending slave certainly had the deck stacked against him or herself. At the close of the Revolution, on the northern banks of Contentnea Creek, a black slave named Rose killed her mistress, a woman named Sibbey who by common Pitt County account was cruel to Rose and her fellow slave, Shade. Having abetted Rose in the premeditated murder, Shade was summarily sold off farther south, but Rose herself was tried and convicted and, as perpetrator of the crime, was sentenced to be burned alive at the stake. The Pitt County sheriff carried out this sentence at Martinborough, now Greenville.

Though Tom Copper and his supposed black army did not rise against the northern Albemarle as feared in 1802, and though there was no antebellum insurrection in Sound Country Carolina to match the aborted 1822 Denmark Vesey plot in Charleston or the grimly successful Nat Turner Rebellion in 1831, just over the line in Virginia, post–Civil War politicians were waving the bloody stump with the purported black threat in mind when Wilmington erupted in 1898 — the same year my grandfather Page watched the Red Shirts ride through

Jacksonville, downriver of his Tar Landing home, heavily armed with horse pistols, rifle- and shotgun-butts to their thighs, the year Carolina Democrats disenfranchised blacks and routed Republicans. What novelist Philip Gerard called the *Cape Fear Rising* torched Wilmington's black newspaper, left ten blacks dead, and installed a white martial government of scant legality led by lawyer-orator A. M. Waddell, a thespian who, playing a lighter role before the war, once strode the boards of the jewel-box Thalian Hall.

More mysterious than Waddell in Wilmington was the late November 1901 disappearance of Pasquotank River belle Nell Cropsey, who stepped onto the front porch of her family's riverside home to say good-night—or more likely goodbye—to her beau of three years, Jim Wilcox, the ex-sheriff's son. Eluding an exhaustive, crusade-like search of Elizabeth City, the Sound Country, and beyond, Miss Cropsey was next seen by two fishermen thirty-seven frigid days later, floating face down in the Pasquotank, and the county coroner—conducting her autopsy in a windowless barn with doors thrown and two thousand men looking on—declared that she had been struck on the head and then drowned. Jim Wilcox, who protested his innocence in the affair, escaped a lynch mob's wrath, and then sat silent through two murder trials, pulled fifteen years for second-degree murder before being pardoned by Governor Bickett in 1918, after which Wilcox returned to Elizabeth City and years of drink and bitterness, a self-inflicted twelve-gauge shotgun blast to the head in 1934 ending his life but extending the mystery of Beautiful Nell Cropsey forever. A ninety-four-year-old woman named Nettie Murrill once sought me out in a Morehead City waterfront bookstore to sing for me an energetic waltz-ballad about the ill-fated romance of Nell and Jim, saying, "You could dance all *night* to that one!" and telling me, too, that she had grown up here in the Sound Country, near the water, and that when she was a young woman and courting—around 1920, when the memory of the Cropsey mystery was still strong, particularly in eastern Carolina—her mother had always warned her to make her date see her safely inside the house, "'Lest you wind up out there dead in the sound, like that Nell Cropsey!" It was an efficacious admonition: in Dare County in 1967, *Lost Colony* actress Brenda Joyce Holland failed to turn in on time or even late, and it was weeks before anyone knew what had come of her. Like Beautiful Nell, she met her end in Sound Country waters and was discovered in the Albemarle near Roanoke Island.

In Tyrrell, one county west of Dare, another 1970s shallow-grave affair came to light. An unhappy Montgomery County, Maryland, man fled his State Department career and took his family with him. He buried his wife and children in a Tyrrell County woods before fleeing farther west, leaving his car and doing away with himself somewhere in the Smokies. I think my cousin Thomas Yerby,

Ruin of the *Daily Record*, black press burned by white mob, Seventh and Church Streets, Wilmington, 1898

the Tyrrell sheriff during the 1960s and early 1970s, had died just before these murders, and I don't believe Thomas was, during his tenure, overrun with such as this—this was clearly imported trouble only nominally connected with Tyrrell County. But I do remember—it was a night one July when I was on the way to Nags Head, and had just dropped in for a few minutes—Thomas's telling me that not too long after he took office, he was called to go arrest a man for bestiality.

"Here?" I said, incredulous. "In Tyrrell County?"

"Right here," said the sheriff.

"Bestiality?"

"With his neighbor's cow."

"Damn," I said. We were standing out in the street in Columbia, about a block and a half from the dark Scuppernong River and just around the corner from the Victorian gingerbread house where my great-grandmother Spruill had sat weeping in her bedroom throughout her daughter Evelyn's wedding to my grandfather Page, two days past Christmas, '09. Somewhere out back of Thomas's house a small dog set up a high, gargling chop.

"Henry's beagle's jumped a rabbit," Thomas said, cocking his head in the direction of the yelping dog. "Yeah, his neighbor's cow."

"How'd he get caught?" I asked. "Don't reckon she turned him in."

"No. Neighbor went out to the barn, and there they were. He stood and watched em a minute to make sure he was really seeing what he thought he was seeing—then he went back in the house and called me."

Not long ago, my friend and student Amy Pritchett from Windsor brought in a report from the week between Palm Sunday and Easter, 1994, when a forty-year-old man and a sixteen-year-old boy teamed up and robbed a pizza joint in Suffolk, Virginia, kidnapping a twenty-year-old pregnant woman and her brother in the bargain. "Just let me get my drink and my cigarettes," she was heard to say. This party headed on off into the northeastern Carolina night, winding up in Windsor about 7:00 A.M. and dropping the older robber off at the local hospital, he with a shot foot.

They then made a stop at a grill on the Williamston highway, where the woman's brother made a run for it and got shot dead. The kid roared east, passing Sheriff Carey who was on his way in to the crime scene from Colerain on the Chowan River, and now a high-speed chase ensued, the result being the kid slammed into a westbound vehicle—driven by a CIA man who had a top-secret document handcuffed to his wrist—and Lord knows what came of the woman and her unborn child. This, too, was imported trouble, as was the Chapel Hill travel agent's shotgun suicide down by the Sans Souci ferry, and the execution killings at the nearby Williamston Be-Lo grocery store, carried out during a robbery a few years ago.

But an astonishing old story from down around Woodard in Bertie was remarkably homegrown. One evening along about 1920, visitors to the White home were stunned to find Mrs. White slashed to death, her infant boychild lolling helplessly on the floor in his mother's blood. Older heads in Windsor still recall being rounded up as children, kept off the streets and not allowed to play outside, while a posse coursed over the fields, woodlands, and swamps of Bertie in an unsuccessful search for Mr. Leroy T. White, the supposed and apparent killer, who disappeared the day of his wife's death and of whom postcard-sized wanted cards with his photograph and physical description were handed out around the county and beyond. But he had completely vanished, it seemed. Nearly twenty years later, returning with friends from a football game at Wake Forest, when college and town were still one, young orphan White met his own death in a car wreck. Graveside in Windsor several days later, an older, bearded man no one knew stepped through the crowd and insisted on having the casket opened, that he might see the dead youth, and for some reason no one now remembers the stranger's request was granted. He stood looking at the boy's corpse for several minutes, then turned without a word and strode right back out of that crowd and was gone. By the time the dazed mourners spoke up to each other about this mysterious stranger and confirmed their eerie suspicion that they had just witnessed full-on the return of the father and wife-slayer, he had vanished a second time just as fully as he had the first, and that was that for all time.

So much blood in the ground?

A while back at the fishmonger's in Carrboro, domain of Atlantic native Tom Robinson, I was studying the shrimp and king mackerel Tom had brought up from Fulcher's and Billy Smith's in down-east Carteret County, the bushel-sacks of oysters from Mill Creek off the Newport River, and the little tubs of crabmeat from Luther Lewis's down at Davis, remembering: Ann's family years ago kept a houseboat on the creek near Lewis's crabhouse, and one night, with the Kindells all asleep inside, a great blue heron roosting on the houseboat scrawked with all his primitive power, awakening them and convincing them there was a mad killer or at least the shade of one atop their craft. Into this memory at the market Tom's assistant Niko Boothby leaned, and over the soft-shell crabs asked me:

"Hey, did you hear about all those ancient skeletons they started finding down around New Bern, washing up in the Neuse?"

"*How* ancient?" I said.

"Seventy, eighty years," said Niko. "Like Prohibition times. *You're* interested in that kind of thing—what do you think?"

Too much blood, is what I think. Certainly there is enough—and just as certainly there will be more.

The roughest stripe on the Sound Country's rough side may well be the broadest—the real and literal crime against nature that in scope of impact and in some cases outright venality soars over Sheriff Yerby's bestiality call thirty years ago.

When my children saw the spotlit fountain at Corolla a few years back, the light on the spray shifting color every few seconds as it ran through the rainbow spectrum, they shouted, "Daddy, what's *wrong* with that water?" Well might they have asked. What is wrong is this: we have been poisoning the greatest inside fishing grounds in eastern America, nursery to half our East Coast's fish and shellfish, wasting the marine life—once not merely productive but prodigiously so—in the sounds great and small and in all the vast marshes that fringe them. From the millfoil grassbeds in the Currituck and the algae blooms in the Chowan all the way down to the CLOSED TO SHELLFISHING signs in the Mad Inlet marshes of Brunswick County, the greatest waters of a great state are ill—

and it still remains for the living to decide whether or not it is a sickness unto death.

In the middle 1990s the single most popular culprit is our old friend, the hog. When 25 million gallons of hogsludge and porcine shitporridge poured through a broken lagoon dike and into the New River in June of 1995, people hereabouts suddenly noticed that so rapidly had the big pig business boomed there were now more hogs than people in the state, and they were cleaning up after themselves no better than we were. The daily environmental demands of the pork processors the industrial farms served were no small or laughing matter, either. One abatoir operator hoped to increase his *daily kill capacity* from 24,000 to 32,000 hogs, the flushee being the Cape Fear River in Bladen County. Another hoped to locate an industrial pork manufactory in our lax, lucrative coastal plain in Edgecombe County, near Tarboro. Edgecombe County commissioners engaged a respected, retired general, the sitting squire of Coolmore plantation, to give the community an objective version or vision of the proposal, and the general attempted so to do, reading to his people from a tipsheet prepared for the occasion by a publicity firm that was also in the employ of the prospective massive slaughterhouse. The general left the hearing immediately upon ending his presentation, taking no questions and making no other comment, but one member of the outspoken opposition *did* have further word, concluding:

"With all due respect to the general," he said, "we're just not that stupid." *Vox populi, vox dei.*

In 1997 the pace of the pork fight picked up. Craven County placed a one-year moratorium on the establishment of new industrial pork spreads, whereupon hog producers promptly sued the county. Fifteen or twenty armed citizens faced down a bulldozer that was all set to start on a hog farm near Vanceboro. Vandals smashed pipes on a farm near Little Washington, spilling 75,000 gallons of hog waste into the adjacent swamp. By early April, the governor himself embraced a state-level moratorium on these heavy-duty hog farms. Something was rotten in the Old North State, and few failed to smell it.

We could spot the pipes of deficient sewerage plants, like Rocky Mount's, which forced the state to levy thousands of dollars daily in fines against the system that ultimately spiked the Pamlico River with toxicity and led to DO NOT DRINK THIS WATER signs on taps and spigots all over Little Washington; we could come to understand what nearly thirty years of mining and extracting phosphates and France-bound wealth with it on the south banks of the Pamlico in Beaufort County had done to the water, the fish and crabs there; we could see that the vast pinestands of loblolly may as well be so many thousands of acres of straws sucking Sound Country groundwaters up into the sky that sweats it out of the trees. But it was far, far easier to point to any and all of these than to bring under control the ordinary run-off from towns and, particularly, chemically addicted farms, the flows that fertilize the submerged deltas and grow the grasses and algaes that choke the oxygen out of the water and belly-up the fish by the millions, flows that feed the dinoflagellates that attack the fish, the oysters, even the people who in 1995 swam in the diseased waters of the Neuse where the toxicity was so high and virulent these swimmers almost immediately developed welts and sores and lesions.

Against these inauspicious tides, I have watched a gathering of the clans drawn together in coastal confederation, inspired by both deep affection and old-time practical appreciation for the Sound Country and its many waters. As *Save Our Sounds*, convened by Berry and John Greene, they came to Raleigh, putting on a stage that looked for all the world like a Frog Island fishing shanty such acts that weren't *acts* as Earline Snow from Currituck who in her sixties could still by backing up eight or ten feet from the mike and honking like a Canada goose about to come in pin listeners to the rear wall, and the Menhaden Chanteymen seated in semicircle and wearing suits, too old now for purse-seining pogyboat fishing for them to be strong into it and there being not nearly the call for it like the days even thirty or forty years ago when Beaufort harbor on Taylor's Creek was wall-to-wall with crow's-nested menhaden boats, still singing with the same lust or with something close kin to it *Bye-bye, Sweet Rosie Anna* and in mime dragging in those nets all hands curled clutching them and all backs bent to the task. And I remember going through a fried-fish line manned and womanned by Todd Miller and Julie Shambaugh and Dot and Larry McGee and sitting eating with the Snows and Mrs. Snow's husband bragging on her (beyond her human goosecalling) as stockcar driver supreme, telling how they used to test their hot-rod out by running quarter-miles on an old concrete airstrip over at Maple in Currituck, and bragging too on a home-made speedboat they once roared around the sounds in.

They were the real thing, but the figures of decline, diminution, and disease we were all there to fight were no less so, figures like those that told the tale of Sound Country oystering: a turn-of-the-century annual oyster catch of 5 million pounds, down to a million pounds by 1989, under 200,000 in 1994. "Used to be the folks up in Cedar Island could go out and it wasn't anything for them to get three, four bushels of oysters," said north Core Sounder Dr. John Kindell of Sea Level, Ann's father. "But not anymore. Not anymore."

It was all stunning, infuriating. Fisherwoman Lena Ritter of Stump Sound would march on the legislature in Raleigh in support of the strong protection of marine resources, and have her declamatory placard confiscated at the door of the Legislative Building before she was allowed admittance. Out riding with this Coastal Federation on the *Mystery* in Taylor's Creek one night (the same evening

I met faux–bull rider Don Bailey), I asked her: "What'd they think you were gonna do with the sign, Lena? Slice their heads off?" and she reeled back, laughing: "I don't know, but I tell you one thing—there's a few of em up there that I'd *loike* to do that to!"

Recent works as different as *The Fish Factory*, Barbara Garrity-Blake's insightful look at the lives of the menhaden seiners, and *Shooting at Loons*, Margaret Maron's eventful, entertaining Harker's Island murder mystery, explore the hostilities between commercial fishermen and sport—two groups with everything to gain by uniting to protect and defend a healthy Carolina fishery. Nor is there total union even *within* these groups—one younger Harker's Island man said to a friend of mine in Beaufort: "I keep tellin my daddy and my uncle, 'You hangin yourselves in your own ropes, thinkin you can still go out and catch anything you want anytime you want just because that's the way you've always done it all your life.' But they won't no more listen to me." And on the sport-fishing side, a sectional blow-up occurred late in the summer of '96, when the mid-Atlantic and New England states lost bluefin tuna-fishing after Southern fishermen, particularly those off the Carolina coast, had already caught that fishery's limit for the season.

One of the state's most serious marine conservationists lamented to me that he thought it a massive shame, the way commercial and sport fishermen had fallen into fighting instead of joining to protect the resource itself. Perhaps 'twas ever thus: a century ago, Roanoke Island shad-netters had their fishing grounds and nets literally overrun and torn up by illegal, well-armed oyster-dredgers down from Chesapeake. In the modern moment, the vitriolic conflict between these different groups of fishermen could result in a general public disgust that might show itself here as it had a few years ago in Florida, with a ban of *all* nets. For not everyone regards the Sound Country with charity, or sympathy.

Once on the courthouse steps of the piedmont county seat of Monroe, a fellow from Charlotte and I were talking in fairly friendly fashion about the Great Dismal Swamp. When I said something about the larger coastal plain, about "eastern Carolina as a whole," suddenly and with the least expensive of wit, he said:

"Yeah, well, that's how most of us up here in the piedmont think about eastern Carolina—as a *hole*!"

No one thinks that when they look for lumber, for feed, for cotton, for scuppernongs or blueberries or Irish potatoes or yams or strawberries, for flounder to drift-fish the inlets, for snapper or clams or scallops or 24-count shrimp, for spot and pompano in the surf and for a clean coast to bolt to when king mackerel and the blues are running, when the mullet practically want to jump into the nets, onto the grills, and into the smokers out on a hundred thousand decks.

Old fishing shack, Core Sound, Carteret County, late 1970s

I can see Clam Bob of Beaufort leaving his Cape Carrot scow and rowing over to Front Street, pedaling his bicycle around town and peddling clams, and I can see Jack Herrick and his daddy Big John digging them in the Bird Shoal sloughs, and I can see Joseph Darden from Beaufort who showed up unbidden with a trunk-full of oysters at the Front Street cottage we kept for a time, and I *know* no one thinks of the Sound Country as a hole when he looks for a bushel or two from Newport River.

Back in the fall of 1987, talk was abroad from Willis' Drum Inlet Seafood down east to the front page of the *Carteret County News-Times*, from the tables at Mike's just plain mainstreet restaurant in Beaufort and out from there a hundred miles north and south, from Wanchese to Wilmington, and it was talk of the tiny fly-speck of life that in astounding, poisonous, and 1,200-mile-out-of-range aggregation had idled the clammers and the oystermen: the algae bloom called the red tide.

By Christmastime when Ann and I returned, it was pandemic, and the talk now was a cascade of questions. What would kill it? How long would it last? Would it close the coast? Welcomed once again into Doctor Kindell's Sea Level home where Ann had grown up, this time we had holiday goose and deer steaks, but there was no oyster dressing. A fellow named Joe Huber (and nicknamed Joe Hardcrab) stopped by the house, a lithe middle-aged man of great humor and warmth who is now a clam aquaculturist. He talked then mostly about the six hours a round it took him to check his two hundred Core Sound crab pots. But there was no shying away from the first tideland topic of the day.

"I don't know what it is, Joe," a down-east woman said, "but I sure would like to get a hold of a peck of clams, just a peck."

"Can't find any, can you?" said Joe.

"No, I can't. You got any idea where I could get some?"

"Oh, yeah," said Joe Hardcrab, grinning fatalistically with plank-walking humor. "Talk to me—I got all the *red-tide* clams you want!"

Later that night, when Ann and I drove from down east back in to Beaufort, we were both silenced by the sight of the seafood house whose owner had paint-ed across the plate glass in front this legend:

CLOSED UP—THIS LINGERING RED TIDE IS KILLING ME.

Perhaps in the face of a plague like this we were all helpless, and none but the fates were at fault. Or perhaps our own carelessness and recklessness with the waters had created a climate where the plague could thrive, blossom even, and sufficiently weaken the oysters and clams to where they could not withstand its effect. I did not know, but I surely know this:

Until the poisons and the powerful fertilizers are out of the ground and groundwaters and great sounds for good, and quit going in to begin with—by law and design, by main and moral force, and by the way and practice of our farms, forests, our manufactories and towns—we are the poorest of poor rela-tions to the Sound Country, and worse: we are like the infant out in that Bertie County farmhouse, whose sad and violent end in a hill-country collision was harbingered by his idle, ignorant dabbling in his own mother's blood.

There were ducks and geese on the sound in those days.
I counted ten thousand Canadas crossing Church's Island for
their night's resting place in Coinjock Bay . . . only a small
part of the myriads frequenting the sound.

—H. H. Brimley, of his first trip to
  Currituck Sound, "Old Times on Currituck,"
  February 1884

Coratank

. . . .

Northeasternmost

Having successfully flown my mother's bought-in-Manteo 1964 Ford Galaxie 500 Country Squire (with the 352 and four-barrel carburetor) from Kitty Hawk down the ribbon of N.C. 12 to Ocracoke and back, the three of us— my friend Bobby Schwentker, a fellow sixteen-year-old, and my younger cousin Steve Lamborn and I—were ready for *more* adventure, as in *heightened* and *increased*. Since we'd found the first batch of independence and thrill in our daytrip south down Hatteras way, we now looked to the north, borrowing the car just after lunch and, against all advice any of us had ever heard about driving cars in sand, proceeded up Currituck Banks, intending to make it all the way from Duck up to Corolla village and back before dark. It was the summer of 1965 and "Help" was the most popular song in America, including the Carolina east, and perhaps that anthem of pleading and needing of aid should have been omen enough for what befell us.

At that time, the town of Duck had one clapboard store, a small white soundside Methodist church, no oceanfront development at all; and, after the hardtopped road stopped there, a damp and marshy sand road ran right along the sound, frequently within inches of it. There was also just above Duck a small navy installation, a cinder-block hut really, with a few bunks and a phone and radio in it, which was there to maintain targets for a navy air bombardment range. If you saw a red flag flying when you got to that point on the sound-side road above Duck, you were to stop or risk submitting yourself to naval strafing.

After a few more shanties and the cottage-conversion of an old Coast Guard station, there came a grave announcement, in black letters on a white field:

STATE

MAINTENANCE

ENDS

and then two parallel tracks, or slight indentations, running off into the loose sand and myrtle jungle of Currituck Banks. So off, too, went we, and I was immediately relieved and surprised at how well the heavy V-8 Ford handled on this sandy safari. We were thrilled, exclaiming as if we had just rallied well in some off-road gymkhana—we would be in Corolla in an hour, standing in the short midafternoon shadow of the dull red brick spindle, Currituck Light. This jubilance lasted perhaps a half an hour.

Then we reached Poyner's Hill.

There, just south of the old Poyner's Hill lifesaving station, the sand ruts veered oceanward, crossed the primary dune, and continued north along the high-tide line of the Atlantic Ocean. Even the sixteen-year-old captain thought better of it—I stopped abruptly, and the Ford sank instantly to its frame.

None of us said a word, but turned our attention to a cheerful inspection of the old Coast Guard ruin, a tour that showed us little but broken glass, old newspapers, silverware encrusted with salt-weather corrosion, a chamber pot. In the company of my father, or my Lamborn cousins, I must have rambled through a dozen of these old heroic relicts—at Chicamacomico down on Hatteras, at Kitty Hawk, the small former station that Daddy owned for a spell. The real men of the roiling surf had lived here in these haunts, and there is no telling how many thousands of people have lived on in the world because men named Meekins and Etheridge and Midgette waited year-round in stations eight or ten miles apart up and down our coast ready at the captain's call to hit the worst surf a March nor'easter or an October hurricane could swell and gale their way. To linger for a bit where these fellows had waited and worked and roistered was great fun and adventure, and it was humbling, too.

When we went back outside to face the Ford, we were doubly humbled. No amount of backing and filling, no digging out of wheels, no slipping of slabs up under the rubber as best we could, no pushing, rocking, cajoling, begging, letting air out of tires, nothing moved the car. It was stuck in the sand, sunk, and so, I knew, were we.

Presently, after about an hour, along came the all-time vernacular vehicle of the shifting sands, the jeep, this one a modified jeepster truck or truckster jeep outfitted for and in the service of the local phone company. There were two men in it, laconic but friendly when they stopped, sized us up, along with our situation, and the driver said:

"Y'all in a fix, hunh?"

"Yes, sir," I said. "We were headin for Corolla, but—"

"Didn't nobody never tell you, you cain't make it up there cept in a four-wheel drive?"

"Yes, sir. Pretty much everybody."

"Well, they were right. Good thing you stopped where you did."

"Yeah," said the second lineman. "Ocean'd just *love* to swaller that Ford."

I felt I deserved every bit of this chastisement, felt greener than the myrtle bushes. They didn't prolong it, though, just poured it on for a minute or two, then offered to help push us around and aim us south toward Kitty Hawk and home. For such salvation as a jeep could offer us in this forlorn place, I could take a little ribbing.

They got the jeep angled on the Ford's front bumper at about forty-five degrees, the idea being just to push the front end around, as if the jeep were a tugboat and the Ford a luxury liner. This worked for about five seconds and a foot or so of sideways motion, but then one or the other of the two vehicles shifted with the sand and the push-board—a 2x8 bolted to the jeep's front bumper—slipped up and over the Ford's bumper and broke one of the station wagon's headlights. We all shook our heads, and the telephone men gave it up for a bad job, but not before the leader put on his boot spikes and clambered up a short telephone pole—there was a line of them just soundward of the primary dune—and tapped the line and called the navy base at Duck.

"How bout y'all send somebody up here to hep these boys out?" I heard the phone man say. For a moment I thought we were saved again, but that was just a moment of naiveté. "Oh, is that right? Well, okay, then—sorry to bother you," he said, then came back down the pole. "Navy cain't hep you," he said. "Against the regalations."

So we three then got in the back of the jeep and rode glumly, desultorily down to Kitty Hawk, where my mother watched us as we disembarked and from the cottage called down to us, showing a vivid and heightened sense of curiosity as she said, "Where's the Ford?"

From there, once she was debriefed and astounded, we headed back up to Anderson's Supermarket, right across from the Kitty Hawk Fishing Pier, where Bill Anderson the Barefoot Peddler, a scroungy and bombastic fixture, sold groceries and canvas floats and held forth on topics usually not of the day. When he heard, out in the parking lot, what I had gone and done with the family car, he leveled his most penetrating gaze my way (it was like being judged by a bootlegger who, for the sake of womanhood, had suddenly developed a sense of justice that had to come down hard *some*where) and said simply,

"What in the hell did you go and do *that* for, boy?"

Oh, the vainglory of it all, I thought, feeling every bit of my ridiculous age as he pondered how to spring me and the '64 Ford. Just then up sauntered a fellow in his early twenties, and Anderson hailed him before he slipped past us and into the store: "Tommy, come here, I want you to help these folks out." Tommy turned out to be a navy man who worked at the Duck navy station, and, when he realized we were the same people who had already entreated his outfit by way of wire-tapping, he gave me the sort of look, as they used to say, that would draw a blister on a washpot. But he didn't *say* anything. He let Bill Anderson state the case and then nodded in a dull affirmative, and off we went.

About two and a half hours later, after a wild ride up the Currituck Banks in an outsized Dodge pickup truck painted battleship gray and called a Powerwagon, and after this selfsame Powerwagon had popped us aright and followed us back down to the Duck navy base, I pulled the Ford into Bill Anderson's to ask him to charge a case of beer for the navy boys (there were three or four of them on our mission) to my mother's account, her idea of a nice gesture which in fact it was. I couldn't help myself:

"You know," I said, "we called those fellows hours ago. From Poyner's Hill. And they turned us down. But then you got em to do it, just like you were their commanding officer. I don't get it."

Anderson laughed heartily, till he was wheezing, then laid his big weathered hand (he was copper-colored in all seasons) on my shoulder and explained the frankly corrupt and oddly loyal world of a fixer. "One time in Hillsborough, this'd a been '35 or '6, your granddaddy was representin me, kind of a touchy situation, and it looked pretty bad in the mornin, but then your granddaddy had lunch with the district attorney and he came back to me and said we could go on home now, it was all right. And you come in here thirty years later needin help, and I know where it's to be had, don't you think I'm gonna find it for you? These navy boys, when they come around bangin on the door of my rusty tin trailer out back, two, three in the mornin wantin cold beer, and showin up on Sundays wantin more cold beer, who sells it to 'em? *I* do. So, hell yeah they'll do what I asked him to, favor like that, to help a friend of mine. Way the world works, son, and don't forget it. You may *want* to, but don't. Now I'm gon put your mama down for a case of Bud—it costs a little more than Blue Ribbon, but that's what these boys want to drink, so that's what she wants to buy em, you follow me? And don't go drivin your mama's car off to Corolla again—don't be doin your mama that way, she's a fine woman and you can tell her I said so—you understand?"

I understood.

And part of what I understood was that when I tried again and finally *did* go to Corolla it would not be overland. It would be by skiff and by water, by God.

Coratank is the Indian word from which our *Currituck*—sound, county, courthouse—was long ago derived. "Where the wild geese fly," it meant, and so prodigiously did they once fly here that even hunters going after the decimated remnant flocks of the 1960s believed they were seeing all the birds in God's creation. Precious few now living can recall the geese and ducks flying so thick and voluminous over Currituck that they darkened the sky, but there are still a few of the old clubhouses and hunters' halls about the sound: Pine Island, Swan Island, Whalehead, and modest Monkey Island. It was Monkey Island for which I was bound one June Friday evening in 1984, with fellow traveler Jim Seay.

"How much to use your boat ramp?" I said.

"What do you mean—you want to go out *now*?"

"That's right."

It was about a quarter past seven, too late in the day to be held up and still get where I was heading. But I stood in the trailer-camp commissary at Waterlily, high on a bluff looking out on Currituck Sound, shuffling as the old man considered my case.

"Where did you think you were going?"

"Monkey Island," I said.

"At *this* hour? Awful late getting started. Most everbody's come back in already. You ever been out there?"

"No, sir, never have."

"Why, look out there, son—wind's whipping up a real chop, dangerous, and people—why, all the time we're having to call the Coast Guard to haul em in. And they're the lucky ones—see this here"—he pointed to a framed letter on the wall—"there's folks just glad to be *alive today*, thanking the Coast Guard, *thanking em!*"

Just then lean, lanky Jim Seay, my fellow traveler, came crashing through the camp-store door, saying, "What's going on? What's the matter?"

"Man's going on about the chop, Jim."

"What?! We just want to use your ramp."

"Kind of boat you got?" said the old man.

"Boston whaler," Jim said, and then he urgently turned up the volume: "Listen, mister, there's a man *waiting* on us out at Monkey Island, and we just want to use your *boat ramp*, all right?!"

"Oh, oh, well, I didn't—that's two dollars a night," said the old man, and as we made our way out the door he called after us:

"You mind, now, I'm telling you, there's folks still thanking the Coast Guard, thanking em, even *today*."

The camp commissar had cost us five minutes, at least. By the time Jim got the boat down to the ramp, and we got our food and gear stowed away in it, it was quarter of eight. Jim roared the Whaler out into the broad shallow sound with a strong sense of mission and urgency.

Monkey Island was a small mound, a clump of green cleft slightly at its center, several miles away across Currituck. Light was fading, the red sunset disc falling down behind us, as we cut through the milfoil grassbeds that choke the sound. We stopped every so often for Jim to throw the Mercury into reverse and kick off the grass that steadily entwined the propeller, and we weren't entirely sure that the island for which we were bound was the right rise, for there were others both north and south of our candidate for Monkey.

"How bout that chop, how *bout* it!" Jim yelled irreverently over the outboard roar. "There's folks still thanking the Coast Guard, thanking em!"

We pressed on for most of forty minutes, in the last failing light nearing what surely must be Monkey Island: egrets wheeling high and low over the water were pure white against the island's pines and live oaks, dark green and nearly black in the gloaming. This little seven-acre figure-eight was one of the greatest egret rookeries in the American East.

Jim slowed and curled us around the south end of the island, through more grassbeds and alongside a rotted bulkhead, and saying: "If this ain't Monkey, whatever it is, it's where we're staying tonight."

We had come to the right place. As we docked at a short pier with missing planks, I could smell, then faintly see, the new-mown lawn. Up the island's slope was the lodge house, its front door open and its living-room light ablaze with welcome.

Across the front of the white clapboard lodge was a long screen porch. Inside, the main living room was nearly twenty feet square, with a sofa and a few chairs near the fireplace and an odd gauge upon the vaulted ceiling. A lone two-dimensional metal duck on a pipeshaft—connected to two weathervane ducks above the roof outside—creaked and turned with the wind, the duck's bill pointing at crude compass points painted on the ceiling to show the wind's direction.

Off the main room to the south was an eight-bedroom wing; to the north two bedrooms, named "Goose" and "Swan," joined by a very low-ceilinged bath.

"This ends the myth of the tall hunter," said six-foot-two Jim.

Egret rookery, Monkey Island, Currituck Sound, early 1980s

It was a terrific place, a tumbledown hunting lodge well lived-in over most of this century, and we were rejoicing at having by grace of the Nature Conservancy, the island's owner at that time, a whole weekend on this verdant dot in Currituck Sound. At the height of our celebratory moment, the caretaker knocked at the door.

Earl Baum was a short, fit man in his late fifties, his white hair brushed briskly back. He had come over from his cottage next to the lodge to shake hands, and to help us move Jim's Whaler up the island shore a few dozen yards into a lagoon-like boat slip. He also left us with a warning:

"You're walking around out here at night, you watch out for the *lifers*." And he told us, too, about his favorite blacksnake, Rufus, who had a white spot on his side—"Somebody from the Nature Conservancy said that's where a tick bit him"—and about the regular route the cottonmouths ran between the old and established egret rookery on the island's north end and the new rookery many birds had created on the south end just last year.

After Earl said good-night and left, we puzzled over the lifers we were to be on the lookout for. An hour later it came to us that we had heard him wrong, and that his warning's word—though antique—was no less accurate:

"Vipers."

After supper in a dining room that would seat sixteen, we sat out on the

screen porch and looked east, at the Currituck Light beaming out short warn-
ings of its own every seventeen seconds from Corolla across the way, at the big
red Friday-night moon rising over the Outer Banks and shining on the sound.
The evening was well along now, and just enough of a breeze and chill came up
to send us inside, where we sat near the hearth as if there were a fire going, and
sipped gin and talked low about the spirit of the place.

"Don't you know these walls have seen some sights?" Jim said. "You know
they have, you *know* it!"

"Long way to come, not to have a big time," I said, and I thought about the
many old Currituck clubs there were, or had been—and about others down at
Mattamuskeet and Pamlico Sound, Core Sound, too, and down on New River in
Onslow. Isolated places where hunters had gathered, hunkered down together,
and then set forth from in the damp and icy dark, paired in blinds about the
sound awaiting the *V*s of geese and the ducks at dawn, sipping coffee maybe
laced, maybe not, or maybe just sipping the lacing itself (but not too much, for
the man who did was a dangerous fool unlikely to be asked back and thus dis-
honored by his own hand and gullet) just enough to beat back the absolute chill,
breathing the heat of their lungs into their gloved hands and, if they spoke at all
as they shivered in the shallows and the dim day came clean and took its shape,
joshing each other with the old familiar good-natured saw, *Now don't this beat
laying up in a warm bed with a naked woman?*

The ghosts were upon me again. Among the hunters here at Monkey Island
was my own father, years dead now, who with his full-choked Browning twelve-
gauge was in the gunning world of Currituck Sound. During duck season, when
he was in school at Chapel Hill, my father used to take the train east to join the
hunt, to get out here on the waters of *Coratank*. You know this place, I thought,
though you never set foot here before tonight, and so does the man with you,
big Jim from Panola County in the deep Mississippi Delta. So we huddled there
at Monkey in the comfort of the old lodge and in all its good warmth, well pro-
visioned and for a few illusory moments carefree. If it were a small and short-
lived peace we felt, it was no less true, and ours, too, was the accessibility of the
palpable and living past.

The wind-duck on the ceiling was creaking more vigorously now, shifting itself in harmony with the winds playing over the rooftop above. We called it a
night, Jim turning into the bedroom called Goose, myself into the one called
Swan.

Early the next morning Earl Baum was out about the grounds, flinging handfuls of cracked corn to his little flock: two hens, one chick, a duck, and a white
dove. After a while he walked down to his workshed beside the boat slip, fired up

his chainsaw, and started cutting up a live oak that had lost its footing in the spongy ground near the water and now, uprooted, lay over on its side.

The island was long ago a fish camp for the Pamunkey Indians, and Earl said he always kept an eye out for their potsherds. As he showed us around the scant two acres of high ground in Monkey's middle, he recalled a time when there was a cabin-cruiser boathouse where our pier was rotting away, and when the pond just below the pier was a holding pen for live decoys. Out behind the lodge house was a small building with two generators on an iron frame, the tabby walls three feet thick to kill the engine noise, and on shelves trays of old batteries that with those motors had been the source of DC power for the island. Now a cable lain upon the sound's floor brought electricity to Monkey, and none of this rusting, corroding gear saw any use.

Back at the boat slip we admired Earl's craft, a cabined twenty-six-foot Harker's Island flare-bow with a big, fast Chrysler inboard. "It'll do forty-three," Earl said.

The slip was cut into the island right at the cinched-up middle of its figure-eight shape, and the sound on the other side was only fifty yards away, beyond a marshy bed of reeds. Earl Baum said that if Currituck Sound came through this narrow waist and sheared the island in two, the northwest winter pounding would tear it apart.

"We get some real windstorms out here—blows the tops out of the trees. Yeah, if the water cuts through, you can kiss her goodbye, she's done for," he said.

Jim walked on up to the lodge house to make ready for our day's expedition over to Currituck Banks, but I lagged back to talk some more with the keeper of Monkey Island. Earl Baum was taken in and raised by folks at Waterlily, after his mother died when he was four. He had spent a dozen years on a Texaco tanker running from Port Arthur to Norfolk, but the man with the *hoightoide* speech had never really left home.

"I been working, messing round this sound all the rest of my life," he said.

I asked him about the Penns of Reidsville, the family that owned the island for years. Frank Penn and I had once met briefly, at a Kill Devil Hills hotel during a breakfast to celebrate the vaunted Currituck Plan in the 1970s—a controlled development plan for Currituck Banks that was to have allowed small clusters of cottages, accessible by passenger ferry like the villages of New York's Fire Island. Vaunted, yet abandoned in less than a decade—these banks were doomed to be developed in intensive strip fashion just as others to the north and south and with a mid-county bridge set in the '90s to put a belt across the great sound. Back in the summer of '73, while shaking my hand Frank Penn had said warmly, "I think I took your daddy out duck hunting the last time he ever went." What did Earl Baum know of the Penns?

"Well, they sold this island *twice*," he said, once to Texas developers who paid a million down but reneged on their million-a-year for three years' note when it turned out they weren't going to be able to develop it, and then again, for three million dollars, to the Nature Conservancy. Then he said cryptically:

"Ed Penn died, but he's still here."

I had no idea what to say to this, so said nothing, and Earl went on:

"Now the Nature Conservancy wants to sell it to the Fish and Wildlife. And the Fish and Wildlife doesn't want Monkey's Island—they only want the coast and marsh that goes with it." He looked off at the Currituck Banks three-quarters of a mile distant to the east, then back at me and said again: "Yeah, Ed's still here."

"What would Fish and Wildlife do with Monkey Island?" I said.

"Lock it up, I reckon," Earl Baum said, "or tear it down one."

"Tear it down?"

"Well, they might—they tore down the lodge at Mackey's Island. See, all they're interested in is the habitat." He was chagrined over the potential loss of this good and useful compound, sad over having the old ghosts roused and routed out. "Thing about Ed Penn is, when he died, they scattered his ashes all around Monkey Island—so that's why old Ed, he's *still here*."

It was a 45-minute trip in the whaler, south from Monkey past treeless Mary's Island, over to the Whalehead Club, the massive 1920s huntclub built by a man named Knight who, fueled by ire at his inability to register his wife as well as himself in any of the other Currituck gunning clubs, created an impressive redoubt with five chimneys, tawny walls, and dormers everywhere on the huge, steep green-copper roof that we could easily see from Monkey Island miles away.

We tied up to a piece of the rotten bulkhead that ran along Whalehead's neglected airstrip, a broad rectangular protrusion into Currituck Sound, made our way up to the deserted old duck hunters' castle, and went in without knocking through a broken-glassed door. In the big sound-side room we first entered was a grand piano and precious little else, and I sat down at it for a moment to play a tune. The old instrument was so out of tune and repair, its broken tones so dull and dead, that it was too sad to play beyond a few bars, and I quickly gave it up. A long baronial hall on the north side led to a central foyer that fed a large dining room, and there were small rooms off every whichaway, debris and clutter everywhere. The kitchen was a mess of old utensils and heavy white china, many monogrammed *US Steel* and *Mercy*, doubtless after some hospital. Upstairs was an endless progression of bedrooms, single and double beds, mattresses all over the place—it could have slept sixty—and all these quarters were tied together by a maze of hallways two feet wide. Whalehead looked like it had been abandoned in a hurry by people fleeing the hundred-year hurricane.

Earl and Mary Baum, on Currituck Sound near Monkey Island, early 1980s

On an upper outdoor balcony we dug into a sack we'd brought along, had a cold lunch of Creole chicken and cream ale, enjoyed our sweeping broadcloth view of Currituck Sound, and kept a careful watch on the big Carolina sky as the day became gray and blustery and made us measure our time on the Currituck Banks more closely than we might have wished.

Still, there was time to troop over and walk a mile or so up the sea beach, to stumble into the Corolla canteen, where one of Jim's former poetry students recognized him and offered us a truck ride back down to Whalehead. The way back went right by the red-brick Currituck Light, built in 1875, making it nearly as old as Cape Hatteras Light and, there on the sound side, far more secure. The fellow with the truck offered to carry us on around Whalehead's lagoon and boathouse and drop us at the castle, but we wanted to cross an elaborate high-backed wooden footbridge over the pool's mouth into the Sound.

"I don't believe I'd do that," the fellow said.

"Why not?"

"It's real shaky, and rotten. Whole damn thing could collapse any minute. Real snaky place, too."

"Aw," one of us said, "it'll be all right."

"Well, I warned you, anyway," he said, and drove away.

So we traipsed gingerly up the old honeysuckle- and poison-ivy-covered bridge. I made it all of twenty feet before punching my right leg through a plank and dropping up to my hip, like the bridge had taken a bite of me. It *was* very rotten, terribly shaky, and it should have collapsed under me just to teach me a lesson, but it didn't.

We shoved off from the Whalehead airstrip and cleared the grassbeds coming out of Corolla, Big Jim now running the 40-horse Mercury wide open. Shirtless and a black patch over one eye, he was the pirate poet, grinning and holding the stainless-steel steering wheel in one hand, just flying over the Sound and the wild goose Currituck wind laying his dark hair down.

Later in the day, back at Monkey Island, I walked down to the workshed by the boat slip. In the shed were Canada goose decoys and olive-drab float blinds, the stuff of the huntclub that was then leasing Monkey for $18,000 a year. There were some gray and green haul nets with cork floats, too, but these were Earl's.

"I made eighteen hundred dollars net-fishing Currituck last year," he said. "Mostly mullet, white perch, catfish."

The more he talked, the more frustration he revealed over the state of Monkey Island, and its fate. "I don't have the money to spend, can't fix things, make repairs. And I don't know anymore about what the Nature Conservancy is doing, or going to do, today than I did the first day I came to work for em." He said that someone had estimated it would take a quarter of a million dollars to put a new bulkhead all around the island, but that that was what it needed.

"It would take a hell of a lot to get this mess back right," he said. "Maybe the best thing is just to forget about it, and let the birds have it."

After a bright and shining morning, a storm blew up Sunday afternoon, and for a while the rain and sun went back and forth. Across the way on Currituck Banks, the sand mountain called Penneys Hill was by turns darkened by clouds and lit up gold and glowing. We left late in the day and, back at Waterlily as we were trailering the boat, an old-timer came down the bluff, aimed himself at Jim, and announced authoritatively to us:

"I watched you all going out Friday evening, with my binoculars from up there on the bluff. I could tell you knew what you were doing. I knew when you cleared that last grassbed that you were going to make it out to Monkey Island all right."

We *had* made it out, and back, all right. Since that time, the Fish and Wildlife Service first bought the place, and now the county of Currituck has gotten ahold of it, intending to fix it up for the use of school groups and scouts, like some sort of county park. Children not yet conceived or conceived of either one will stroll the old grounds and look in wonder at the big white birds wheeling about the island and its tiny woods. So we had left our shades to commingle with those of the old hunter roisterers, the long-gone Indians, too, and I have often thought with peace and pleasure of my own ghost meeting my father's from a time when he was half my age, the two of us just shades at a tumbledown hunting lodge on this inner island in the shallow sound that once never was and someday nevermore will be.

One autumn Friday, the night sky had a glowing cloud in it from the tall football lights at Northeastern in Elizabeth City, then another one once Ann and I had crossed the dark Pasquotank and the Causeway to Camden, where the boys in green scrimmaged with the boys in white, yet again at Coinjock, where now maroon and white did battle. When we were approaching Coinjock—well past my Ferebee cousins' old potato-grading sheds at Belcross and Cuff the bear's old station—from way out in the flat wide-open farmlands we were able to see the Coinjock aura miles ahead and the Camden aura way behind, and it was good and reassuring to see the small towns pulling together against the chill of coming winter.

Some were communing differently and elsewhere: a six-foot plywood isosceles with flashing colored lights drew our eyes to a small, packed-tight pool-room on U.S. 158 just west of the Currituck Crab Company. It was only September, and Ann shook her head: "Tell me that doesn't have anything to do with Christmas."

Then we passed Judge Morris's white two-storied home, with its broad screen porch where as a small boy I had learned what visiting was all about, and with its horse pasture to one side, a dirt training track to the other. In the kitchen there the judge's elderly mother-in-law had once fed me strawberries and Coca-Cola till I was full to overflowing. I remembered other old times, too, when I was a boy and my father used to take me down through Camden and Currituck to our cottage at Kitty Hawk, he to check the damage of winter winds and storms and to replace ripped and whipped-off shingles, to repair loosened window shutters, while I, his tiny companion, combed the chilled and vacant beach. Bundled up and set to rambling, I grew to love the empty strand and those times as its sole citizen.

Now the road down through Currituck was four- and five-laned, with a bevy of billboards gigantic and obtrusive. The store at Coinjock—Bishop Coke visited in 1785 and called it Coenjock, but it has also been Cowenjock and Cornjack—had its big, telling *we got all you need* sign:

BLOODWORMS

CIGARETTES

Near where there had long been a silver, steel side-draw bridge was now a high flyover, named for *Collier's* publisher Joseph Palmer Knapp, one of many wealthy Northerners who favored and patronized the county back during its waterfowling heyday. I showed Ann our favorite stops of yore, Anna Gallop's vegetable stand that always had the ripest tomatoes, the Powell's Point carver from whom I'd bought a brace of small unfinished cedar ducks and a bright-white Canada goose whirligig, and one other stop memorable though for ill reason: North River Peaches, where a sailor in a convertible with his arm wrapped around a blonde and his eyes much upon her as well rear-ended our family's Kitty Hawk–bound station wagon, nearly flipping us, in 1964.

Even in the dark I strained as I had all my life to see the pines where the far and narrow forests beyond the fields became only one or two trees deep there by Currituck Sound, signaling our approach to the southern tip of the county, to the mainland's tapering away. Soon we were at Point Harbor, where the Currituck empties into the Albemarle and where my folks and I had always stopped for the best cheeseburgers on earth, and then we were sailing across the Wright Brothers Bridge to the banks far more easily than the Wrights themselves ever traveled in this corner of creation. Duck to the north was now Duck Village, all latter-day prettified with shop*pe*s and proclaiming itself the "Fashion Capital of the Outer Banks," words that to sound-siders like myself had a hard time butting up to each other and making the least bit of sense at all.

Yes, it was a hard road now where once I shimmied a car along on a sandy trail, all the way to Corolla and above, and, yes, there were colored lights on timers changing through the spectrum as they illuminated the entrance fountain at a housing development wherein what people still called *cottages*—without irony—went for a cool half million dollars each. And there were newcomers to this strand, so new they would virtually adopt the local wild ponies as pets and then turn on them just as soon as the ponies began to devour their lawns and shrubberies and then further try to foist these ferals off on the biological reserve on the sound-side marshes, which politely at first but then more stringently refused them as exotics and disruptive to the pursuit of what they wanted to know about the diminishing actual and authentic environment of the banks. Yes, all that was now true in the 1990s.

But other things were true, too. From the small cottage near Pine Island where we were bound, over time Ann and I came to witness these wonders: a phosphorescence in the rolling curl of the breaking nightwaves that was a bright, glowing gold in the moonlight; a 300-foot cargo ship that appeared at first light, nosed aground just a mile to the north of us, a modern reminder that Maple over in mainland Currituck got its name from the Union transport *Maple Leaf*, which, filled with Confederate prisoners, foundered here on the banks, too; threads, ribbons, and clumps and whole hawsers of spindrift lighting up the Currituck Banks of a gray, winter-storm morning. When I flew over these banks twenty years ago in a swift King Air, I saw none of this, though I had seen clearly from two hundred feet that the strand was so thin it seemed one might easily reach out and pinch it between thumb and forefinger and form an inlet on a whim, letting the salty Atlantic into the sound for the first time since the old New Currituck Inlet closed in 1828 and the sound's oystering went all to hell and died out and gave way to freshwater fish and grass and wild celery on the sound bottom and waterfowl drawn by the millions to the new feeding grounds and Northern hunters drawn by them.

One October afternoon Ann and I walked over from the ocean through the Pine Island dunes, the myrtle and small pines, sat down on the sound-side shore for a couple hours, and simply stared at shallow, magnificent Currituck Sound. It was still, glassy, and, most of the time while we were there watching the sun drop toward the mainland, swimming back and forth, north and south, twenty or thirty yards offshore was a solitary teal. Tomorrow we would see from the high channel-span of the Wright Brothers Bridge the sun setting a band of molten gold westerly upon the Albemarle, but today there were a few high clouds and the light was gauzier on the Currituck glass. We spoke, when we spoke at all, about other times on these waters, about juniper skiffs and duckblinds and Daddy's dawn hunts and the still August night when Ann, after following the Currituck loggerheads, lay out on the pier at Monkey Island watching the stars fall from Perseus as stars simultaneously flew upward from the water to meet them, lights both source and mirror rushing toward a moment of incandescent match.

It was like the last act on a set stage. It was the
beginning of the end of something, he didn't know
what except that he would not grieve. He would be
humble and proud that he had been found worthy
to be a part of it too or even just to see it too.
—William Faulkner, *The Bear*, 1942

Haystacks

. . . .

Heart of the Coast

One stormy summer night seventy-odd years ago, my aunt Sister
and uncle Joe traveled by train from Wilmington to Beaufort. Ten and eight
then, they came up the seaboard and on in through Morehead City on the shot-
straight Old Mullet Line, the name the North Carolina Railroad got for hauling
so many million pounds of fish out of the Sound Country and into the world,
but the train would not cross the Newport River that night—a nor'easter had
weakened the railway bridge, washed some of it out. So the Beaufort passengers
were met on the Morehead City side of the river by men with slickers and a dory,
who then boated the children across the water. My aunt and uncle thought this
was the standard way to get to Beaufort, and, moreover, that it was great fun.
Their uncle Bill Rumley met them where Broad Street hits the water at Gallants
Channel, took them on down cedar-lined Ann Street to the home at 824 where
their tearful, near-hysterical aunt Roxie—one of the Tyrrell County Spruills—
awaited them on the porch, crying "O my babies, O my babies!" When Roxie
had calmed, Sister gave her the little bag of figs she had bought her aunt for
a nickel on the train. Roxie set them aside with scant notice, and Sister was
mystified and more than a little hurt, till in the balmy sunshine the next morn-

ing when she saw in the backyard the Rumleys' enormous and productive fig tree.

In the dark of that long-ago night, the dory had passed the Haystacks, the big broad western marshes of the Newport River, falling between the river's channel and Crab Point Thorofare, by Phillips Island, where the egrets wheel and roost around an old brick chimney. Well since then, in skiff, canoe, runabout, and eight-foot sailing pram, we have boated often and all throughout these tidal lanes, though never with the need to make up for a washed-out bridge. Now the train tracks in Beaufort are no more, torn up from Gallants Channel to the fish-meal plant in the summer of 1995, and though the small blue diesel of the train-building Beaufort & Morehead RR moves constantly from the Jefferson Motor Hotel in Morehead (where a possum has been known to run amok in the lobby, deviling the night clerk and raising hell with incoming clientele), past the rickety river pier of L. T. Smith's Fish Camp and Shark Island Skiffs and Sonny Lane's Discount Marine and the diminutive, arched Piver's Island bridge, the diesel is busy with trains that haul not fish but aircraft fuel into the Radio Island depots that serve Cherry Point Marine Air Station and with others that are in huge hoppers bringing the Southern forests chip by chip into the holds of Oriental freighters that will bear them across the bar out Beaufort Inlet and to the other side of the world.

And now from upstate we come home to the Haystacks down the long strip of highway that parallels the Old Mullet Line and the bemused cedars that flank it, too, and the laughing gulls that haunt the live oaks and curb-service lot of El's Home of the Superburger, and the big blue marlin in the glass case across the street all welcome us. On past Promise Land, as folks call the cottage settlement on Bogue Sound to our right, as their predecessors called it when the awesome San Ciriaco hurricane blasted them in 1899 and they gave up whaling and everything else at Diamond City out on Shackleford Banks a century ago and came on in to make homeport here, or at Harker's Island to the east. On past the state port, the phosphate semiglobes, and up the double-high Newport River Bridge from the top of which we can see the whole Haystacks basin lying summergreen or wintergold to the north below, and out to the east and south small Beaufort on Taylor's Creek, Carrot Island, Shackleford Banks, the ship channel and the sea. Then over the small sturdy drawbridge into town, the Grayden Paul Bridge that doubtless will be replaced someday soon by yet another high span, which prospect once prompted from our friend Jimm Prest the barefoot innkeeper this query, so similar to the question others ask about Gore's old pontoon bridge to Sunset Beach far south of here:

"If people're in such a hurry that they can't stand to wait five minutes for the bridge to open and a boat to go through, then what're they doing down here?"

Beaufort waterfront, from Piver's Island, about 1900

The Haystacks are open to heart and eye at all hours, in all weathers, and their pull equals that of any swamp, any lagoon I have ever known and thrown myself into. Once I sat on a wrought-iron balcony in the Hotel St. George in Algiers, from which Eisenhower commanded North Africa, looking out upon the dark-lit harbor and the Mediterranean and loving it but at the same time as a son of the Carolina swamps and sounds wishing with all my heart that I were gazing out upon the Haystacks from the stern of my skiff, or sitting instead behind Ann's mother's house on Orange Street, beneath the pecan trees of Pat Kindell's backyard. Ann and I have been lucky enough to partake of it all, to walk the flat near-empty streets at midnight and sit secretly in the dark of the Ann Street

Girls with horseshoe crab, Beaufort, early 1900s

Methodist Church steps, to commune at the draughty Back Bar with such port-towners as we have fallen amongst and to eat steamed shrimp and chalk a cue at the Royal James, to be down here in both fair weather and squall, just plain at home.

The Christmas blizzard of '89 fell hard upon Beaufort, as it did all across the Sound Country, and we were lucky then, too, to beat it there, if only by half an hour.

We came upon the snow just outside Goldsboro, at the western edge of the storm, early Saturday afternoon two days before Christmas. It was not even falling there, but was forming and hanging in the air, a crystalline mist that gauzed December's stubble-fields and the dark green pines beyond. As we drove east it fell, then fell more heavily, small powdery flakes that swirled in long thin curving lines in the trailing winds of cars and trucks as they passed us — even so, it was scarcely sticking and gathering itself on the road shoulders at that time, and not at all on the roads.

Up in the red clay hills it had been a gray morning, and no weather. But there was already a dry frosting down in Beaufort, Pat Kindell had said when she called about eight. If we were coming, we better come on. Ann and I hadn't planned to head east for another six hours. Wait that long, we figured, and likely there would be no Carteret County Christmas for our clan. In the coves of my heart this thought ran aground:

Her gift is already there, has been there since last night by her brother's hand. My plan, his cheerful collaboration in a theatrical holiday surprise.

Grandparents' tales of Albemarle Sound frozen over and the mail truck driving shortcut across the ice came to mind, and we moved out—grabbed Hunter and Susannah, our then four-year-old twins, strapped them into the backseat and hurriedly tarped over the unassembled bicycles in the way-back of our big white woody station wagon, and roared off into the coastal plain. We would drive as far east as we safely could, stop and stay in a motel if we had to, then see what it was like Christmas Eve. We made Kinston, gassed up at the Neuse Sport Shop, that great eastern tacklebox, glided easily down the four-lane where in warmer times we see deer browsing at the reaching edges of swamps, and passed New Bern.

At Havelock things changed abruptly.

Slocum Creek was the border—over the bridge the snow was thick on the road. I cannot imagine what shift of nature was occurring in the great pinelands of the Croatan Forest, but shift it did, and we had to figure again. If we stayed on N.C. 70, even if the Newport Bridge from Morehead to Beaufort were open now, that high vaulting span could easily be closed due to snow and wind during the hour or two it would take to get that far. The sure and safe road to Beaufort would be N.C. 101, the back way, the flat way where only Core Creek Bridge over the Intracoastal Waterway presented any elevation. It was the right road.

Just before dark we pulled in at the house on Orange Street, and the twins were ecstatic. The wind had grown steadily as we moved east, and the powder was gathering quickly in big drifts. They had been in snow that deep, but not since they could remember. Now they wanted it all, to dive into it, roll in it, swim in it, eat it, throw it (though it was far too dry to clump a snowball at all). After dinner Ann's sister Carolyn and Ann's aunt Betty took them on a promenade, and when they returned, the twins' faces were bright red, burnished by the cold, and they couldn't say enough good about it:

"It's wonderful out there!" they went on and on. "Just wonderful!"

Next morning, from her Front Street cedar-tree perch three feet above the snow, Susannah shouted, "I want to stay here forever!" It was Christmas Eve, and we were out surveying the cold gray harbor of blizzard-bound Beaufort. The snow had piled higher than the door handles of the station wagon, and the children in their snowsuits shrieked gleefully, "Throw me in, throw me!" There was not a tire track on Orange Street, and just after we got the little redhead down out of the tree, we all spied the most effective traffic of the day, cousin Sue gliding down Front Street on cross-country skis, alternately pushing with her poles and waving at us as she approached, passing an eight-foot drift at Clawson's lamp post.

They were skiing cross-country down in Wilmington just then, too, though other news from around the East was less sporty. There was gale-force wind all up and down the Sound Country, and Nature dropped three cottages into the winter seas at Kitty Hawk. Power was out in Pender, and hundreds lost heat, light, and water in this first-ever Outer Banks white Christmas—a Coast Guardsman called it "Your basic Siberia effect."

By Christmas morning there would be four inches of snow in Robeson County, five inches in Fayetteville, fifteen inches and zero degrees in Wilmington, where fish and a pelican were reported dead. Twenty-five miles north of Kitty Hawk a 600-foot navy tanker ran aground. There was nearly as much snow in Myrtle Beach and Charleston, and the same cold in Florida was killing the citrus and sugarcane and strawberries.

But all that was far away from four-year-old Hunter, who had unshakeable faith that Santa Claus would find him wherever he was. He dropped off easily on the eve of the big day, but his twin sister worried over this very point and stayed awake, which worried her even more. (I fretted some, too, over Ann's present that was still twenty miles farther east, down at Sea Level on Core Sound.) When Susannah finally fell asleep around two, we helped Santa Claus wheel the pair of little bicycles—one black, one pink, that we had helped him put together above the garage out back—into the house and under the tree.

Then it was our turn to embrace and regard the Christmas we had been given, to rejoice that our holiday found us happy with family and friends in the land of poached fish and oyster dressing, in a realm where some still remembered such tideland traditions as Christmas Eve flounder-gigging:

"Next day," said Wilmington's *Star-News* that snow-bound Sunday in '89, "the unfortunate flounders, lovingly stuffed with native delicacies such as oysters, crabs, collards and grits, graced Christmas tables all over the area. Non-Baptists who could afford it and knew a reliable bootlegger accompanied the humble dish with a jelly glass of high octane cheer."

Boats were frozen atilt, masts askew, in the rimy ice of Taylor's Creek, in North River too (where brother Tad had nearly been blown off the bridge with Ann's present three nights earlier), on our way as we traveled farther down east in Carteret. The tawny marshes were vast plains of snow, and the duckblinds and small shacks that dot them were lifeless, lonesome in the long, slanting western sunlight. So different was the look of the place now that Ann and sister Carolyn, both of whom grew up here, frequently had difficulty figuring right where we were as we crawled toward Sea Level and their father's home along U.S. 70. "This is where Ann saw the bear," we said, just past the Harker's Island turnoff. No bruins abroad today, but near Williston, home of the world's first scallop-shelling machine, we did catch a glimpse of a solitary goose hunkered down in an icy ditch beside the road.

At Doctor John's the fire was all ablaze, as Ann says it always will be on Christmas, even if it is balmy and all the windows have to be thrown open. The fire was no decoration this twenty-degree holiday, and the only thing thrown open was our collective spirit. We warmed ourselves at that hearth, took turns, very much for real, and Tad warmed as he took me aside and told me of the re-markable voyage down, with Ann's gift strapped to his car.

"Nearly lost that thing on North River Bridge," he said, laughing but with a serious turn of the head that said, It may be funny *now* but it sure wasn't when it happened. "Only had it tied front and back, not over the top—it started to go sideways. I mean it was a gale! Had to get out and re-tie it on the bridge, in the dark, with *all that wind*!" Men happy of heart do not light long at such places. Together Tad and I acknowledged his trial, but did not let our spirits darken. The living room was full—Doctor John is the only physician east of North River, and has many friends. Outside, beyond the snowdrifted deck, the waters of the sheltered cove off Core Sound lay settled in the cold blue evening light.

It would be dark in twenty minutes. Now was the time.

After a brief, whispered instruction to Hunter, I slipped outside with the jovial, brawny fisherman Duke Daugherty, and together we took the present in hand, all seventeen feet of it, brushed the snow off it and carried it from beneath the live-oak tree around back, where in a moment we would come into view of all those on the warm side of the living room's wall of glass. I stopped, peered in, saw Hunter standing still behind Ann, he not moving till he saw me, then reach-ing around the corner and retrieving the ash paddle and putting it in her hands and pointing our way, just as Duke and I slid the long, gleaming white canoe up onto the snowy deck, Ann's expression one of thorough surprise and unequivo-cal delight as she smiled at me and looked around at all of us and over and over again at the graceful flatwater craft come to rest in the drift of powder at her childhood home.

White Christmas in Carteret was a midwinter night's dream that we relive often in our hearts, where a towheaded boy will always be half the height of a boat paddle and a snowy redheaded girl will sit in a Beaufort cedar tree *forever!* and a down-east man and woman will float the Sound Country ever after in a canoe as white as the driven Christmas snow.

For several years Ann, the children, and I stayed a great deal in a small, slant-floored cottage near the sunset end of Front Street. From an old black-and-white taken from what is now marine labs and wharves on Piver's Island, this cottage seems to have been a turn-of-the-century boat- or nethouse that since has had an extra bit of living and sea-staring space *L*-ed onto it. It was the only house on the water past Barbour's Marine, a machine shop, and there was nothing else along this quarter-mile of shore except a few piers and small craft. We were living in the custom house, and our watch was Beaufort Roads: the confluence of Gallants Channel, Taylor's Creek, and the main channel down between Carrot Island and Radio Island to the Morehead City ship channel out to sea. From our small cottage porch we had a powerful, unobstructed view of sail and powercraft moving in and out of Taylor's Creek, of the shrimpers coming in and out from their Gallants Channel wharves, of the doings over at the Piver's Island marine labs, of great freighters moving portward and seaward behind the Bird Shoal sandbanks in such a way that they seemed to be crossing a desert. We could see the rolling breakers at Beaufort Inlet as they came crashing in at Fort Macon Beach, and beyond all of this the huge high-piling cumulus clouds that stood tall in the heavens and marched steadily in summer-sea formation out over the Gulf Stream — next to the heat and the daycrowds in town the most powerful declaration of the season that we knew.

The first night we ever spent there was a Friday evening before the Big Rock King Mackerel Tournament, and the town was full of hopped-up big talkers (the twins called them "the *Ya*-hoo boys") stomping about their 28- and 33-foot cruisers with the flying bridges, shouting out to Taylor's Creek and the seas beyond — with much Dutch courage, of course — how bad they were going to slay em the next day. If they were noisy and over-amped, they were also harmless and entertaining.

The best boat in the harbor, though, besides our own Buddy boat, which spent its nonnavigational time on the forty-foot beach next to the cottage, was the research vessel *Cape Hatteras*, warped up alongside the big pier over on Piver's Island. The *Hatteras* was a smart ship, dark forest green painted to well above the waterline, bright navy-white railings and decks and superstructure.

(opposite) Ghost tree, Sea Level, November 1996

Front Street cottage, Taylor's Creek, Beaufort, with the *Cheryl Jean* and Carrot Island beyond, August 1996

We watched her throw off her lines in the morning and head down the channel and out to sea, and when she returned a week or ten days later, there were a dozen dolphins plying and plunging about her bow wave.

In season there were always two or three enormous powercraft drawing gawkers to the boardwalk, sleek and not infrequently menacing, slit-windowed oceangoers with full-sized skiffs for dinghies above decks — one craft even had a single-seat aircraft under wraps right behind the cabin. These boats always struck me as failed audition pieces from James Bond films, and they were poor stand-ins for the forest of crow's-nested pogyboats that for decades crowded this harbor, when fish houses backed up to the water where now there was the broad open promenade along Taylor's Creek.

Occasionally Hunter and I, when he was just eight, would slip from the cottage at dawn, boating up the creek after a newspaper for Ann and passing the sleeping sloops and cruisers. One low-tide morning we nosed in at the dinghy-dock and Hunter stepped upon the jonboat's bow and tried to hoist himself up onto the dock. But we weren't yet fast, and his motion kicked the jonboat back and sideways from the boy just as his life jacket kept him from flipping forward onto the dock. Hunter fell noisily off the dock into Taylor's Creek, and when he bobbed up screaming with laughter at the cold, unintended ablution, I knew we were in Huck Finn heaven.

But Injun Joe and the floating House of Death were part of Huck's world, too. Once we came home from a summer afternoon walk to find a tall, disoriented thief wandering around the cottage, pilfering our camera and pocketknives and small change. He slipped by us, but I followed him up Moore to Ann Street to Orange till the police collared him easily at Broad—he was a strung-out addict from Pitt County. More serious was the day the two killers made a jailbreak at the county courthouse, ran down Craven for Front Street, and leapt into Taylor's Creek. The one that couldn't swim got fished out and recuffed, but the other, the leader, hid out all day on Carrot Island in the thick myrtle and cedars where the wild ponies sleep. A deputy moonlighting as a night-watchman at the Piver's Island marine labs kept watch down by the bulkhead, on his strong hunch that the killer would swim the channel that night and try to make it out of Morehead by jumping a freight car bound back to some remote eastern Carolina woodyard or another. The deputy was right. Along about midnight he heard the escapee splashing around, exhausted, trying to climb the bulkhead. When the sheriff of Carteret County showed up shortly, the killer refused to come out of the water. The sheriff jumped in after his quarry, thrashed him, and got reelected.

So we kept our eyes out on Beaufort Roads. From the cottage porch we watched Billy Smith's big, black-hulled shrimpers move in and out of harbor; watched the slender, six-man rowboats the Maritime Museum had built, replicating old ship tenders, as they glided around, skirting larger traffic; watched the EJW bait-barge go after floating trade, the big skiffs and runabouts ferrying foot-passengers from Beaufort docks out to Shackleford Banks several miles seaward.

And from our small purchase on Taylor's Creek we, too, were always setting out for somewhere—shelling with the children on the small beach at Gallants Point near the Beaufort airport, on across the Newport and back up into the Haystacks, night-boating around Piver's Island, canoeing the sloughs between Carrot Island and Bird Shoal where Clam Bob would be out walking and stalking bivalves. Most often we went on over to Carrot Island, where the children played on the beaches to either side of Cape Carrot, slowly approaching the wild ponies when they appeared looming up over the dune sides. Let out like marooned sailors or Indians, the twins came to play over on the island for longer and longer periods of time. When we would return to pick them up, they would present us with shells, pony hair, white socks full of seed ticks.

One spring evening Cary and I crossed, just the two of us, for a sunset walk, and literally strode into a quarter of the pony herd, all six of them, grazing atop

Venus on Taylor's Creek, Beaufort, August 1996

the high hill across Taylor's Creek from Liveoak Street; one of the mares was heavy, and when we saw her again in August her foal was keeping tight beside her, grazing with her now in the salt grass along the creek.

Years ago Hunter and Susannah and I took the jonboat way up Taylor's Creek toward North River one summer afternoon, and Susannah, when she saw the channel marker where creek met river, asked with intensity:

"Daddy! Are we going to the triangle?" The daymarker was three-quarters of a mile distant yet.

"Sure, sweetheart," I said. "Then we'll turn around and come back down the creek."

"Not the triangle!? Please not the *triangle*!" she started wailing, crying, and shifting her weight in the boat to such an extent I came about and beached us across the creek just east of the menhaden plant, the astonishing wired- and braced-together batch of piping, boilers, conveyors, net reels, and tall thin smokestacks that has bought and paid for Beaufort, black and white, for generations. But I had a squawling seven-year-old redhead aboard, and could not dwell just then on industry and ingenuity. I grabbed her out of the skiff and held her tight.

Gregory Poole moored at Beaufort Fisheries, Taylor's Creek, Beaufort, August 1996

"Honey, what is it? Are you hurt?"

"Not the triangle, not the—"

"What are you *talking* about? What's wrong?"

It took several minutes for her to regain her composure, and when she did she told me, between sobs:

"Boats . . . disappear . . . in the triangle . . . and never . . . come back!"

Now it came clear. We had been heading straight into the Bermuda Triangle and I as captain had steered us recklessly, heedlessly forward, even as one of my mates sought stridently to warn me. Well, once settled on that, we then turned our minds and hands to diverting water out of a shallow tidal pool there on the creekside of Carrot and channeling it down into the creek, a thing far more mysterious than any Bermuda Triangle, water running through the fingers of children and seeking the nearby sea—only to have the moon pull it back again to pools and sloughs where plovers might stalk in it, where sand ponies might gallop and graze.

A summer or two later, Susannah and Hunter both were all too eager to thread themselves through the bowrider of a nineteen-foot whaler bound down Taylor's Creek, past *The Triangle*, for Harker's Island and the Lighthouse Channel. Jim Rumfelt, the athletic bicycle-shop entrepreneur who hailed from Salty Shores over on the mainland Bogue Sound side, was piloting us out for a late-afternoon picnic at Cape Lookout Light, the shoal-warner whose spindle of black-and-white diamonds is a ubiquitous emblem around the central coast. As we made the turn at Harker's Island and headed down the Lighthouse Channel, down The Drain, I asked Jim how long he'd been in Carteret County this visit. His business was in Chapel Hill, and he was by his own admission playing hooky.

"About six weeks."

"Six weeks!" I said. "Man, you're doing something right."

"I don't know," said Jim, cracking the head off a cold frosty, "I think I'm developing a bad attitude towards work."

He dropped the twins and me at the lighthouse, which is only a few dozen yards from the inside waters of Lookout Bight, the bay inside the hook of the cape. While the children swam and tried to wash the black lighthouse paint from the flat of their palms (it was "bad paint," someone told them after they'd run over to touch it, "coming off way too easy") Jim took off around the tip of the hook to go fishing outside in the rip-roaring surf of Lookout Shoals, the churning waters he called "the washing machine."

"It's where the fish are," Jim always said. "See, I don't believe in fishing. I believe in *catching*."

I lazed with the twins in the waters of Lookout Bight and watched the old red disc slide down the sky toward Shackleford Banks, toward the Diamond City Hills there, the long-gone whalers' domain, and the spots of marsh and shoal behind the banks—the Bunch of Hair, the Hard Working Lumps, the Shooting Hammock, Sam Windsor's Lump. During that golden hour in the shallows I kept thinking: What I would give to fix, capture, encapsulate this little moment and give it back to these noisy innocents when they were fifteen, or fifty. It was as sublime as the Sound Country gods can make it, which is substantial. But the couple who had ventured out with us, a pair of sociable Northerners trying and not entirely succeeding at fitting into the power and society of contemporary New Bern, began to get nervous over the increasing length of Jim's absence. The sun was almost sitting on the horizon, and he was gone now nearly an hour longer than he'd proposed.

"You think he's all right?" they worried.

"I reckon he is," I said.

"What could be keeping him? He said half an hour."

"He'll be here in a minute," I said. "He got into some fish, is all."

Presently the whaler came in from the ocean and made for us, skylit by the sunset. When he pulled up and killed the engine, Jim was whooping, "Hey, give me a hand with this cooler—I got a mess of *Spanish!*"

We threw the cooler down in the water at the little beach, where Jim fileted them swiftly, and was done in twenty minutes. He washed the filets in the waters of the bight, handing the fish guts to Hunter who, as Susannah moaned and shrieked, threw entrails to the hovering gulls, and for a few moments we were in a primitive ritual of ruck and gore that tied us to islanders in Greece, New Zealand, the Seychelles, their knees down on the beaches of other globe corners faraway, their hands grabbling over the fruits of the sea.

It was dusk as we cruised the light seas just off Shackleford, dusky dark by the time we came around the wreck where those banks taper off into Beaufort Inlet. The Spanish mackerel would be the feature of the feast at several Orange Street fish fries in the coming days, and Cap'n Jim, as the twins now called him, would be out again tomorrow, this time before dawn with his uncle over at Harker's Island, clamming somewhere on the eastern end and literally raking them in, as he most always did—part of his bad attitude about work, I later reckoned. We lolled briefly beneath a rusty tanker's ten-ton anchor over at the state port, then moved slowly in the dark back up the channel, now bound for the live-oak landing at the menhaden plant in Beaufort, first passing Piver's Island and the little Front Street cottage and rounding Cape Carrot to enter Taylor's Creek, and were followed that slow rolling way into Beaufort Roads by a host of dolphins.

We cleared Lenoxville—or rather Lenox Point where the never-built Lenoxville was supposed to be—about three o'clock on a hot late July blue-sky day, with Hunter at the whaler's helm until that point. Ospreys were still roosting in the hulking old boiler and rusting guts of a fishing boat that burned years ago on a shoal at the mouth of North River. San Juan sailor Carl Spangler was reading the chart, Pat Kindell and now Hunter too (honorably relieved of command) were riding, and I was trying to stay off the bars and give a wide berth to Harker's Island (where in backyards and garages and fair-sized hangars by rack of eye they lay out and cobble and craft and fit out the flarebow boats that kick back the surf and spray of the bow-wave and that are first among equals in the boatyards of the world, small craft and large, and where theirs is a generally healthy and always skeptical disdain of outsiders they've long called *ditdots* and *dingbatters*, and where plaintalk could be no plainer—"It was so ca'm this mornin," said an old islander to fisherman Tom Earnhardt once, "you could hear a loon fart clear to Egypt"). A sea turtle surfaced briefly in the channel as we plied around the island's west end, and soon we were passing under the island bridge and I watched Hunter as he craned his neck upward toward the underpinning of the bridge, remembering when I was his age and my father was less than my age now and the water was Pasquotank and the horsepower 1¼ instead of 90 but the boyhood thrill of a motor-drone echoing off a bridge bottom was precisely the same.

Then we were through The Straits at Marshallberg, where the only boat traffic this particular Friday was a pair of men fishing in a jonboat, and were out upon Core Sound, to my mind the central coast's reflection of Currituck. A white mansion stood out grandly at Davis Island—an old duck-hunting club built a century ago by a Brooklyn man who plowed up the island's cemetery and threw the grave markers into the Sound—but little else of human hand obtruded, outside of net stakes and channel markers, and, as we were early to meet Ann and our daughters at Davis Shore, we stopped and drifted in the light waves of the Sound, and I radioed Ann back in Beaufort from Red 34 while Carl and Hunter swam for a spell off the boat.

At the Davis docks where we met the rest of the family, I went momentarily aboard the tall ferry *Captain Alger* and got a fix on how to get into the camps over on South Core Banks from bearded, tattooed Ronnie Willis, who drew a map and talked as I sighted my binoculars in on the two high-stilted cottages across the miles of Sound: "Y'go in at a pole with three faded orange slats, they're horizontal, with a yellow sign with a bicycle illustration on it just below the three slats, and follow that line of white PVC on it, the ferry channel, and you'll go right on in."

And so we were off again. Willis's way sounded easy enough, and it was, but I am always mindful that the water is wide, and one's depth perception walks the plank on big waters and simple sights can be deceptively tough to spot and draw a bead on. The western sun was lighting the marshes and shoal waters of Great Island Bay, plating them in a summer gold as we found the bicycle on Core Sound and went on in to the small wharf at Willis's Fish Camp. At sundown the clouds that filled the open bowl of sky were every shade of white: Dover chalk, oyster shell and ash, and lavender too, with a green and light lavender fleck of rainbow at the top of one high-piling cumulus cloud. Later on, after reading by candlelight to the children Judge Whedbee's account about the wreck of the *Carroll A. Deering*, the ever-mysterious ghost ship of Diamond Shoals, we all trooped out onto the nighttime beach and found in the night sky shooting stars by the dozen.

In our shanty on Core Banks, where a century ago mullet fishermen built the same crude, efficacious brush-and-thatch camps their forebears had made back in Africa, everything was meet *and* right. A raccoon clawed around under the shack by night, and the children awakened next morning convinced they'd survived nocturnal visitation by some platoon of bears, looking out the back screen door across sand and myrtle here called *myrkle* and marsh and Core Sound spread out forever like all creation and shimmering in the morning sun. Doctor John and Tad and Linda boated down from Sea Level for the afternoon, bringing us a spaghetti pot in the bargain, and Susannah got a red badge of courage—a bashed and cut lip—while swimming in the heavy curl of surf. And then it was time for more flashlight tag in the dunes, for more of the judge's legends read by the light of a single candle flame.

Davis Island Hunting Club, Core Sound, August 1996

All just as we had done two years before up at Don and Katie Morris's Kabin Kamps on North Core Banks, in tarpaper and tin and crusty-screened shack #13, where Cary took her first steps. This was where Ann had grown up, learning to drive an old stick-shift Peugeot in the sand, and nowadays our big-boat tours with Doctor John and his 21-footer always started at Don and Katie's sound-side marina, whether we were going north and swimming at Rumley's Hammock on the near side of Cedar Island, or drift-fishing Drum Inlet and pulling in two flounder at a time on a high-low rig, or circumnavigating the landmass of Sea Level and Atlantic through the cut connecting Nelson's Bay and West Bay — where the massive military firing range made the old Duck set-up in Currituck seem like something children had built, and where the porpoise swam alongside by the score.

Well I can remember coming in from one frigid Core Sound trip, Susannah shouting through a swaddling about her face, "Yo, Don Morris! It's *freezing* out there!" to Don who was bundled in a mechanic's dark suit and walking along the bulkhead. And I remember, too, Cap'n Glenn, the big genial dark-haired fellow, running us out to Cabin #13, piloting the four-car ferry *Green Grass* in a warm, driving rain and blinding fog one April, the twins with little Lizzie Dodds and Baylor Gray in tow for the weekend.

Drum Inlet Coast Guard station at Core Banks, burned in 1970s, with Core Sound in foreground, Atlantic Ocean beyond

A thousand times I have asked Ann what it was like to grow up out here in the original down-east country, walked with her wondering just that as we collect-ed net floats and whatever other flotsam the latest hurricane or nor'easter had cast up on the little beach outside of Doctor John's cove, where the short pines and cedar live heartily with some of the most convoluted live oaks one could ever imagine, walked with her down the wildlife road near the Thorofare where the purple gentian blooms in midwinter, lifting itself just enough to blossom forth in the wiregrass of the Carteret flatwoods, the pine savannas. What was it like to be a girl and come of age in Sea Level, a place by name and common par-lance more down to earth than all others, to become Miss Mariner at seventeen and own it all—from the Haystacks to Lookout Shoals, from Drum Inlet to Portsmouth Island to Point of Marsh, all of it?

She told me about all the fish fries near the big dock at Sea Level and great billowing fires on the marsh at night where the causeway goes across to Cedar

The Thorofare, Cedar Island marshes, Carteret County, November 1996

Island, about times when she was eleven and twelve when she and a gang of her cohorts would get dropped with their bicycles at the Cedar Island ferryslip in the morning and then be met when the last ferry crossed Pamlico Sound returning that night, bringing them home from a day swimming and messing around Silver Lake and Ocracoke, about times, too, not long thereafter when she and some of these same cohorts would be tenting sound-side in the woodsy yard of someone's folks' fish camp at Tusk, wide awake and electrified at the notion that some boys, not bears, from nearby Marshallberg might sneak up on the tent and pay them an illicit nocturnal call.

And she reminded me of a more recent date, when in the fishing boat a bunch of us toured Core Sound on Thanksgiving Day, ducking into Monroe Willis's store at Atlantic for gas and ice, then cruising up and into the harbor of refuge there. We'd admired a camouflaged, scow-built boat recently completed and intended to haul duck hunters' gear to Tad's two-story houseboat anchored up a creek on the back side of Core Banks across the way. The talk among us was about all the boats at mooring there, who owned this one now and didn't so-and-so used to and what was the new fellow rigged for, all these generations of ownership such second-nature knowledge to those who were reared here that I knew in this safe water the book of the life of the little town, and Core Sound as well, lay open wide, if only you had been around long enough you knew how to read it. When we were under way again, the sun was all gold and diamonds on the water till it fell behind the clouds, and we skirted and raced a squall back down to Sea Level and the small cove off Styron's Bay.

And this time in July at Willis's on South Core Banks, we all admired the aborning fascination of Brooklynite Caroline Parsons with the thin spindle of Cape Lookout Light as it kept courting her, cajoling her, and winking at her, beckoning her from eighteen miles distant, its power and appeal such that, as we rode the whaler back down the Sound toward Beaufort on a sunny Sunday afternoon, passing men with a fully laden scow of empty crabpots and a boy fishing off the stern of a shrimper in the Straits, Caroline resolved that one of her goals in life was to return to Willis's and to hike the shoreline to the cape and back.

Good that there was still a state-of-nature *somewhere* like Core Banks where young and old alike could dream dreams and see visions: of striding the sandy, sea-beach world like a titan and no one and no thing standing in one's way, of shouting to the seas like Demosthenes, of making love on the beach and drawing no more attention—whether celebratory or derisive—than that of a laughing gull, because there was no other creature abroad from whom or which to draw it. Good, too, that one might strive for the northernmost point of Core Banks, above the Swash (the strand all empty, still and always, like the Currituck Banks once were and might have remained) and cross the tidal flat toward Portsmouth, the ghost village, and be turned back by high-wind mosquitoes that are undaunted and undeterred by stiff breezes and that hold the faded, myrtle-shrouded town fast, as if there *were* a war on, by clouding its entryways and stunning intruders, clogging them ear eye nose and throat till they fall away, no chemical capable of quelling such swarms. If that also was the state of nature, then so be it—and let the pilgrim from New York or Ontario, from California or even Carolina stall out, stand, and wonder how those who once lived there did it, stood it, made it.

On my desk at home are two small clay ponies that my daughter crafted years ago from the thick gray mud of Carrot Island. They are a bit over an inch long, maybe a half inch high, with tawny manes made of grass seed from our Front

Street cottage yard. Perhaps to some eyes they would look as much like slugs as horses, but I swear if I had smooth, to-scale wooden models of these animals, with mane and musculature realistically fashioned by the best carvers Down East could put forward, they would be nowhere near as evocative of Carrot Island and Beaufort Roads as these lumpy equines Susannah formed up in the summer of '93.

She had, after all, been gazing up at the Depression-era Federal Arts murals in the Beaufort Post Office on Front Street six blocks east, and one of the four oil-on-canvas pieces portrays three of these creatures, which the *émigré* artist Simka Simkhovitch called "Sir Walter Raleigh sand ponies." With a ship's ribbing and channel markers behind, a colt is nursing, and I well remember the pregnant mare of Carrot Island over the winter of '93–'94, the spindly foal of summer '94, and the stocky colt of early '95. Simkhovitch may have been from Chernigov, a Russian river town ninety miles north of Kiev, and he may have been painting in Greenwich, Connecticut, a half century ago, but he caught the small Beaufort beasts well enough to make my little girl want to take a turn at pony portraiture, and so she did, in a medium all her own and from the source.

That was when we were staying off and on in the Front Street cottage, keeping our jonboat tied to a huge rusty anchor that had gotten away from its craft at least a decade or two ago and washed up on the forty-foot beach beside the cottage. From this small purchase on the harbor, we lit out I don't know how many times to make the four- or five-minute crossing—Taylor's Creek to our left, Piver's Island and usually the big green-and-white *Cape Hatteras* to our right—to the beach beyond the northwest point of the island, a myrtle-and-willow tangle known to at least a few of the locals as Cape Carrot.

That beach was one of the best places in the known world. Sitting on it, eyes left, one could see across Bird Shoal, Rachel Carson's Bird Shoal, where the great, lyrical student of the seas once strode, across the tidal flats and bars oceanward of Town Marsh and Carrot Island, to the breakers at Beaufort Inlet, the old Fort Macon on Bogue Banks beyond. One Doctor True came upon a very rare whale out on Bird Shoal back in 1912, and got to name it: True's Beaked Whale. Now the wild ponies, singly or in groups of up to four or five, often appeared in the distance in the shallows, or right behind us, from out of the cedars on the grassy sandhill that rises behind Cape Carrot. Just down the channel from the Cape Carrot beach, low tide always exposed a long, slender oyster-shell bar, and for some reason known but to the hand that guides the swirling ebb and flow of this place this shell bar always caught more than its share of bottles, so Hunter and I were given to prowling it. Mostly they were clear, flat pint bottles, but many were small square-shouldered old-timey medicine bottles, being dredged up and revealed to us from what Neptunian apothecary, who knew?

Susannah, though, always showed more interest in the clumps, balls, and gobs of gray clay on the beach, and I don't think we ever left the beach to cross back over to town without a handful or two in the floor of the boat. The two ponies on my desk, one grazing, one staring down the coast, have proven to be the most durable of her creations, just as feral ponies (as well as goats, cattle, and pigs) have persisted in the margins of the Sound Country, from Carrot Island and Shackleford Banks northward to Ocracoke and Currituck and, similarly, on up in Virginia's Chincoteague and Assateague and down upon Georgia's Cumberland Island, these small, woolly ponies being endlessly proclaimed as the latest generation of offspring deriving from shipwrecked Spanish horses centuries ago rather than from what somebody's granddaddy might have stuck out there on the island in the 1920s for free range, browse, and pasture.

One of the most highly visible craft on Taylor's Creek in recent years is a sixty-foot lunker with a garish steamboat superstructure, the *Crystal Queen.* Many nights Ann and I have watched it come roaring in from down the channel, blasting into the harbor with a bow-wave that seems of greater swell than most boats in Beaufort could create astern, raking a 300-watt beam over Carrot Island as if jacklighting the ponies, while a disembodied voice thunders out over Taylor's Creek, telling all and sundry that "sometimes you can even see wild ponies off to our right, the descendants of horses from Spanish shipwrecks!" The *Mystery*—with a name that far better fits the Sound Country—and the headboats *Capt. Stacy V* and *Carolina Princess VI* all look like they *belong* to be moving about the Beaufort waterfront, in contrast to this theme-park barge. Most evenings at least a few people moving slowly along the boardwalk shake their heads and cuss the breach of peace. One night as the boat cleared Cape Carrot coming in, I overheard two fellows who were leaning on the boardwalk rail:

"Aw, hell," the first one said.

"What?" said the second, and the other replied:

"Aw, nothin. It's just that goddamn *riverboat* again," as just then the *Crystal Queen* drowned them out:

". . . descended from shipwrecked Spanish horses!"

Now the lights are shining upon the waters, the many waters of the Sound Country. They are shining from the small dunes and summer surf of Core Banks where the children play tag with flashlights on a late July night, from the thousand-yard beam of a pushboat searchlight shining down upon the old pontoon bridge across the waterway at Sunset Beach, and from the jetty lights at Little River in the south to a cabin lamp on Knotts Island in the north, and from the wheeling spokes of Oak Island Light to the points of beacons both steady, like Old Baldy and Price's Creek Light on the Cape Fear, and revolving, like Lookout and Hatteras, Bodie Island and Currituck. Coming into Elizabeth City along the Camden Causeway one dusky Christmastide evening, I have seen the lights to my left in homes across the Pasquotank, some of them built on stilts out over the river itself, and before me, past the small tower lights on the bascule bridge, the old watertower lit crisscrossed with holiday red; and I have sat on the waterside porch of our old slant-floored cottage at Beaufort Roads staring at the faint lights atop the sailboat masts in Taylor's Creek and at the channel markers red and green out in the main ship channel beyond Cape Carrot and Bird Shoal, the glowing white-golden work lamps of Fort Macon Coast Guard Station out there too, the nearer lights of the jaunty-green *Hatteras* docked at Piver's Island.

Through Ann's eyes I have seen shrimpboats and smaller craft moving through Nelson's Bay and Core Sound, men on the nightdecks living and breathing diesel and unaware how festive their dingy workboats might look across the Sound, and I can see her on the short dock at Monkey Island and through her eyes again see the brief but stunning phosphorescent chalkings of the Perseid meteor shower falling over Currituck and mirrored in that Sound, and, for all that, I have given her the ultraviolet sundown moment when, out in the jonboat in the Haystacks, I watched a full sky-sculpture appear, the planets Mars, Mercury, and Venus coming all in a straight line out of the concavity of the slender new moon one May, celestial signals from that silver parabola high over the Haystacks. By these lights see all that it is and remember: phosphorescence glowing in the curl of rolling surf one Currituck oceanside night; bright spindrift catching all the light ashore on a wintry-gray Outer Banks morning; a year's-end sunset over Pamlico Sound, from a fire on the horizon to the light eggshell blue and green high above, a long, low molten cloud now a golden reef, in fifteen minutes a ridge of ash. Of the little line of islands at the head of Core Sound—Chainshot, Harbor, Wainwright, and Shell—Harbor Island and the huntclub there with its tabby foundation are nearly no more, and the old screw-pile Harbor Island Light is on the charts but a *pile*. In fifty years or a hundred perhaps, not even an eyeblink in God's time, this green and golden coastal plain, field forest swamp marsh and sound, may be half or all beneath the waves of the sounds or of the sea herself. But for now, if only for now, the Sound Country, this ephemeral, water-loving land, is ours, our title to it as true as our blood and our beating hearts.

Gazing out at the sunset one November night near the waterfront marker honoring Beaufort's Michael Smith, captain of the *Challenger*, I thought of a navy captain from another challenge, another time, Otway Burns of the *Snap-dragon*, who braved the British in the War of 1812 and now slept in a sepulcher with a huge iron cannon atop it in the old Ann Street burying ground a couple

Wooden grave markers, Sea Level, 1996

hundred yards away; and, too, of another navy, the victims of the *Crissie Wright*, sailors whose schooner foundered on Lookout Shoals in a gale 111 years ago and who wrapped themselves in the jib sail and froze to death off Shackleford Banks and now lay in a mass grave not far from Captain Burns. Near the tall pines of Sea Level, on Nelson's Bay twenty miles to the east, unnamed and unknown men women and children of the Sound Country had on the ground above them simple wooden slabs carved with full rounded tops like heads upon shoulders, mere shades of what they were in life but markers nonetheless of times passed here on this land that rides the waters. In the west the evening redness deepened, as I stood watching the night herons come in swiftly and in silhouette swiftly light and grasp the tops of pier-pilings in Taylor's Creek, taking their places, each to his own.

Selected Sound Country Sources

BETSY

My parents moved back to Elizabeth City, my father's hometown, in December of 1948, when he was admitted to the bar and began to practice law; our life there—including time with my grandmother, Jeannette Foster Simpson; my great-aunt, Jennie Bland Simpson Overman; and great-uncle, Harold Speight Overman Sr.—informs "Betsy." Further architectural and historical information about Betsy town and Pasquotank can be found in: Thomas R. Butchko, *On the Shores of the Pasquotank: The Architectural History of Elizabeth City and Pasquotank County, North Carolina* (Elizabeth City, N.C.: Museum of the Albemarle, 1989); Catherine W. Bishir and Michael T. Southern, *A Guide to the Historic Architecture of Eastern North Carolina* (Chapel Hill: University of North Carolina Press, 1996); and the *Pasquotank Historical Society Yearbook*, vol. 1 (N.p.: n.p., 1954–55), vol. 2 (N.p.: n.p., 1956–57, edited by John Elliott Wood), and vol. 3 (Baltimore: Gateway Press, 1975, compiled and edited by Lou N. Overman and Edna M. Shannonhouse). Regarding other lives in this place: *Narrative of the Life of Moses Grandy: Late a Slave in the United States of America* (London: C. Gilpin, 1843) is a remarkable portrait of one black man's upper Sound Country experience, no less powerful for its brevity; the great American poet's pilgrimage through the Great Dismal and Betsy is drawn from *Robert Frost: A Biography* (New York: Holt, Rinehart and Winston, 1982), by Lawrance Thompson; novelist Doris Betts, during her writing of *The Sharp Teeth of Love* (New York: Alfred A. Knopf, 1997), told me of Tamsen Donner's teaching tie to Elizabeth City. Accounts of the inventor-aviator Wrights include those by: Thomas Parramore, *Triumph at Kitty Hawk: The Wright Brothers and Powered Flight* (Raleigh, N.C.: Division of Archives and History, 1993); Stephen Kirk, *First in Flight: the Wright Brothers in North Carolina* (Winston-Salem, N.C.: John F. Blair, 1995); and John Alexander and James Lazell, *Ribbon of Sand* (Chapel Hill, N.C.: Algonquin Books, 1992). Forester Gerald Frazier has answered many of my questions about the big eastern woods over the years, and B. Culpepper Jennette Jr. and David Harris, two of my oldest friends on earth, reminisced with me about our younger river-town days on the old racetrack of Williams Circle.

SCUPPERNONG

"This Brief History of My Ancestors" (unpublished manuscript, ca. 1964), by my great-aunt Catherine Spruill Yerby, describes and delineates much of our Spruill family history in Tyrrell County, as do John William Melson's "Benjamin and Nancy Spruill Lineage" (unpublished manuscript, 1964–65) and Jerry L. Cross's "Site 31Ty9: The Spruill Home Place" (unpublished manuscript prepared for the Archaeology Branch of the N.C. Division of Archives and History, dated April 16, 1984). Boatloads of memories about Scuppernong River life have also come to me by way of my mother and my aunt Sister (Evelyn [Spruill] Page Burdette, namesake of my Alligator, N.C.–born grandmother, Evelyn Spruill). The history of our native muscadines and wines is largely drawn from Clarence Gohdes's slender, erudite *Scuppernong: North Carolina's Grape and Its Wines* (Durham, N.C.: Duke University Press, 1982), with comments from John Brickell's *The Natural History of North-Carolina* (Dublin, 1737), from Samuel H. Perkins's diary, edited and presented by Robert C. McLean in "A Yankee Tutor in the Old South" (*North Carolina Historical Review* 42 [January 1970]), and from George Higby Throop's novel *Nag's Head; or Two months among "The Bankers." A story of sea-shore life and manners* (Capt. Gregory Seaworthy, pseud., Philadelphia: A. Hart, 1850). I met Rose Hill vintner David Fussell many years ago at his Duplin Wines booth in the agricultural building of the North Carolina State Fair, and he has since graciously corresponded with me regarding the scuppernong.

HULLS

America 1585: The Complete Drawings of John White, by Paul Hulton (Chapel Hill: University of North Carolina Press, 1984), offers the earliest European graphic look at Sound Country watercraft. David Stick's *The Outer Banks of North Carolina* (Chapel Hill: University of North Carolina Press, 1958) and Gary S. Dunbar's *Historical Geography of the North Carolina Outer Banks* (Baton Rouge: Louisiana State University Press, 1958) are both excellent, essential texts toward an understanding of our coastal waters and the boats that have floated them, and Stick's *Graveyard of the Atlantic* (Chapel Hill: University of North Carolina Press, 1952) tells us what vessels sank where and when. More is to be had from *Sailing with Grandpa*, by Sonny Williamson (Marshallberg, N.C.: Grandma Publications, 1987); from the chapter "Traditional Boats of North Carolina," by Mark Taylor in *Wildlife in North Carolina*, edited by Jim Dean and Lawrence S. Earley (Chapel Hill: University of North Carolina Press, 1987); from Rodney Barfield's *Seasoned by Salt: A Historical Album of the Outer Banks* (Chapel Hill: University of North Carolina Press, 1996); from the works of Michael B. Alford, who comments on such Carolina craft as the periauger (in "The Tool Bag," *Tributaries* 2, no. 1 [October 1992]) and other sailboats (in "Shad Boats and Sharpies: Traditional Watercraft of the Carolina Coast," *Tar Heel* 9, no. 6 [June 1981] and in *Waterline: Newsletter of the North Carolina Maritime Museum* 20, no. 2 [June 1995], on spritsail skiffs); from *When the Water Smokes: Tides and Seasons on a Wooden Boat*, by Bob Simpson (Chapel Hill, N.C.: Algonquin Books, 1983); from "Workboat" by Lawrence S. Earley in *Wildlife in North Carolina* 56, no. 11 (November 1992); and from *The Carolina Watermen, Bug Hunters and Boatbuilders*, by Richard Kelly and Barbara Kelly (Winston-Salem, N.C.: John F. Blair, 1993). The story of the *Paragon* is drawn from a John Parris piece in the *News and Observer* (Raleigh, N.C., February 13, 1949), reprinted in B. A. Botkin's *A Treasury of Southern Folklore* (New York: Crown, 1949). Few traverses of our coast, inside or out, can match the true *tour de force* of Nathaniel Holmes Bishop, recounted in his *Voyage of the Paper Canoe: A Geographical Journey of 2500 Miles, From Quebec to the Gulf of Mexico, During the Years 1874–75* (Boston: Lee and Shepard, 1878). Showboat tales take the stage in W. J. Overman III's "James Adams Floating Theatre," *Pasquotank Historical Society Yearbook* 3 (1975), in L. A. Squires's "Little Washington and Show Biz," *The State* 47, no. 6 (November 1979), and in Edna Ferber's memoir, *A Peculiar Treasure* (New York: Doubleday, Doran & Co., 1939). Two wonderful works — *A North Carolina Naturalist, H. H. Brimley: Selections from His Writings*, edited by Eugene P. Odom (Chapel Hill: University of North Carolina Press, 1949), and *Adventures in Bird Protection: An Autobiography*, by Thomas Gilbert Pearson (New York: D. Appleton-Century Co., 1937) — show the Sound Country wilds of the late nineteenth and early twentieth centuries, as Brimley and Pearson, the amazing naturalists and friends, sought the deepest possible comprehension of our coast and its many resources. An informative and engaging depiction of contemporary Carolina sailing is Fred Powledge's *A Forgiving Wind: On Becoming a Sailor* (San Francisco: Sierra Club Books, 1983). Current seekers after the mysteries of the Sound Country deep include: East Carolina University's Program in Maritime History and Nautical Archeology, with its Nautical Archeology Conservation Lab, Greenville; the North Carolina Division of Archives and History's Underwater Archeology Unit, Kure Beach; and the North Carolina Maritime Museum, with its Harvey Smith Watercraft Center, Beaufort.

SUNNY SIDE

Burgwyn history can be found in Archie K. Davis's *Boy Colonel of the Confederacy: The Life and Times of Henry King Burgwyn, Jr.* (Chapel Hill: University of North Carolina Press, 1985); in Jack Temple Kirby's *Poquosin: A Study of Rural Landscape and Society* (Chapel Hill: University of North Carolina Press, 1995); and in Henry Wilkins Lewis's *Northampton Parishes* (Jackson, N.C.: n.p., 1951). Particularly helpful to Ann and me in Windsor and Bertie County were the H. Mack Bells and the Cullen Dunstans. "Rockfish on the Rebound," by Kent Nelson (*Wildlife in North Carolina* 58, no. 3 [March 1994]), and "Bears in the East," by Vic Venters (*Wildlife in North Carolina* 60, no. 1 [January 1996]), are clear status reports on these two important creatures of the Roanoke River and its 150,000-acre hardwood bottomlands. Porte Crayon's "The Fisheries" ran in *Harper's New Monthly Magazine* 14, no. 82 (March 1857), George Higby Throop's exclamations about "Cypress Shore" appear in his novel *Bertie, or, Life in the Old Field, A Humorous Novel*, Capt. Gregory Seaworthy, pseud. (Philadelphia: A. Hart, 1851), and Elizabeth Lawrence's piece on Scotch Hall is in her *Through the Garden Gate*, edited by Bill Neal (Chapel Hill: University of North Carolina Press, 1990).

GHOST POCOSINS

Our rough, wondrous Carolina pocosins draw comment from John Lawson in his 1709 *A New Voyage to Carolina*, edited by Hugh Talmage Lefler (Chapel Hill: University of North Carolina Press, 1967); from Curtis J. Richardson, editor, et al., in *Pocosin Wetlands* (Stroudsburg, Penn.: Hutchinson Ross Publishing Company, 1981); from B. W. Wells in *The Natural Gardens of North Carolina* (Chapel Hill: University of North Carolina Press, 1932; reprint, 1967); from Douglas Neil Rader in *Carolina Wetlands: Our Vanishing Resource* (Raleigh, N.C.: North Carolina Environmental Defense Fund, 1989); and from Jack Temple Kirby in *Poquosin: A Study of Rural Landscape and Society* (Chapel Hill: University of North Carolina Press, 1995). Observations on the recent turn of topomorphic fortune in the Albemarle and Pamlico peninsula come from Vic Venters in "A Look at Our Newest Refuge" (*Wildlife in North Carolina* 55, no. 8 [August 1991]) and Lawrence S. Earley in "Can We Build a Wetland?" (*Wildlife in North Carolina* 58, no. 7 [July 1994]). For more of Blackbeard, Hugh F. Rankin's *The Pirates of Colonial North Carolina* (Raleigh, N.C.: State Department of Archives and History, 1960) and Alexander and Lazell's *Ribbon of Sand* (Chapel Hill, N.C.: Algonquin Books, 1992) both look into the pirate's groggy legend. A strong illustrated portrait of logging in the Albemarle and Pamlico peninsula can be found in *American Lumberman*'s "A Trip Through the Varied and Extensive Operations of the John L. Roper Company in Eastern North Carolina and Virginia" (April 27, 1907) and in *Steam Logging Machinery* (Pine Town, N.C.: Surry Parker, 1912), a catalog of Parker's manufacturing operation before he took on the Arbuckle tract in the Great Dismal Swamp between 1918 and 1925. Ornithologist and naturalist Brooke Meanley studies Pinetown Pocosin in his *Swamps, River Bottoms and Canebrakes* (Barre, Mass.: Barre Publishers, 1972). Other reflections on Lake Mattamuskeet are in Rachel L. Carson's *Mattamuskeet: A National Wildlife Refuge* (Washington, D.C.: U.S. Department of the Interior, Fish and Wildlife Service, 1947); Phillip Manning's *Afoot in the South: Walks in the Natural Areas of North Carolina* (Winston-Salem, N.C.: John F. Blair, 1993); and Jim Dean's "Mattamuskeet Memories," in *Wildlife in North Carolina* (Chapel Hill: University of North Carolina Press, 1987), edited by Dean and Lawrence S. Earley. My cousin Nancy Meekins Ferebee of Camden shared with me the chilling story of her father Nat's transit down the Alligator as an infant.

CROATAN

Years ago, Dan Neil of the Raleigh *News and Observer* directed me to one of his favorite haunts, Brice Creek in the Croatan National Forest. Michael Alford writes of "The Ferry from Trent: Researching Colonial River Ferries" in *Tributaries* 1, no. 1 (October 1991). Johann David Schoepf, a German doctor, appraises Tryon Palace in his *Travels in the Confederation, 1783–84* (Philadelphia: William J. Campbell, 1911). John Lawson charts his progress as an early-eighteenth-century eastern Carolina pilgrim in his 1709 *A New Voyage to Carolina*, and Lefler's introduction to the 1967 edition helps explain the events of the energetic, ill-fated surveyor-general's life here (Chapel Hill: University of North Carolina Press, 1967). Lefler and Albert Ray Newsome's *North Carolina: The History of a Southern State* (Chapel Hill: University of North Carolina Press, 1973) shows what a troubled time in the life of the colony that was. Our great central stream is the domain of—among others—the Neuse River Foundation and River Keeper Rick Dove ("Keeper of the Neuse," by Sarah Friday Peters, *Wildlife in North Carolina* 59, no. 7 [July 1995]) and of author and naturalist Janet Lembke, whose *River Time: The Frontier on the Lower Neuse* (New York: Lyons and Burford, 1989), is a deft and lovely depiction of her life at remote Great Neck Point. Jack Dudley tells of Babe Ruth at Camp Bryan in his *Carteret Waterfowl Heritage* (Burtonsville, Md.: Decoy Magazine, 1993), and wildlife advocate Manley Fuller has spoken often with me about Ellis Lake and its resident gators. Ospreys catch Roger Tory Peterson's eye in "High-Diving Fish Eater" in *Water, Prey, and Game Birds of North America* (Washington, D.C.: National Geographic Society, 1965) and David Lee's in "The Complete Osprey" (*Wildlife in North Carolina* 58, no. 3 [March 1994]).

TAR

In William S. Powell's *The North Carolina Gazetteer* (Chapel Hill: University of North Carolina Press, 1968) and in his "What's in a Name? Why We're All Called Tar Heels" (*Tar Heel* 10, no. 3 [March 1982]), one finds plenty to ponder regarding tar on our maps and tar in our culture. Doctor Johann Schoepf looked at us and our ways with the woods during his *Travels in the Confederation, 1783–1784* (Philadelphia: William J. Campbell, 1911); Frederick Law Olmsted's observations appeared in his classic *Journey in the Seaboard Slave States* (New York: Dix and Edwards, 1856); and Porte Crayon pictured "The Piny Woods" in *Harper's New Monthly Magazine* 15, no. 84 (May 1857). Chemist A. W. Schorger and engineer H. S. Betts called for "improved methods" in their highly illustrated collaboration *The Naval Stores Industry*, bulletin no. 229 (Washington, D.C.: U.S. Department of Agriculture, 1915). B. W. Wells's *Natural Gardens of North Carolina* (Chapel Hill: University of North Carolina Press, 1932; reprint, 1967) is excellent in this area, and an intriguing and highly informative document is *Longleaf Legacies: A Calendar for 1995*, by Julie Moore and Carol Goodwin (Gainesville, Fla.: Long Needle Press, 1994). Brooke Meanley, who loves the Croatan, spoke to me long ago of the Millis Road savanna; Janet Lembke writes of the "Small and Most Particular King," the red-cockaded woodpecker that lives there, in her *Dangerous Birds: A Naturalist's Aviary* (New York: Lyons and Burford, 1992); and more on this woodpecker is in Garnet Bass's "Ghosts of the Pinelands" (*Wildlife in North Carolina* 56, no. 4 [April 1992]).

THE BIG EMPTY

William S. Powell's *Gazetteer* sketches the history of the Welsh Tract and Penderlea, and Jack Riley's entry on Hugh MacRae in Powell's *Dictionary of North Carolina Biography*, vol. 4

(Chapel Hill: University of North Carolina Press, 1991) tells of MacRae's wide-ranging entrepreneurship. All voyagers who take on coastal-plain waters are well met by *A Paddler's Guide to Eastern North Carolina*, the work of Bob Benner and Tom McCloud (Birmingham, Ala.: Menasha Ridge Press, 1987).

MACO

Two tales of the Maco Light are John Harden's in *Tar Heel Ghosts* (Chapel Hill: University of North Carolina Press, 1954) and Nancy Roberts's in *An Illustrated Guide to Ghosts & Mysterious Occurences in the Old North State* (Charlotte, N.C.: Heritage House, 1959). Clare Johnson Marley's *Crusoe Islanders* is in the *Carolina Play-Book* 17, no. 1, edited by Frederick H. Koch (Chapel Hill: Carolina Playmakers and Carolina Dramatic Association, March 1944); Ruark's remarks are drawn from *The Old Man's Boy Grows Older* (New York: Holt, Rinehart and Winston, 1961). Franklin Burroughs is keen and amusing in *Horry and the Waccamaw* (New York: W. W. Norton, 1992). Venus's-flytrap and its territory are treated in Wells's *The Natural Gardens of North Carolina* (Chapel Hill: University of North Carolina Press, 1932; reprint, 1967) and in Edwin Way Teale's "Prehistoric Trapline" in *North Toward Spring* (New York: Dodd, Mead, 1951). More on the southeastern river valley are in *The Cape Fear*, by Malcolm Ross (New York: Holt, Rinehart and Winston, 1965), and in the program "River Run: Down the Cape Fear to the Sea," narrated by James Leutze, written by Philip Gerard (Wilmington: University of North Carolina, 1994, broadcast by UNC Center for Public Television, Research Triangle Park, N.C., 1994). The great coastal historian David Stick turns his gaze to the Southeast in *Bald Head: A History of Smith Island and Cape Fear* (Wendell, N.C.: Broadfoot, 1985).

ROUGH SIDE

Life at the Collins family plantation is explored by William S. Tarlton in *Somerset Place and Its Restoration* (Raleigh, N.C.: Division of State Parks, Department of Conservation and Development, 1954) and, more recently from an African American perspective, in *Somerset Homecoming: Recovering a Lost Heritage* (New York: Doubleday, 1988), by Dorothy Spruill Redford, with Michael D'Orso. Notes on James Johnston Pettigrew appear in his entry by Clyde Wilson in Powell's *Dictionary of North Carolina Biography*, vol. 5 (Chapel Hill: University of North Carolina Press, 1994). Folklorists Michael and Deborah Luster helped reunite the Menhaden Chanteymen, who recorded "Won't You Help Me to Raise 'Em" at St. Paul's Episcopal Church, Beaufort, N.C., December 2, 1989 (New York: Global Village Music, 1990). David Stick's *Roanoke Island: The Beginnings of English America* (Chapel Hill: University of North Carolina Press, 1983) sorts out the English efforts and explorations and their dealings with Indians in the Sound Country of the 1580s, up to and including the disappearance of Sir Walter Ralegh's Roanoke colony. Twentieth-century hardships concern Linda Flowers in *Throwed Away: Failures of Progress in Eastern North Carolina* (Knoxville: University of Tennessee Press, 1990) and David S. Cecelski in *Along Freedom Road: Hyde County, North Carolina, and the Fate of Black Schools in the South* (Chapel Hill: University of North Carolina Press, 1994). Literature on lowland runaways abounds and includes: *Roll, Jordan, Roll: The World the Slaves Made*, by Eugene V. Genovese (New York: Pantheon Books, 1974); "Runaways: Slaves Who Stole Themselves" in *Black Majority: Negroes in Colonial South Carolina from 1670 through the Stono Rebellion*, by Peter H. Wood (New York: W. W. Norton, 1975); parts of Samuel H. Perkins's diary, presented by Robert C. McLean in "A Yankee Tutor in the Old South" (*North Carolina Historical Review* 42 [January 1970]); *The Black Experience* in *Revolutionary North Carolina*, by Jeffrey J. Crow (Raleigh, N.C.: Division of Archives and History, Department of Cultural Resources, 1977); "Lost in the Desert," in my book *The Great Dismal: A Carolinian's Swamp Memoir* (Chapel Hill: University of North Carolina Press, 1990); and "The Shores of Freedom: The Maritime Underground Railroad in North Carolina, 1800–1861," by David S. Cecelski (*North Carolina Historical Review* 71, no. 2 [April 1994]). Ruel Tyson gave me the story of the slave burned at stake, having turned it up in *Sketches of Pitt County: A Brief History of the County, 1704–1910*, by Henry T. King (Raleigh, N.C.: Edwards and Broughton Printing Company, 1911). Daniel W. Patterson sang "The Night the Boozeyacht Ran Ashore" to me years ago; and Alec Wilkinson captured Garland Bunting's northeastern revenuing in *Moonshine: A Life in Pursuit of White Liquor* (New York: Alfred A. Knopf, 1985). John Harden wrote "The Mysterious Death of Beautiful Nell Cropsey" for his collection *The Devil's Tramping Ground and Other North Carolina Mystery Stories* (Chapel Hill: University of North Carolina Press, 1949), and I took another look through that glass darkly in *The Mystery of Beautiful Nell Cropsey* (Chapel Hill: University of North Carolina Press, 1993). Cullen Dunstan in Windsor told Ann and me the strange story of Leroy White and family. In the environmental area, *Troubled Waters*, by Glenn Lawson (Swansboro, N.C.: Hadnot Creek Publishing Company, 1990), is a close observation of our degraded estuaries and of citizens' efforts to overcome government failure to protect those resources, particularly the creation and early work of the N.C. Coastal Federation; Sarah Friday Peters's "Caring for the Coast" (*Wildlife in North Carolina* 59, no. 10 [October 1995]) is an update on the work of the Federation. Our fisheries are dealt with, and in each very differently, by Barbara J. Garrity-Blake in *The Fish Factory: Work and Meaning for Black and White Fishermen of the American Menhaden Industry* (Knoxville: University of Tennessee Press, 1994) and Margaret Maron in her novel *Shooting at Loons* (New York: Mysterious Press, 1994).

CORATANK

More on the Sound Country's hunting clubs can be found in: "Currituck's Historic Sporting Clubs," by Lawrence S. Earley in *Wildlife in North Carolina*, edited by Jim Dean and Earley (Chapel Hill: University of North Carolina Press, 1987); *Waterfowl Heritage: North Carolina Decoys and Gunning Lore*, by William Neal Conoley Jr. (Wendell, N.C.: Webfoot, 1982); *Carteret Waterfowl Heritage*, by Jack Dudley (Burtonsville, Md.: Decoy Magazine, 1993); and *A North Carolina Naturalist, H. H. Brimley: Selections from His Writings*, edited by Eugene P. Odom (Chapel Hill: University of North Carolina Press, 1949). Intricacies of the 1970s Currituck Plan's failure to prevent the dense strip development of this county's coast are in Thomas J. Schoenbaum's *Islands, Capes, and Sounds: The North Carolina Coast* (Winston-Salem, N.C.: John F. Blair, 1982).

HAYSTACKS

Ann's family moved to Sea Level and a home on Nelson's Bay in 1962; her life there in downeast Carteret County and, later, Beaufort informs "Haystacks" throughout. Claiborne S. Young's *Cruising Guide to Coastal North Carolina* (Winston-Salem, N.C.: John F. Blair, 1983) is an entertaining, illustrated, indispensable book for Sound Country boaters. Excellent articles by historian David S. Cecelski vivify two coastal sites: "The Hidden World of Mullet Camps: African-American Architecture on the North Carolina Coast" (*North Carolina Historical Review* 70, no. 1 [January 1993]) and a nineteenth- and twentieth-century African American settlement in Carteret ("The Last Daughter of Davis Ridge" in *Coastwatch* [September/October 1996]). Stick, in his *Outer Banks*, devotes a chapter to Diamond City on Shackleford Banks, and he covers two other vanished communities—Portsmouth and Shell Castle Islands—as well; Gary S. Dunbar's writing on Shell Castle in his *Historical Geography of the North Carolina Outer Banks* (Baton Rouge: Louisiana State University Press, 1958) is also of interest. More of Carteret can be had in Grayden and Mary C. Paul's *Folklore, Facts and Fiction: About Carteret County, North Carolina* (Beaufort, N.C.: Beaufort Historical Association, 1975); Karin Safrit and Jean Bruyere Kell's *Historic Beaufort, North Carolina: A Pictorial Profile* (Greenville, N.C.: National Printing Co., 1977); Jean Day's *Cedar Island Fisher Folk* (N.p.: Golden Age Press, 1994); Nancy Tilly's novel *Golden Girl* (New York: Farrar, Straus, Giroux, 1985); and Sonny Williamson's *Sailing with Grandpa* (Marshallberg, N.C.: Grandma Publications, 1987). Marcus B. Simpson Jr. and Sallie W. Simpson offer the densely detailed *Whaling on the North Carolina Coast* (Raleigh, N.C.: Division of Archives and History, Department of Cultural Resources, 1990). Sarah Friday Peters reports on Banker ponies in "A Haven for Horses: Horse Love Steers Debate over Outer Banks Herds" (*Coastwatch* [May/June 1994]). Rachel Carson has given us *Under the Sea-Wind: A Naturalist's Picture of Ocean Life* (New York: New American Library, 1941), *The Sea Around Us* (New York: Oxford University Press, 1950), and *The Edge of the Sea* (Boston: Houghton Mifflin, 1955); and in the tradition of T. Gilbert Pearson and Rachel Carson is John O. Fussell III's *A Birder's Guide to Coastal North Carolina* (Chapel Hill: University of North Carolina Press, 1994).

Acknowledgments

Together over the years we have gone deeper and deeper into the Sound Country, and we have been helped at every bend in the river, at every turn in the road. We wish to thank: the North Carolina Collection in Chapel Hill—Robert Anthony, curator, former curators H. G. Jones and William S. Powell, and Alice Cotten, Jeff Hicks, and Harry McKown, as well as Jerry Cotten of the Photographic Archives; the Museum of the Albemarle in Elizabeth City—Brenda O'Neal, director, and Don W. Pendergraft; the North Carolina Maritime Museum in Beaufort—Rodney Barfield, director, and Connie Mason; two excellent photographers—Scott Taylor of Beaufort and Bill Bamberger of Mebane; Visions Laboratories of Santa Fe, New Mexico; Homeport in Beaufort—Pat Kindell, Candy Rogers, Kerry Smith, and Judy Weaver; Dr. John R. Kindell of Sea Level; the North Carolina Coastal Federation in Ocean—Todd Miller, director; the North Carolina Coastal Land Trust in Wilmington—Camilla Herlevich, director; the North Carolina Environmental Defense Fund in Raleigh—Steven Levitas, founding director, and Doug Rader, senior scientist; the Pamlico–Tar River Foundation—David McNaught, former director; the North Carolina Wildlife Resources Commission's magazine *Wildlife in North Carolina*—Jim Dean, editor, and Lawrence S. Earley, associate editor; the University of North Carolina Press in Chapel Hill—Pam Upton, editor, Suzanne Comer Bell, copyeditor, Rich Hendel, designer, Heidi Perov, cartographer, Johanna Grimes, sales manager, Lisa Dellwo, publicity director, and David Perry, editor-in-chief, who has in spirit come along on this whole eastern Carolina ramble; two wonderful writers who both share our love for the eastern region and who gave this work their best critical regards—Janet Lembke of Great Neck Point and Jack Temple Kirby of Miami University in Ohio; and our dearest of friends, Rachel and Jerry Leath Mills, who read this manuscript in the middle of a move to their own home on the river, the Pamlico at Washington.

To all those who speak through these pages we offer our thanks, to all the living and the dead.

M.B.S. III
A.C.S.

Illustration Credits

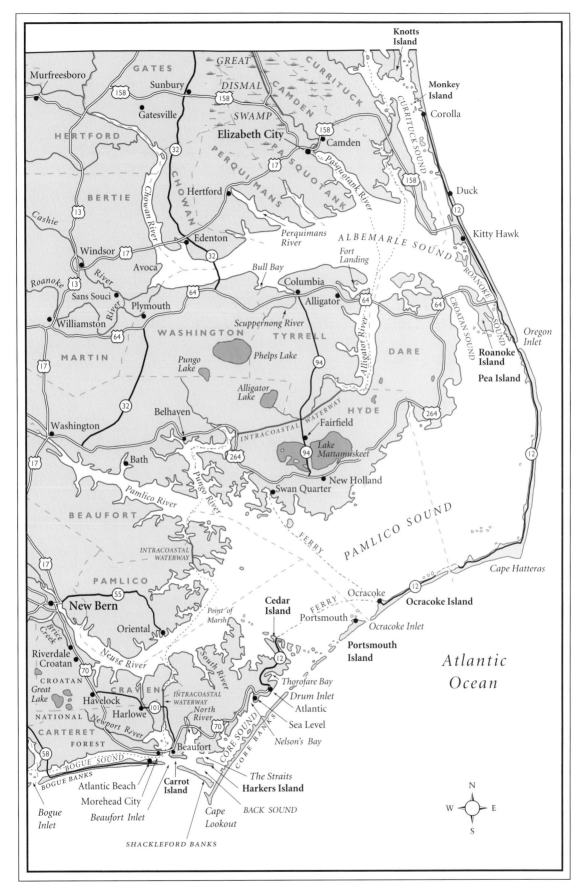

North Carolina's Central and Upper Coast and Coastal Plain

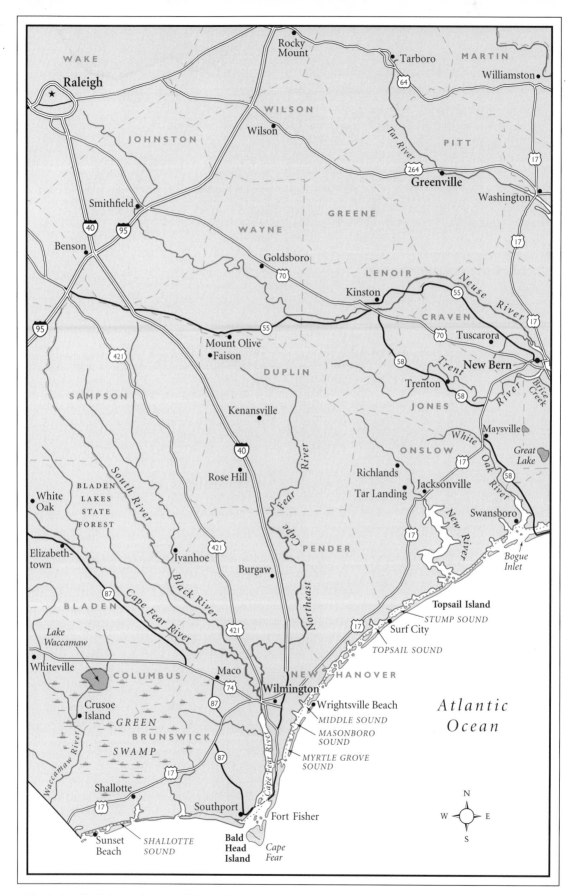

North Carolina's Lower Coast and Coastal Plain

Index

Entries in italics are watercraft, except where otherwise noted.
All places listed are in North Carolina unless another state is specified.